SIMPLY
THE BEST

SIMPLY
THE BEST

A BIOGRAPHY OF
RONNIE O'SULLIVAN

CLIVE EVERTON

First published by Pitch Publishing, 2018

Pitch Publishing
A2 Yeoman Gate
Yeoman Way
Worthing
Sussex
BN13 3QZ
www.pitchpublishing.co.uk
info@pitchpublishing.co.uk

A CIP catalogue record is available for this book
from the British Library.

ISBN 978-1-78531-444-5

Typesetting and origination by Pitch Publishing.
Printed and bound in India by Replika Press Pvt. Ltd.

Contents

Introduction

RONNIE O'Sullivan is the finest player in snooker history, a genius who can make the game look preposterously easy. At his best, he is simply the best.

Despite an erratic career trajectory, he has (as at November 2018) won five world, six UK and seven Masters titles but his most important victory has been over himself, over the inner demons that threatened the fulfilment of his prodigious talent.

As with John McEnroe and Tiger Woods, Ronnie's boyhood driving force was his father. When Ronnie senior was sentenced to 18 years in prison, it left him without his anchor and shattered his sense of innermost security.

Snooker had come easily to him (although he still had to work at it) but coping with real life often did not. He endured bouts of depression. He did not always act wisely. Top-notch performances mingled with episodes of mediocrity that disgusted him.

He turned to drink, drugs, overeating and even religion in doomed attempts to alleviate what he described as his 'treadmill of turmoil'. He was tormented by his aspiration for perfection or, at any rate, a rarefied level of excellence of which he knew he was capable but was mentally blocked from achieving.

As a television commentator and editor of *Snooker Scene* since its inception in 1971, I have followed Ronnie's life intimately on and off the table, chapter by chapter, year by year over the switchback of a life course that has only recently, through his work and friendship with Dr Steve Peters, achieved a settled equilibrium.

It has been good to see Ronnie emerge from the days of dark shadows to regain his love of the game and his appetite for its challenges.

Through long involvement in the snooker world, I know Ronnie about as well as anyone other than his close friends can know him. He is, at his core, warm hearted, a sportsman neither vainglorious in victory nor a whinger in defeat. He is extensively quoted in this book from published sources, mostly *Snooker Scene*. These quotes portray him in triumph, despair and everything in between.

Ronnie politely declined to co-operate in this book, perhaps feeling that some long-ago matters might receive another airing but, if so, they are part of his extraordinary story and an illustration that genius is not an impenetrable shield against what life can throw as you.

Clive Everton, July 2018.

Chapter 1

[1991]

O N 12 October 1991, Ronnie O'Sullivan was playing in a tournament in Amsterdam while his father, Ronnie senior, was enjoying an increasingly raucous night out at Stocks, a nightclub in the King's Road, Chelsea. It was the date on which his life was to change irrevocably.

'Big Ronnie', as he was sometimes known in reference not to his sleek figure but to his professional reputation, went to Stocks with Edward O'Brien. At a nearby table there was a birthday party for Angela Mills, a former girlfriend of Charlie Kray, brother of the notorious Kray twins, Reg and Ronnie, who had been locked away for many years for murder, extortion and various other crimes.

The trouble started, a court heard a year later, when Ronnie senior and O'Brien started singing football songs and making abusive comments that included racial taunts directed at Bruce Bryan, formerly Charlie Kray's driver, and his younger brother, Kelvin.

Kelvin Bryan was to state that he and his brother were out with four girls when, late in the evening, O'Sullivan and O'Brien approached their table, trying to chat up the girls and waving a £250 drinks bill 'under their noses to be flash'.

'Then they started getting nasty and called one of the girls a nigger lover and started taunting us with "you black cunts" and "nigger, nigger, nigger".

'They said "who do you think you are, coming in here with four white girls? Do you think you're Nigel Benn or something?"

'One of the girls was slapped in the face. There was a lot of panic and people started running away.

'Then O'Sullivan produced a [six-inch] hunting knife and stabbed my brother. I smashed a [champagne] bottle over his head to get him away from Bruce. Then he stabbed me in the chest and stomach.

'I could see Bruce was badly injured, there was blood everywhere. He staggered to the door to escape and when I got outside he was slumped to his knees. I screamed at him to run but he just looked at me and said: "I'm finished. I'm dying".

'I held him in my arms. He shook his head one last time and died.

'When O'Sullivan came out, he kicked Bruce in the head as he lay dead on the ground.'

The O'Sullivan family's version, as Ronnie was given to believe and as he described it in his first autobiography, was that Ronnie senior and O'Brien had been arguing over who would pay their bill and that the Bryan brothers misunderstood and thought they were refusing to pay at all. A row started in which one of the brothers picked up an ashtray. In protecting himself, two of Ronnie senior's fingers were severed by the ashtray as it broke and the other brother struck him with a champagne bottle.

'Dad then picked up a knife that was on the side of the bar and that was it,' Ronnie was quoted as saying.

This version of events was never to be tested in court because Ronnie senior declined to give evidence in his own defence, so what a six-inch hunting knife was doing on the side of the bar in the first place was a question that did not arise.

After the murder incident, Ronnie senior spent four days in hospital. Understandably, the family tried to shield young Ronnie from the unpalatable facts and sent him out to the World Amateur Championship in Bangkok a few days earlier than planned. Johnny O'Brien, Edward's brother, who had been sent along as Ronnie's minder, was no doubt worried about the trouble his brother was in and did not prove to be a source of emotional support when Maria O'Sullivan rang late one night to tell her son that Ronnie senior, as feared, had been arrested and charged with murder.

Young Ronnie was understandably shattered, although curiously it did not affect his game immediately. He was a hot favourite for the title and continued to brush aside all his opponents in his round-robin group. There was a Volvo on offer for a 147 break and he was not far from claiming it until he missed a double after potting 13 red/blacks.

Perhaps his matches were refuges in which he did not need to think about his father's situation but the dam of his emotions collapsed in the last 16, the first round of the knock-out phase. He could not keep his concentration together and from 4-2 up lost 5-4 to a capable but not outstanding Welshman David Bell. His dominant emotion was guilt that in some way he had let his father down. This was to be a recurrent theme during the 18 years' imprisonment to which he was to be sentenced. He wanted to win as much, probably more, to boost his father's morale than he did for his own sake.

Back in England, there was further trauma. Straight off the plane, he visited Brixton prison and there was his father in prison uniform looking as rough and unhealthy as any other inmate. Maria O'Sullivan held things together; Ronnie's school, Wanstead High, agreed to let him have time off. He was in his GCSE year but never went back. Snooker and the exhilaration of his relationship with his first real girlfriend kept his spirits up and overcame for a while the sense that a shadow was creeping over what had always been his normal, carefree life. Emotionally, this shadow was to become a darkness that he had never known existed.

Chapter 2

[1975–91]

THE O'Sullivans came from tough stock. Micky O'Sullivan, Ronnie's grandfather, was a boxer, as were his brothers, Danny, who was British bantamweight champion from 1949–51, and Dickie, who was known as 'The Toy Bulldog'. Boxing circles knew them as The Fighting O'Sullivans.

Ronnie's father was a chef and his mother, Maria, a chalet maid when they met at Butlins. They were soon married, she at 17, he at 18. They lived in Dudley, West Midlands, near Maria's family, the Catalanos, whose main business was ice cream. Maria Catalano, Ronnie's cousin, has been one of the top female snooker players for several years.

Ronnie was born in Wordsley Hospital, Stourbridge on 5 December 1975. His parents wanted to be in London, put their names down for a council flat and secured one on a notoriously grim estate in Dalston. Both Ronnie senior and

Maria cleaned cars in a car park in Wardour Street, Soho. Both soon had second jobs, Ronnie senior in a sex shop, Maria as a waitress. Until he was about seven years old, Ronnie himself saw little of his parents because they were always working. Often, he felt separation from them keenly, though this was to prove no preparation for the long, enforced absence of his father that was to come later.

When Ronnie senior opened his own sex shop, it turned over £360,000 in its first year. Financially, he was on his way. Through his company, Ballaction, he had built an empire of 20 shops by the time he was jailed in 1992.

Much of the stock was kept in the garage at home. 'When I was 11, I'd be in the garage saying: "What's this then? This is great."' According to Ronnie, some tapes in luridly promising boxes were actually blank, whether by accident or design. These sold at £50 each but it was correctly assumed that embarrassment would deter purchasers from demanding refunds.

It did not strike Ronnie that this was an unorthodox childhood: 'My dad wasn't breaking any laws. All he was doing was putting dinner on the table for his kids. He just wanted to be a family man.'

As many players have, Ronnie took to snooker when he was given an undersized table for Christmas. When he was eight, his father, now flush with cash, built a snooker room for him at the bottom of the garden in the large house to which they had moved in Chigwell. He made his first century, 117, when he was ten, but regardless of his exceptional degree of hand-eye co-ordination and instinct for the game, Ronnie has on occasion emphasised how hard he has still had to work on his craft.

Virtually every moment he was not at school, Ronnie could be found in snooker clubs in Barking and Ilford. His father made it clear that he was not there to mess about. If he was going to make something of his life through his exceptional natural talent, he would not do so by playing cards or the fruit machines.

From an early age, Ronnie bore a heavy burden of expectation: 'I was meant to be the youngest ever world champion from the age of 11 or 12,' he said in a BBC interview. The corollary that loomed large in Ronnie's mind was that anything less than this was failure: 'It was obsessive but I think you need to be.

'It was inbred, y'know, get up, go for a run, get down the club in the morning, bottle up and get on the table, because I wanted to feel I was putting my part in. When I had a bit of time and I could help brush tables, I did it. When the girls behind the bar needed helping out, I'd do it, so I started work a lot earlier than most people start. I started my career when I was eight.'

For parents of talented children, there is often a fine line between keeping them focused on the field in which they excel and force-feeding them to the extent that they want to give it up. The O'Sullivans seem to have handled it about right and young Ronnie, of course, would never have persisted unless he had been fascinated by the game and the promise of what it could deliver, not only financially but in terms of fame and satisfaction.

The only problem he had with his father that was to have long-lasting effects was that he was extremely sparing with his praise. Victories were immediately brushed aside: the next match was always more important than the last; not a bad maxim up to a point, except that it seemed to breed an excessively self-critical attitude in Ronnie. He was to set himself virtually impossible standards, even for him, and punish himself with criticism if he fell short of them.

When he was ten, Ronnie was selected to play for England in the Junior Home Internationals at Pontins, Prestatyn in a week that also hosted open and junior events, attracting the better part of a thousand entries in all. Ronnie was lively, cheeky, naughty, certainly not above flicking beans off his plate or throwing bread rolls. Getting into an altercation with an older boy, he threw a glass of coke over him and ran. He threw the glass on the floor to slow down his pursuer but was reported by an elderly lady, who thought he had thrown the glass at her. Ronnie was expelled from the site forthwith and suffered his first but by no means last official disciplinary sanction, suspended for a year by the English national governing body. Eloquently represented by his father, he appealed and the ban was reduced to six months.

The precocity of his talent soon meant that Ronnie tended to have few friends his own age. He won his first pro-am — an event held in a single day, often with a late-night finish, in which amateurs and low-ranked professionals competed —

when he was 12. Not much later, his prize money earnings were annually well into five figures. The best times were when his father, as fathers do, ferried him here, there and everywhere. At other times, he was with 'mates', all older than him.

When Neal Foulds, then a top-eight player, first saw him at Pontins he thought he was 'ridiculously good' and was not looking forward to playing him in the tournament: 'I didn't want to lose to a 12-year-old, even giving him 21 start.' In fact, Foulds won 4-1.

Ronnie senior realised as his son grew up that he needed the best quality of practice opponent he could find. Ken Doherty, six years older than Ronnie, was Irish amateur, world under-21 and world amateur champion. In 1997, he was to become world champion at the Crucible. His heart was in Dublin but he too needed better day-to-day practice opposition and moved with some less talented Irish hopefuls to Ilford, where he and Ronnie frequently practised together.

Sometimes Ronnie senior would send a taxi to pick him up to be driven to the O'Sullivan home to play on Ronnie's table. One day, when Ken beat him 10-2, Ronnie said that he had had enough and had to do his homework. Ken went outside to his taxi but returned when he realised he had forgotten his cue towel. There was Ronnie practising, homework or not.

'He hadn't liked losing but he couldn't stop playing,' Ken recalled.

The 12-year-old Ronnie was, Ken said, 'spoilt rotten'. Everything was laid on a plate for him, except his father's praise. In a few years, Ronnie and Ken drifted apart and later became rivals. 'He got in with the wrong people, got into drugs and wasn't a very nice person for a while. I didn't speak to him for a couple of years over an incident with a girlfriend of mine but we eventually patched it up.'

Ken found Ronnie senior, as most did, a mixture; 'flash and cocky but also funny and warm, the sort of person you'd be a bit wary of but also happy to be friends with and have him looking out for you'. Very generous with money, Ronnie senior helped out many a young snooker hopeful without wanting to be repaid, although violence sometimes came to the surface.

Mark King, who was to achieve a career-best ranking of eleventh, was another Essex boy, 18 months older than Ronnie, hoping to make it in snooker. His father, Bill, once admonished Ronnie for some misdemeanour or other and was promptly knocked to the floor by Ronnie senior.

One day, Ronnie came home from school with a bloodied nose from a playground scrap. Next day, his father was waiting with a baseball bat for the boy who had inflicted it. He did not use it but it nevertheless sent a message.

Ronnie was naturally bright, often producing a vivid turn of phrase, but school interested him only sporadically. Beyond the basics, and like many others, he could not immediately see what education was for since he was going to be a professional snooker player anyway. He was a moderately talented footballer, good enough to train later with Tottenham Hotspur and Leyton Orient without making a fool of himself, and at the instigation of his father, who appreciated the importance of fitness even for a not very aerobic sport like snooker, he was a dedicated runner.

One of his school friends, two years ahead of him, was Andy Goldstein, a useful player himself and subsequently a talented television and radio sports presenter.

'When he was about 15, I used to drive Ronnie to Ilford [Snooker Club]. One night, he was on a maximum. He got to 140, finished straight on the black, about nine inches behind it – and started pulling the balls out of the pockets for the next frame.' What was he doing? What about the 147?

'Not boastfully at all but just very matter of fact, Ronnie said, "I wasn't going to miss it, was I?"'

In February 1991, Barry Hearn promoted a £1m World Masters tournament that included a world under-16 Junior Masters. Its field of 32 included three future world champions, Ronnie, John Higgins and Mark Williams, and several others who became respected professionals. Ronnie almost did not get to the starting line. He was sitting at home believing that his first match was the next day when a phone call abruptly convinced him otherwise. In best Formula One fashion, his father drove his Mercedes to the National Exhibition Centre on the south side of Birmingham so that Ronnie made the deadline with just a few minutes to spare. Only 38 minutes later, he was rounding off his 3-0 first-round win with a break of 106, the highest of the competition. Foreshadowing the countless battles they were to have as professionals, he lost 5-4 in the quarter-finals to Higgins, who beat Williams 6-1 in the final.

Shortly afterwards, in the quarter-finals of the Southern section of the English Amateur Championship at Aldershot, while still only 15, Ronnie became the youngest player and only the third amateur to make a 147 in competition.

When he won the tournament, *Snooker Scene* wrote: 'Twice British under-16 champion, it has become apparent since his first appearance on the scene at the age of nine that O'Sullivan is in the [Stephen] Hendry/[Jimmy] White class for natural ability. That does not make it certain that he will emulate their achievements but he is certainly proceeding well on schedule and appears to have the necessary attitude and commitment.'

It was widely assumed that Ronnie would beat Steve Judd, the Northern section winner, in the national final at Leeds and thus, at 15 years six months, supersede White as the youngest ever amateur champion, but it did not work out that way.

As a professional, Judd never made the top 100 but in that two-day final he potted like a demon and went 5-1 up. It was 8-8 going into the final session but Judd won its first two frames, was always at least a frame in front thereafter and clinched victory at 13-10.

'I didn't think I could get beat before the final,' Ronnie admitted. '[But] every time I left Steve a pot, he knocked it in. I couldn't get in front the whole match. I'm not too down about the record.

'I've got a lifetime ahead of me. I've had a lot more good days than bad.'

On his way to Leeds for that final, Ronnie had called in at the Crucible, where the World Championship was under way. Such was his air of confidence and maturity that it was difficult to believe that he was only 15. One incident did strike me, though. Ronnie picked out 15 first-round winners in an accumulator. Common sense argued that he would still win quite heavily if he laid off his selection for the last match, but he let everything ride on it and lost the lot. It was perhaps a demonstration of Ronnie's all-or-nothing temperament, which on the snooker table could be satisfied only by peak performance, not just by winning.

Just before that final, Barry Hearn signed Ronnie to a three-year management contract. The World Professional Billiards and Snooker Association (WPBSA) had announced that the professional ranks would be open to all for the 1991/92 season but, with a minimum age limit of 16, Ronnie was not among the new intake of 443 aspirants.

In the meantime, Ronnie became the youngest ever world under-21 champion in Bangalore, outclassing the opposition in every match except for a tight 5-4 in the last 16 against a New Zealander, Mark Canovan.

Back home and still an amateur, there were tournaments to compete in every weekend. Ronnie won first prizes of £800 at Stevenage and £2,500 at Pontins, Prestatyn and on his form in the early rounds of the World Amateur Championship in Bangkok, Ronnie would have become its youngest ever champion but for real life intervening in the form of his father's arrest.

Chapter 3

[1992]

ONCE the initial shock of seeing his father in prison garb had eased, even more so after he was granted bail, Ronnie was putting the future to the back of his mind when he suffered another devastating emotional blow.

Chris Brooks, who was 16, was his best friend and a good player. They won the Essex doubles together three times in succession. They were driven up to Birmingham for a tournament and when Chris lost he was ready to go home, either immediately or if Ronnie, whose match stood at 2-2, lost the fifth-frame decider.

Ronnie won, there were other lifts available and so he played on while Chris and another young player, Martin Carolan, went home. They never got there. Both were killed when the car in which they were travelling crashed on a notorious bend at 70mph. As Ronnie could so easily have been in that car, some residual survivor's guilt possibly became a component in the savage depressions that he was later to suffer.

Ronnie lost 3-1 to a young professional, Jason Whittaker, in the quarter-finals of that tournament and was accepted on 1 January 1992 as a professional eligible for the summer qualifying competitions for world ranking events. He wanted to complete his amateur commitments by winning the English Amateur Championship but from 4-1 up he lost 8-5 in the southern final to 17-year-old Stephen Lee, later a world number five and later still banned for 12 years for match fixing. The longer that competition went on, the worse Ronnie played. He was already no stranger to the immense pressures of fulfilling the expectations of others and perhaps himself. Jimmy White, by a margin of four months, therefore remained the youngest ever English amateur champion.

Ronnie spent the summer of '92 at the Norbreck Castle Hotel, Blackpool, where tables had been erected in 22 grey three-walled cells for pre-qualifying and qualifying matches for the 1992/93 season's ten world ranking events. In the second year of the WPBSA's open house policy, its membership had grown to 719 and results were churned out on an industrial scale, more than 5,000 of them. In his first professional match, in UK Championship qualifying, Ronnie made a break of 115 in beating Jason Scott 5-2. Somebody pointed out that because of the arcane exemption system based on previous rankings, he had to win 11 more matches to reach the televised phase.

Many of the new aspirants were destined to remain non-earning professionals. How some of them could ever have imagined that they could make a living, or even part of a living, from their snooker skills was a mystery, but they had paid their £500 enrolment fee, £200 subscription and £100 entry fee per tournament and their money was as good as anyone else's.

In Rothmans Grand Prix qualifying, Ronnie superseded by 34 seconds Jimmy White's record for the fastest 5-0 win in competition by beating Jason Curtis in only 43 minutes 26 seconds. He won his first 38 matches, overtaking Stephen Hendry's record of 35, although the quality of Ronnie's opposition was frequently not up to much. As fit as he was, though, he found it tiring to play a best-of-nine virtually every day.

Getting out of bed for his first-round qualifying match in the British Open, he moved awkwardly and cricked his neck. Despite playing in a neck brace, he won his first two matches 5-0 but his winning streak ended in the sixth round with a 5-3 loss to Sean Storey who, a few years later, qualified for the Crucible and also earned a measure of fame within the sport by making two 147 breaks in the same day in a pro-am at Mexborough, Yorkshire.

After 51 matches, Ronnie's record stood at 50 wins, of which no fewer than 21 had been whitewashes, with 17 5-1 victories for good measure. He had made 14 centuries. His father spent most of that summer at Blackpool, disbursing various loans he never expected or even wanted to be repaid.

He also put £100 behind the bar for the late Eddie Sinclair, a notoriously thirsty Scottish player, although even this had to be topped up before closing time.

Ronnie's sixty-fifth match at Blackpool ended in a 5-0 defeat by Dave Finbow but the Blackpool snooker factory continued beyond the qualifying competitions to reduce fields still further if only 16 or 32 players were required for an event's final venue.

When Ronnie beat Jimmy White 5-1 to earn a place in the 16-man field for the final stage of the European Open in Tongeren six months later, he was elated. 'I knew I had the ability to beat someone of Jimmy's class if I hit form,' said Ronnie. 'I feel a hundred miles an hour. I'm still pumping with adrenaline.'

Generous as ever, White said: 'My safety just wasn't there and the way Ronnie was playing it was certain heavy punishment. I like the way he plays, fast and fearless.'

Having won 70 of his 72 matches at Blackpool, Ronnie faced four more best-of-19s to qualify for the televised phase of the World Championship at the Crucible. He never looked like losing and in the eleventh and final qualifying round beat Mark Johnston-Allen 10-4 to become the youngest ever qualifier for the Crucible – although he was to be two months older than Hendry had been on his debut when he first hit a ball in snooker's most famous arena.

Any euphoria Ronnie was feeling vanished swiftly. His father had been on bail for several months but was back in jail just before and during his three-week trial at the Old Bailey.

Ronnie kept unpleasant reality in the back of his mind but the day after qualifying for the Crucible he was back home in time for the verdict. Sitting in his grandfather's house, he learned from his aunt Barbara that his father had been sentenced to life imprisonment, with a recommendation that he serve a minimum of 18 years, to run concurrently with other convictions for wounding with intent, assault and affray. His friend, Edward O'Brien, was sentenced to two years for affray.

With excessive optimism, Ronnie senior had rejected the chance to plead guilty to manslaughter and had expected to be acquitted. During the trial, he bought another sex shop. The likely outcome was never properly faced and he declined to give evidence in his own defence, which was that he had not stabbed anyone. He had the right to silence, even though the jury was entitled to interpret this as an admission of guilt. He could have said, 'There was a fight. It was him or me.' But he said nothing, nor did he accept offers from the boxer Nigel Benn and others to give evidence that he was no racist.

The perceived element of racism may have added as much as six years to the sentence passed by Mr Justice Hobhouse, who said, 'Drink is no excuse for any crime. This was a very unpleasant attack, which included elements of racial harassment and quite gratuitous and disproportionate violence.'

Certainly the words Ronnie senior had used prior to and during the assault were racist, although when fuelled by drink and anger, words are not always carefully picked. Rather, as expressions of dislike, there may have been a tendency to attack the victim through focusing on the most obvious characteristic, in this case, his colour.

When the sentence was passed, friends and family of the victim cheered. Opposing factions in the public gallery traded abuse. The police were called to restore order. Ronnie senior took it all impassively. Next morning, young Ronnie noticed how eerily quiet the family home was.

Chapter 4

[1992–94]

RONNIE senior was sentenced on 21 September 1992. Only three weeks later, while still trying to come to terms with this, Ronnie was being tested in a higher league of competition.

Beaten 5-3 by Gary Wilkinson in his first match in the Rothmans Grand Prix at Reading, he admitted that he would need time to adjust to the special pressures generated by competing in a large public venue: 'I know that nerves are part and parcel of a competitive match but they stopped me playing naturally. I looked round the audience a couple of times and it felt special. It's completely different to Blackpool.'

Wilkinson, world number eight at the time, said, 'I felt like the underdog. I know he's only 16 but he's going on 28. It's like he's been playing all his life. He's definitely got the game to win titles – even this season.'

The influence of Barry Hearn, who had managed him since April 1992, saw Ronnie included in invitation events like the Humo Masters in Antwerp, where he beat Peter Ebdon and Mike Hallett before losing 6-5 to James Wattana, then the world number seven, in the semi-finals. He then became the youngest player to win a professional tournament, a four-man round robin in Bangkok, when wins over Alan McManus and Wattana made his defeat by John Parrott irrelevant. Ronnie pocketed a £10,500 first prize.

At Preston in the UK Championship, he beat the Canadian champion Alain Robidoux, coming from 7-4 down to win 9-7 but, quoted at 1-12 by the bookmakers, was perhaps overconfident against the wily Welsh veteran Cliff Wilson. Neither did it help, when the match got close, that Ronnie became aware that Jimmy White had bet £4,000 on him to win and did not want to let him down.

When Ronnie made a 145 total clearance to lead 4-1, he appeared to be cruising. He had set his heart on playing Stephen Hendry, the world champion and runaway world number one, in the first televised round but the burden of pressure became evident as Wilson levelled at 4-4. Trailing 8-7, he showed his mettle with a match-saving 78 break but failed to convert two chances in the deciding frame and lost 9-8.

'He treated me with contempt at the start,' said Wilson. 'He'd obviously seen me play in the qualifiers at Blackpool. When I started to come back at him he [clearly] thought, "The silly old bugger can play!" Then I saw him sweating.'

There was another setback against Neal Foulds, who beat Ronnie 5-0 in the Welsh Open.

'I thought of myself as the underdog before the match and that helped me get the correct attitude,' said Foulds. 'I was trying so hard, it hurt. Ronnie is going to have all the top players throwing the kitchen sink at him because they know what a phenomenal talent he is.'

A lesson was painfully learned at the European Open in Antwerp, when Ronnie was 3-0 up on Andy Hicks in their quarter-final in only 34 minutes before losing 5-4.

'I should have played a lot tighter when I was 3-0 up,' said Ronnie. 'Maybe I was rushing, maybe the pressure got to me because I did begin to feel it.'

Ronnie's potting and break making were already as formidable as anyone's, except possibly Hendry's, but his tactical game, his balance between attack and defence and simply the need for more experience, meant that his rookie professional season, even though it included 30 centuries, was not a tale of constant success.

In the Asian and British Opens, for instance, he took the worthy scalps of Steve James and Dean Reynolds respectively but lost 5-2 to Joe Swail, who was still ranked above him, and 5-4 to Drew Henry, who was just below. Nor was Ronnie's Crucible debut the triumph some expected as he lost 10-7 in the first round to Alan McManus, who went on to reach the semi-finals and end the season with a ranking of sixth.

Snooker Scene reported that 'for all his maturity and poise, pressure appeared to affect his performance. It is perhaps too easily forgotten that he is only 17. Some brilliant long pots were counterbalanced by unforced errors but he showed true grit and a quality of safety play recently enhanced by practising regularly with Steve Davis.'

Ronnie was still in it at 7-7 but McManus, who had already played many tense matches in the game's chief theatres of war, brought out his best in the closing stages to clinch victory with a three-frame winning streak.

Realistic in defeat, Ronnie said, 'He got stronger and I got weaker towards the end. He potted the crucial balls, I didn't. I'm gutted but I wasn't really good enough. I missed a lot of middle-distance pots and you can't afford to do that.'

Four rookies won places in the top 128 in the end-of-season rankings, thus excusing them from several rounds of qualifying competitions for the 1993/94 season. Able to count only one season's points as opposed to the two that more experienced professionals could, it showed just how good that quartet was and what golden futures lay ahead for them.

Ronnie was ranked 57, Stephen Lee 101, Mark Williams 119 and John Higgins 122. Stephen Hendry, John Parrott, Jimmy White and Steve Davis occupied the top four places.

For all his worries about his father, Ronnie found the challenges and new experiences of life on the circuit sufficiently stimulating to keep him, for the most part, well focused on his snooker but it was nevertheless difficult at times to keep his sense of loss at bay. Nor had he fully comprehended just how wide an expanse of time 18 years was.

His father was his anchor, the one he needed to keep reminding him to do the right things. Ronnie was running every day, going to the gym frequently, trying to eat healthily and not drink or smoke but, on his own, this regimen was not easy to maintain and it grew harder. It was hardest of all in the summer, when there were no tournaments to sharpen an immediate sense of purpose or the need for self-denial.

He was still in good shape for the start of the 1993/94 season, winning all ten of the qualifying matches he played to reach the main venues. In the first of these, the Dubai Classic, Ronnie beat Foulds 5-0, an exact reversal of their Welsh Open encounter, Willie Thorne 5-1 and Peter Ebdon 5-2 before learning another valuable lesson in losing 6-2 to Hendry in his first world ranking semi-final, which was not the match they both expected it to be.

'I didn't feel under a lot of pressure, although I should have,' said Hendry. 'The result revolved around me making several good clearances when they really counted.'

Ronnie admitted that he had been a little too excited. 'I thought I had to play mega. I was surprised I had so many chances but I didn't know what to do with them.'

Hendry had a clear vision beyond that match. 'He's a future world champion and already capable of beating anyone in the game, myself included.'

Ronnie was comprehensively outplayed 5-1 by John Parrott in the Grand Prix at Reading, but in sublime fashion earned a debut appearance in the Masters at Wembley Conference Centre by winning its qualifying tournament in Edinburgh.

His 5-4 win over Ebdon was one of the matches of the season. Ebdon, making breaks of 120, 50 and 114, led 3-1 and then 4-3 by stealing the seventh frame with a 74 clearance from 0-62 before Ronnie scythed through the last two with 98 and 104 to win 5-4. In the next round, he completed a 5-1 win over Peter Francisco with successive breaks of 116, 117 and 138, only the sixth hat-trick of centuries recorded in competition.

There was now no stopping Ronnie and with a 9-6 win over John Lardner in the final he pocketed the first prize of £5,000, plus a guarantee of at least another £7,000 from the Masters itself. Immediately, his thoughts turned to his father, who had kept in touch with the progress of the match by telephone from D-wing, Wormwood Scrubs.

'I can't wait to show my dad the trophy. I'm more pleased for him than I am for myself. Without my dad, I couldn't have done this. He gave me more support than anyone could ask for.'

Within 36 hours, Ronnie had to come down from this emotional high for the UK Championship at Preston. 'I had no trouble getting the adrenaline going because Alan is the type of player I've got to prove myself against,' he said after beating Alan McManus 9-5.

McManus was impressed. 'Ronnie is a top-four player at the moment. I've played against all the big boys but none of them played any better than Ronnie did today.'

Ronnie was not so impressive in his 9-8 win over Nigel Gilbert, an able journeyman distinguishable by wearing a cotton glove on his bridge hand. His memories of the Wilson match were all too vivid: 'It was *déjà vu*. I just had visions of last year all the time.'

Patently edgy and prone to irritation at the slightest distraction, Ronnie allowed himself to be upset by Gilbert's relatively slow pace of play. Relative, that is, to Ronnie, for he was actually no slower than dozens of others.

'He was so slow and bogged me down and I couldn't get going. I wouldn't have said anything if I'd lost because it would have been sour grapes, but there was no way he could beat me on ability and skill.'

Uncharacteristically, Ronnie suggested that his opponent's inadvertent rattling of an ice bucket in the first frame of the second session was an act of gamesmanship, although he admitted an hour after his press conference that this was unjustified.

'If there was anything wrong Ronnie should have told me during the match, rather than go whingeing to the press,' said Gilbert, whose behaviour had invariably been exemplary in his seven years as a professional.

This incident hinted at just how tightly Ronnie was strung and was the first sign of the psychological difficulty he was to have against opponents capable of frustrating him by keeping a series of frames tight and slow. Modest as he has always been, Ronnie knew that his game was far superior to these sorts of opponents but was inclined to become irritated if he could not just sweep them aside. Much later in his career, he had little relish for the sort of matches he could expect from tenacious adversaries like Peter Ebdon, Mark Selby and Graeme Dott. He was unreceptive to the idea that there is sometimes more than one way to win a snooker match and seemed even to believe, at times, that he should be able to beat such opponents without having to try his hardest.

From 6-2 at the interval, Ronnie held off Ken Doherty 9-5 to become the youngest quarter-finalist in the event's 16-year history: 'I know Ken very well and I know he's got fighting qualities, so I took nothing for granted, even with a big lead. I've made a lot of sacrifices I didn't make last season. I realised I wasn't practising hard enough.'

Neither was Ronnie carried away by his 9-6 win over Steve Davis. 'Steve played terrible and I fed off his errors. That was basically it. It was sad watching him, a bit like falling out with your first girlfriend. That wasn't the Steve Davis I'd practised with. He just didn't fire.'

Ronnie was selling his own performance short, a habit that was to become deeply ingrained. His father was far away but nevertheless a voice in Ronnie's head. Winning was rarely quite enough and was not when he beat Darren Morgan, his third top-ten victim of the tournament, 9-5 in their semi-final. 'I'm a bit disappointed,' Ronnie admitted. 'I've played patchy stuff today and in most of my matches but I'm still through to the final.'

In the other semi-final, Hendry played to a standard that, even at his most downbeat, Ronnie would have been pleased with. In the afternoon session against John Parrott, he made four centuries in five frames in establishing a 7-1 lead and went on to win 9-3. He was a heavy odds-on favourite for the final but Ronnie, 6-2 up at the interval, beat him 10-6 to become, a week short of his 18th birthday, the youngest ever ranking title winner, superseding Hendry, who had won the 1987 Rothmans Grand Prix at the age of 18 years nine months.

'Ronnie plays the game like I used to,' said Hendry. 'He's fearless and frightened of no one. I felt good going into the final but he ran away with it. I expected him to miss a few easy balls here and there but he didn't.'

The thunderous reception Ronnie received left him in a state of shock. 'After getting a taste of this, I want more. To beat Steve Davis and Stephen Hendry in the same tournament, I can't believe it. They are snooker. I'm determined not to let this be a flash in the pan.'

Ronnie and his father were always able to keep in touch by phone at certain times of the day and spoke three or four times on the day of the UK final. 'Ten minutes before the final session, he wished me luck and told me he'd be watching. Everybody in the jail was watching the game in their cells and there was lots of screaming and shouting. He couldn't see the end of the game because of lights out but he had reports phoned to him. After I won, he was really choked. I could tell by his voice.

'He gave me very good encouragement. He's the only person who says things that really go into my head. My dad never pushed me but he said, "If you want to do what I did and be a car park attendant for years and clean a few windows, then that's up to you. But if you want to have a good life, like Steve Davis, it takes a lot of practice and early nights and this and that."'

The practice was happening mid-morning until 8pm, with a break for lunch on every non-tournament day at either Upton Park or Ilford. As with a concert pianist, practice is for fusing technique, fluency and feeling.

'It's about ridding yourself of fear,' Ronnie remarked, the theory being that only self-imposed mental barriers stopped players succeeding with shots in matches that they regularly accomplished in practice.

Barry Hearn, his manager, said of snooker's young generation of players, 'They've had ten years of watching Steve Davis on television. They've taken that TV knowledge and added to it the impetuosity of youth. They've removed the nerve ends and added more attack. Ronnie will bring in a whole load of new viewers and also extend the commercial boundaries.'

In the midst of triumph, Ronnie himself maintained an endearing purity of desire. 'Money's not everything. Winning snooker tournaments is what I want to do. It's fine being the best player at 17 but I want to be the best player when I'm 21, when I'm the finished article. I've got a long way to go until then. Your peak at snooker is when you're about 25 or 26. Davis, Parrott, [Alex] Higgins, White – they all hit their peak when they were that age.

'I'm over the worst now,' he said of his father's imprisonment. 'It's a shame but life goes on.' Of course it does but, like a bereavement, he was to feel the pangs of enforced separation sporadically for many years and there was to be much more family trauma to cope with.

More immediately, taking the trophy to show his father, by then transferred to Gartree prison, Leicester, was a joyous occasion. Many inmates gathered for autographs and photographs. Even prison officers entered into the spirit of the day by taking polaroids of father and son with the trophy. Ronnie said, 'Dad was just so proud it made me feel nine feet tall.

'I've grown up a lot since [he went to prison] but I've got over it and come to terms with what happened. I'm a man. I wasn't going to crumble when my dad got sent to prison. The only way he's going to feel strong is if I'm strong. I'm trying to do myself proud and at the same time do him proud. The buzz of doing well for him keeps me going. I listen to everything he says. He's awesome. I don't think I'd have got here today unless it was for him. He's always kept me down to earth. He said to me, "I love you for being my son, not for being a snooker player."'

This day was, of course, a fleeting interlude in Ronnie senior's drab and featureless existence. The inescapable reality was that Ronnie senior would remain in prison for many years and it began to dawn on Ronnie that he would never enjoy the quality years that he expected to share with him. His love for and loyalty to his father, who was even more of a hero to him than most fathers are to their sons, was touching and admirable, and he loved talking about him as if this might in some strange way give him a life separate from his tedious incarceration.

'My dad had the sort of charisma of Al Pacino. He had a lot of style and a lot of class. He could put on a bin liner and look good. I love visiting him. I love seeing him. I love talking to him.

'He's always buzzing and positive. I think he's done pretty well for himself. I know he's ended up where he's ended up … so have a lot of people. That doesn't make them bad people. It's just being in the wrong place at the wrong time. It could happen to anybody.'

Not everybody would rationalise it in these terms and, like any son and many before him, he idealised his father without realising that he did not have to do so in order to love him. Perhaps this was why – or at least partly why – in the bouts of depression he was to suffer he tended to blame others for nothing and himself for everything.

The emotional boost of the UK title and the prison visit was still running through Ronnie's veins when he went to Antwerp for the European Open, where he beat Willie Thorne 5-4, Ken Doherty 5-2, Steve Davis 5-3 and Jimmy White 6-3 before losing 9-5 to Hendry in the final.

'I wasn't in the right frame of mind at Preston. I was waiting for him to make mistakes and for a world number one that's ridiculous,' Hendry said.

'Stephen played really well tonight. I knew he would,' said Ronnie. 'There's a major talent. His long potting just eats them, he's head and shoulders above the rest. I lost frames I should have won, particularly the 12th [when I was trailing only 6-5]. After that, I knew I was vulnerable.'

After Christmas, there were qualifying matches to play at Blackpool. There was a 5-4 loss ('I played like an idiot') to his old Ilford sparring partner Mark King, but he won all the other matches necessary to reach the main venues, even if he found himself 'forced to admit that when you've been in a UK final and won a big title like that, playing here is a bit of a comedown'.

Even world championship qualifying did not quite feel as if it was attached to snooker's blue riband event. Down 8-6 to Andy Hicks, he said, 'I was really under the cosh. It meant so much to me to get to the Crucible and all I kept thinking about was not getting there after such a great season.' He came through 10-8 but had another struggle to beat Tony Jones 10-8 from 9-5 up in the final qualifying round.

All this was emotionally draining. Inspiration was entirely lacking when he went out 5-3 in the first round of the Welsh Open at Newport to Paul McPhillips, one of an army of useful Scots. 'If you play like an idiot, you've got to expect to lose. I'm disappointed with myself. I looked at it beforehand as a good draw but Paul played better than I thought he would.'

There was more to it than just an off day. Indeed, Ronnie may have been experiencing his first bout of depression. 'I just can't concentrate and enjoy it when I go to the club to practise,' he said after making countless mistakes in his inglorious 5-1 loss to Dennis Taylor on his Masters debut.

Later that week, Ronnie went to watch some boxing at Brentwood, just up the road from his home, and received a warm ovation as he was introduced from the ring. At about this time, 9pm, a woman went into Chigwell police station to complain that she had been followed by men who had forced her off the road. As she left the station, a white Rover cruised past and she was bundled into it.

Computer searches revealed that Ronnie owned a white Rover, so four carloads of police swooped on his house in the dead of night. Despite having an alibi that could have been supported by more than a thousand people, Ronnie was detained in a police cell for 16 hours before he was released without charge.

This did nothing to reduce Ronnie's suspicion, right or wrong, that the police's approach to his family was vindictive. In previous skirmishes with the law in the sex shop business, Ronnie senior had not adopted a respectful attitude towards the police and this was perhaps remembered.

Ronnie lost 5-0 in the first round of the Thailand Open to James Wattana, who played superbly and went on to win the tournament. Bad news awaited when Ronnie's flight from Bangkok touched down at Heathrow. The police, again mob-handed, had arrested his mother at the family home at 5am and for four days she had been in a cell at Lime Street police station.

Ronnie senior had continued to run his sex shop empire by phone from prison, oblivious to the printed notice on the wall stating that all calls would be recorded and monitored.

Ronnie's mother, a sleeping director of the family companies and a signatory to cheques and official documents, was charged with a £230,000 VAT fraud. Bail was fixed at £250,000. Young Ronnie put up a (returnable) £100,000 surety, Barry Hearn the other £150,000 and there the matter rested until the trial date of 7 June 1994.

After some fallow months, Ronnie rose above his family problems to win the British Open at Plymouth. In the first round, he beat Peter Ebdon, who was to remain a career-long rival, 5-4. In the eighth frame, with Ebdon needing two snookers, Ronnie very sportingly called a foul on himself when he thought he saw the cue ball make the thinnest of contacts on the adjacent blue. The referee did not think so and Sky's cameras could not confirm it, but Ronnie was adamant. Ebdon obtained the other snooker he needed to make it 4-4 but Ronnie, with impeccable and in the circumstances surprising composure, controlled the decider. Like most professionals on the circuit, Ronnie has always adhered to a strict code of on-table ethics. It is part of his regard for the game.

Next up, he beat Willie Thorne 5-2 and then, from two down with three to play, Ken Doherty 5-4.

'With the World Championship just around the corner, it's good to know you can produce the goods under pressure. It's my best comeback,' said Ronnie, who throughout his career was to win most of his matches from the front. He tended to be behind only when he was struggling for form.

His 5-0 quarter-final win over Nigel Bond in only 68 minutes was a devastating exhibition of everything from delicate touches to piledrivers, and he was too good both for an off-colour Hendry 6-2 in the semi-finals and a subdued Wattana 9-4 in the final.

'I felt vibes that James wasn't enjoying himself. I felt like the daddy out there. I felt I could control things,' said Ronnie, who was naturally pleased to have won his second ranking title but was refusing to get carried away. 'I'm only 18,' he said. 'I've got a lot to learn.'

At the Crucible, Ronnie pulled away from 5-5 to beat Dennis Taylor 10-6, but produced only glimpses of his quality in losing 13-3 with a session to spare to John Parrott, who had won all four of their previous meetings.

'John played better than me in every department of the game,' Ronnie acknowledged. 'His long potting was accurate, his break building was solid and his safety kept me out. You can't ask for more than that.' Ronnie's season thus ended with him ninth in the world rankings, inside the top 16 and therefore exempted from all pre-qualifying and most qualifying competitions for the following season.

Chapter 5

[1994/95]

ALTHOUGH his father was in prison and his mother facing a criminal trial, Ronnie's life remained as stable as these circumstances allowed through the summer of 1994 but he welcomed the start of the new season because the tournaments provided something on which he could focus.

It was to be a season in which, out of nine ranking events, he lost in two finals, two semis, four quarters and a last 16 beside becoming, at 19, the youngest ever Masters champion. It was also to be a season in which he developed his rivalries with John Higgins, with whom he appeared to be disputing the succession to Stephen Hendry as king of the sport, and Hendry himself.

The high-quality consistency and maturely balanced game of Higgins could be contrasted with Ronnie's inspirational flair and brilliance, although there were, of

44

course, times when Higgins could be inspired and Ronnie consistent.

In 100-degree temperatures at the Dubai Classic, Ronnie could usually be found practising in places the sun could not reach and beat Higgins 5-1 on his way to a semi-final he lost 6-4 to Peter Ebdon. At Derby for the Skoda Grand Prix, Ronnie was constantly outmanoeuvred in the tactical exchanges as Higgins beat him 5-0 and went on to win his maiden ranking title.

Ronnie then almost lost in the first round of the UK Championship. Against Mark Flowerdew, who retired from snooker two years later to become an accountant, he was 6-2 down at the interval when he took a furious call from his father.

'Where he is, he needs something and I'm the only thing that's keeping him alive,' said Ronnie, having taken the first six frames of the evening and gone on to win 9-7. 'Defending a title for the first time put me under pressure as well. It's a different ball game when everyone expects you to do well but I suppose in some ways that helped me focus when I was behind.'

The veteran 1979 world champion Terry Griffiths wove tactical webs round him but even after he had been shut out for long periods, Ronnie was able to find his customary fluency within a couple of shots when he did eventually get a chance. Playing such opponents was, of course, an essential part of his snooker education.

'I'm learning more about my game and getting more and more consistent,' said Ronnie. 'Terry's slow and makes the game difficult. I didn't really enjoy it. Frames just kept going on and on and I just couldn't get any rhythm. He's a mega safety player, you've got to give the fellow his due. You've got to scrape him off the table. I felt I didn't want to miss because I didn't want to sit down for another 20 minutes. I knew I had to be alert and stick in or I could have been beaten.'

Griffiths described Ronnie as 'lethal when the balls are open', adding, 'When he's hot, he's practically unstoppable and anyone who plays him at a potting game will come off second best. I had to stop him with hard safety.'

When Ronnie's title defence was terminated by Doherty, 9-7 in the quarter-finals, he took it hard and spoke for the first but far from the last time of early retirement. Doherty had been steadier, cooler and more patient; Ronnie's chief failing had been missing the odd easy ball, invariably a sign of wayward concentration. Talk of retirement was, as *Snooker Scene* said at the time, surely indicative of a deeper malaise clouding his mind rather than of simply losing a snooker match.

After starting the next tournament, the European Open in Antwerp, with a 5-2 win over Neal Foulds, Ronnie said he did not 'really care' about winning or losing. 'If I win, I win. If I lose, I lose. There's too much money to be earned from snooker to pack it in, but it's only a game and I'm not going to pull my hair out over it. I know I'm capable of winning the world championship but I'm not going to put myself through the pain barrier. For two years, I've put in eight hours practice a day and lived snooker but I can win tournaments playing two hours a day. I've told my dad what I've been telling you and he thinks I'm a mug. He's never pushed me into anything but he's sure I'll regret it. Maybe I'm just going through a phase, I don't know.'

Ronnie's mood and outlook was starting to vary from day to day. His 5-1 quarter-final win over Dave Harold prompted the loser to say, 'I've never seen snooker like that before. It was a privilege to watch. Even if I'd played to my peak, I don't think I could have touched him.'

So headlong was Ronnie's pace of play that in the first frame, on a break of 82, he was fouled for not giving the referee time to re-spot a pink before he potted his next red. Hendry, watching on the press room monitor, laughed in disbelief at some of Ronnie's shots.

'I'm strolling, not really trying,' said Ronnie. 'I've come to the conclusion that even if I get beat, I'm going to go out there and enjoy it.'

It was unrealistic to play with the same lack of inhibition in his semi-final against Hendry, a classic he lost 6-5 in a riot of potting and break building that took only 107 minutes in all.

Having made the first mistake in the decider, Hendry later admitted he 'honestly didn't expect to get back to the table because it seemed that every frame was being won in one visit'. However, three shots later, Ronnie missed an easy black off its spot to let Hendry in for his match-winning 76.

'It should be a new word in the dictionary – Hendry. It means more than excellence. You just can't afford to miss, the way he scores. There's no one in the game a patch on him,' said Ronnie. 'I'm learning just by watching how he copes with things.'

Ronnie took the opportunity to explain his remarks about retirement at the UK Championship three weeks earlier. 'At the UK, I was surrounded by idiots who planted bad seeds in my mind. Here has been a nice environment down at the club where I've been practising and I've responded to it by being happier. I really get upset when people say things to have a dig. I'm just fortunate that 99 per cent of people in the game are diamonds and if I keep away from the other one per cent I'm OK. In every sport, there are people who try to make your life a misery. I'm just pleased I'm back in the right frame of mind again and I'm looking forward to the next tournament.

'Anyway, you lot [the press] don't want to take much notice of what I say in the heat of the moment after a match, win or lose. I just get to boiling point.'

Ronnie lost again to Hendry, 5-3 from 3-1 up in the Liverpool Victoria Charity Challenge quarter-final, and survived two early 5-4s in the Welsh Open against Drew Henry, who missed a match ball, and Anthony Hamilton, who led Ronnie 3-0 and 4-1.

'I honestly thought it was going to be Anthony's day the way he was scoring early on,' said Ronnie.

This pitted him against Higgins in the quarter-final, their third clash of the season and one of the many classics they were to contest in the next 20 years.

From 3-0 down, Ronnie recovered to 3-3 and, in play with 73, was in line not only for a 4-3 lead but the £20,000 bonus for a 147 break until he overran position for his tenth black. Hastily and somewhat irritably, he lashed out at a pink that with more care he would have potted and eventually lost the frame after Higgins had needed two snookers.

Commendably, Ronnie shook off this reversal, recovered to 4-4 with a break of 75 and scored first in the decider with 68 but missed a tricky match ball red and had to watch Higgins clear up with 69 to go into the semi-finals.

It was a match in which Ronnie had shown both his extraordinary talent and the all-or-nothing excitability that sometimes undermined it. Higgins, considerably more measured, had shown not only an equivalent talent – if not so dashingly expressed – but exceptional coolness and nerve under pressure.

This was a setback but Ronnie was still in the groove and competing hungrily when he arrived at the circuit's next stop, the Masters at Wembley, although he was fortunate to survive 5-4 against John Parrott, who was leading by 40 in the deciding frame when a ghastly blunder on a dolly blue from its spot killed his momentum. This led to Ronnie getting home on the pink with a match-winning break of 58.

Nor did Ronnie have it all his own way in his 6-4 semi-final win over Peter Ebdon, but in the final against Higgins a seven-frame winning streak, embracing the last five frames of the afternoon and the first two of the evening, left him with a 7-2 lead that he went on to convert into a 9-3 victory.

'When the lights went up at the end, I got a real buzz out of seeing so many faces that I knew,' said Ronnie. 'I relish the big occasion and the big venues turn me on.'

Higgins reflected, 'When he gets on a roll, he's the hardest player in the world to stop. It's not as if you can settle into a match. He wins frames so quickly. He got stronger and I got weaker.'

There was a 5-2 first-round defeat by Mark Johnston-Allen, who had just beaten Hendry for the third time in three attempts, at the Sweater Shop International but a run to the final of the China Open included a 5-2 win over Hendry ('Ronnie played fantastic snooker, pure and simple'), although he confessed to running out of steam towards the end of the week.

The first hints that Ronnie was not cut out for long spells away from home or competing week in, week out began to surface. He thanked Tony Knowles for keeping him company, 'It gets lonely away from home but he's hung around to practise with me. I'm grateful because having him around has made me relax.'

All the same, he felt 'sloppy and lethargic' in falling 6-2 behind to James Wattana in the final. He was within a ball of levelling at 6-6 but Wattana won that frame on the black with a 50 clearance and pulled away to win 9-6.

There was a first-round defeat to Parrott in the Irish Masters but a run to the final of the British Open, where he lost to Higgins for the third time in their five meetings that season, 9-6. In those days, seedings were based for a whole season on the previous end-of-season rankings, so Ronnie met Hendry in the quarter-finals of the World Championship. After the opening frame, Hendry had his nose in front throughout and from 9-8 reached the winning post at 13-8.

After his seventh loss to Hendry in ten matches, Ronnie's admiration for him was clear. 'Stephen is class. He played really well [in the last session] and hardly missed a ball.'

Hendry described Ronnie as 'the most naturally talented player I've ever seen. He's better than Jimmy [White] or I was at that age but he's still got a lot to learn.'

For Ronnie, up to third in the rankings behind only Hendry and Steve Davis, it was a good season's work and he had £285,175 to show for it.

Chapter 6

[1995/96]

IN July 1995, 13 months after her arrest, Maria O'Sullivan was convicted of evading £250,000 VAT between September 1991 and March 1994. The initial part of her sentence of seven months, which was served in Holloway, was hellish. As the mother of a wealthy celebrity, she became a focus for the pent-up rage of many other inmates. She was physically threatened, once with a razor, and was the object of unwelcome lesbian attention. As Maria had paid off what was owing, Ronnie could not see why she had to go to prison at all. With both parents behind bars, Ronnie even had to deal with a couple of family business matters himself.

Ronnie senior's imprisonment had affected Ronnie deeply but, even if it was not for so long, his mother's affected him even more. He felt powerless to help them and whatever was left of his stability had been toppled. Suddenly, he not only had to look after himself for the first time but also his

12-year-old sister Danielle. He had lost his driving licence for speeding – 133mph down the M4 – so he could not even take her to school and his culinary expertise extended only to what he had learned from home economics classes at school.

Visiting his mother was a necessary ordeal. After she had been transferred to the more tolerable surroundings of Drake Hall open prison, Maria emphasised how enjoyable she found classes in keep fit and food hygiene – useful when she and Ronnie opened a bagel shop in Chingford – but Ronnie was in pieces, losing himself in drugs, drink and parties, including some epic ones at the family home.

There were no snooker tournaments to give direction to his aimless existence and he had no heart for practice. For his first match of the new season against John Higgins, in the Scottish Masters at Motherwell, he arrived by taxi with only five minutes to spare wearing the disenchanted expression not just of a certain loser but of someone who wanted to escape from the building as quickly as possible.

Trailing 4-1, 56-0, he threw his cue at a long red, made 41 from it, snatched the frame on the pink and reeled off three more to lead 5-4. At 5-5, a series of fearless pots, including the brown down a side cushion to a distant corner pocket, turned into the 35 clearance that gave him victory on the final pink.

Lost in snooker again for the first time in months, Ronnie brandished his fist in triumph but was subdued and unco-operative at his press conference. The journalists did not know why because reporting restrictions had been placed on Maria's imprisonment.

'Ronnie just went for everything all night as if he was taking the micky or something,' said Higgins. However, his approach took him no further and Ebdon picked him off 6-1 in the semi-finals.

Snooker Scene, as much in the dark as anyone about what lay behind Ronnie's black mood, reported after his first-round exit in the Thailand Classic, 5-4 to Mark Johnston-Allen, that he 'needed to have more respect for the game and for the abilities of his lower-ranked opponents if he is to attain the consistent success his natural talent warrants'.

Ronnie's mixture of superb shots and inexcusable errors left Johnston-Allen, the world number 49, bemused. 'In the early stages, I found it very difficult to play well and concentrate because of the way he was treating the game. You don't expect Ronnie to play so haphazardly.'

He could not quite bring himself not to try at all, even though his mind was elsewhere, partly on his father, primarily on his mother, whose predicaments made snooker seem unimportant almost to the point of irrelevance. After the most non-committal of press conferences, he rushed to the airport to catch the first flight home.

Playing with the same recklessness he had shown in Bangkok, Ronnie then lost 5-2 to Michael Duffy in his first match at the Skoda Grand Prix in Scotland, Duffy describing some of his shot selections as 'mad', but Ronnie was in a better frame of mind for the UK Championship at Preston, albeit able only sporadically to engage his higher gears. After three comfortable wins, he led Andy Hicks 5-3 at the interval of their quarter-final – at which point bookmakers were quoting him at 1-14 to win – but was beaten 9-7.

'He's good under pressure and pots the important balls,' Ronnie acknowledged with the customary fair-mindedness he shows to opponents. As for his own performance, he knew he was relying on his natural ability without underpinning it with a systematic practice regimen. Even at tournaments, his mind was not on it and his heart not in it.

In contrast, Mark King, possessing but a fraction of Ronnie's talent, was practising seven hours a day and beat him 5-3 in the first round of the German Masters in Frankfurt. Ronnie again hastened his own demise by attempting countless ill-advised pots when the odds were stacked against him. It was as if he was telling himself that losing did not really count if he was not trying his utmost to win.

There was even more bad news. Maria was due, with remission, to be released in January 1996 but was informed that, together with other family members, she was to go on trial accused of helping to run the family pornography business on the instructions from jail of Ronnie senior. No sooner had one term of imprisonment been completed than she was facing another.

In the midst of this, trying both for himself and his designated charity, the National Deaf Children's Society, Ronnie beat Ken Doherty 6-4 and John Higgins 9-6 in the last two rounds to earn £30,000 for himself and £100,000 for his charity at the Liverpool Victoria Charity Challenge in Birmingham.

'It's great to win a tournament again, especially one where other people benefit as well as yourself,' said Ronnie.

There was no one to play for but himself at the Welsh Open, where he abandoned all the self-discipline he had shown in Birmingham in losing 5-4 from 4-2 up, to Billy Snaddon, hitting some balls ferociously hard and taking on one risky pot after another.

At last, Ronnie's luck turned, albeit with a farcical twist. Maria's trial had started at Southwark when the judge's attention was drawn to a snooker article in *The Sun*, not something that happens every day. He ruled that some of the O'Sullivan family details in it were prejudicial to her receiving a fair trial. Two jurors had read the piece. Maria was told she was free to go.

This revitalised Ronnie's defence of the Masters title, although he could have lost in the first round. Having totalled only five points in going 3-0 down to Nigel Bond and later 4-1 adrift, he went from poor to brilliant in a trice to score 392 unanswered points, including two centuries, in going 5-4 up. Still a decider was required before Ronnie won it on the pink to go through 6-5.

'This tournament really means a lot to me,' said Ronnie, having played for the previous few months as if snooker did not mean very much at all. 'If I'd lost, I would have been gutted and that's why the last frame was Twitch City. There was a spell when I couldn't miss. But that's the way I can play sometimes.'

Ronnie then shot himself in the foot or, rather, kicked it against a concrete-mounted potted plant after a row with his girlfriend. On a lesser occasion, he would have certainly withdrawn from the tournament. As it was, no one could have predicted that he would move round the table more slowly than his quarter-final opponent Darren Morgan as he eked out a 6-4 win.

'It must have been off-putting for Darren,' said Ronnie. 'I brought him down to my level. That's the only reason I won. If he'd played his normal game, he would have won. I just had to grind.'

Heavy bruising and strained ligaments were diagnosed. A variety of treatments was used, from lasers and cream to painkillers and immersing his foot in an ice bucket for ten-minute spells. As a result, between Thursday evening, when he had to be virtually carried to a car, and his Saturday afternoon semi-final, Ronnie's condition had significantly improved. The ice bucket was still coming into play and he wore a two-piece plaster cast in addition to his normal footwear. He could not play at his usual headlong pace but this did not seem to be to his disadvantage as he beat Andy Hicks 6-1.

'This could be a blessing in disguise because it's making my game more solid and cautious,' said Ronnie. 'I've got a good safety game, you know. I just don't use it very often.'

Next day, with his injury continuing to respond to treatment, he was much less severely handicapped but lost 10-5 to Hendry, who thus won his sixth Masters title in eight attempts.

In his characteristic way, Ronnie was both generous and realistic. 'Stephen deserves everything he gets. He's got tunnel vision, he's totally single minded and he's got a lot more discipline than me. That's why he's where he is in the game.'

All true but could anyone have maintained tunnel vision on snooker in the midst of the family traumas Ronnie had to endure?

Having played in front of a Wembley full house of 2,198 in the Masters final, Ronnie was one of many top players left with a sense of anti-climax when the next tournament on the circuit was played in the more spartan setting of a sports centre in Swindon. The top ten in the rankings all lost early – Ronnie 5-3 to Fergal O'Brien – and Higgins won the tournament. Yet another first-round exit, his fifth in seven ranking events, came when he lost 5-4 to Dave Finbow in the European Open in Malta.

'He's a joy to play at the moment because of the shots he takes on and his speed round the table means you're bound to get plenty of chances,' said Finbow, who was not among those amused by Ronnie clearing the colours left-handed in one the frames he won. 'He's a tremendous player but he should give his opponent and the game more respect.'

As he always had and always would, Ronnie treated Higgins with exemplary respect but still lost 5-3 to him in the second round of the Thailand Open. After another first-round exit, 6-5 to Joe Swail in the Irish Masters, he said, 'I'm low on confidence and everyone can see I'm struggling.'

In addition to any off-table influences that might have been at work the mere fact of losing, for whatever reason, tends to erode confidence. He was also paying a delayed penalty for abandoning his practice and training routine when his mother was in prison.

Ronnie came to the British Open in Plymouth having lost often enough – for whatever combination of reasons – for opponents not to be afraid of him.

'I've got beat by some really bad players, as it happens, but they've played well, you know what I'm saying, and I haven't. And if I'm not playing well, these players aren't scared.'

At Plymouth he won three matches, including beating Graeme Dott 5-1 and Ken Doherty 5-3, and felt he was 'a little bit fresher in the mind … playing a little bit better', but could not help comparing this with how he plays when his mind, and therefore his hand-eye co-ordination, is stuck flush on the right wavelength.

'It's an instinct game for me. I get to the table and just know what to do but sometimes when I'm struggling it's a really hard game and that's where your Hendrys and Higginses are more clinical. I'm more of an on-the-day sort of player, which isn't really good.

'I know you've got to dig deep sometimes and I haven't done that. You've got to be up for it and to be honest I haven't been up for it. I haven't really practised at all. I haven't enjoyed it, you know.

'I can honestly say that there's no adrenalin flowing sometimes and this game is all about adrenalin. I haven't been pumped up going out there. I wanna be nervous, you know, wary, and I'm not wary of anyone.'

In the quarter-finals, Ronnie beat Mark Williams, who made up the trio of competitors in the World Junior Masters in 1991 who were to win world titles, but who was then taking a little longer than Ronnie or Higgins to reach top level. Ronnie's 5-3 victory in a fine, fast-flowing match showed a return to form and a sense of enjoyment. When safely past the post, his last four shots were taken right-handed, left-handed and two one-handed. This was showmanship but why not? Williams was as amused as anybody.

Ronnie lost 6-4 to Hendry in the semi-finals but again did enough to show that he could be a threat at the Crucible, although he let himself down badly, late at night, with toilets available, by urinating against an inner wall of the venue. Whether this was simply oafish, a reversion to infantile behaviour after all the pressures he had endured, or some kind of inarticulate protest against he knew not what is unclear and in a sense immaterial as Michael Ganley, one of the WPBSA backstage officials on duty, reported the matter to his superiors. This report was to contribute to a much more serious incident at the Crucible.

Chapter 7

[1996/97]

FOR Ronnie, the 1996 World Championship was nothing if not eventful, too eventful to give himself his best chance of winning it.

His 10-3 first-round defeat of Alain Robidoux did not end with the customary handshake. Ronnie had just made a typically swashbuckling 126 to go 8-2 up and in the eleventh frame, holding an impregnable lead, played three academic pots left-handed in attempting a crowd-pleasing clearance.

Robidoux, mild mannered and perhaps not appreciating just how well Ronnie could play left-handed, interpreted this as an attempt to belittle him. Therefore, even with the frame beyond rescue, he refused to concede.

Perversely, Ronnie would not pot the pink, which would have ended the frame, even when it ran over a pocket. There was an embarrassing eight-minute impasse live on BBC television.

'I was just enjoying myself when the frame was over and the crowd loved it,' Ronnie said afterwards, only to forfeit any sympathy for this stance when he dismissed the Canadian's performance as 'useless, rubbish ... I didn't give him any respect because he didn't deserve any'.

This lapse from the game's traditional courtesies, for which he apologised a couple of days later, was the subject of an official report.

Ronnie's 13-4 second-round win over Tony Drago occupied only two hours 12 minutes, including 13 in which Ronnie made two centuries, 100 and 120, but prior to the quarter-finals the question of whether he would be allowed to continue in the competition was to arise.

For a few years, Ronnie had been friendly with Del Hill, a snooker enthusiast who had a smallholding in Lincolnshire with a lake suitable for fishing. Ronnie would sit beside it for hours. Though not much of a player himself, Hill was a student of the game and some years later, partly through his connection with Ronnie, he established a reputation as a coach. At professional level, he was at his most useful in saying the right thing prior to a match or during intervals. Several years later, he and Ronnie became quite bitterly estranged but at the time of the 1996 World Championship they were very close.

Trouble arose through the WPBSA imposing a strict dress code in backstage areas. When Hill, Ronnie's guru and friend, appeared in the players' room wearing a pair of jeans, he was asked to leave, not in a few minutes but immediately, by Michael Ganley, who had reported Ronnie for urinating against an inner wall of the venue at Plymouth a couple of weeks earlier.

Ronnie's highly protective instincts towards family and friends were instantly activated as he flew at Ganley, punching him in the testicles and biting through his lip, an assault that fell within a definition of actual bodily harm.

'I just snapped,' Ronnie was to explain. 'I'm ashamed about what I've done but I've apologised to Mike and feel much better. He was very good about everything.'

So he may have been but this could not be allowed to pass. No one challenged his mitigation that he had acted out of character but he had nevertheless acted. A disciplinary hearing was hastily convened to determine whether he would be allowed to play his quarter-final against John Higgins. A wiser course might have been to defer the hearing until after the championship but, as it stood, the disciplinary committee had to consider not only whether Ronnie was guilty as charged but also factors like the desirability of aborting a quarter-final that was a prime television attraction or of unbalancing the event by giving Higgins a walkover into the semi-finals. There was not much doubt which way the preferences of the BBC or Embassy, the sponsors, lay.

Shortly before midnight, it was announced to the journalists and others who were there, including Higgins, that Ronnie would be fined £20,000, plus a 'voluntary' contribution to two charities, a punishment that, as it transpired, still allowed him to make a handsome profit on his prize money of £60,000.

So at 10am next day, Higgins started a quarter-final that he had been uncertain he would have to play at all. He had been appalled by what Ronnie had done, as most snooker people were, and had been honest enough not to subscribe to any romantic nonsense about not wishing to accept a walkover.

Considering the build-up to the match, its quality was exceptional. Higgins led 10-6 going into the final session but in only 47 minutes Ronnie made it 10-10. Higgins went 12-10 up but failed to convert a couple of reasonable match-winning chances as Ronnie took the three remaining frames to go through 13-12.

It was not only due to the immensity of his disappointment that Higgins offered a handshake lacking its usual warmth. Ronnie had done very well in trying circumstances, albeit of his own making, and there was no reason at all why, having been reprieved, he should not do his utmost to take advantage of it. 'I came here to give it my best,' he said. 'There's a lot of pressure at this tournament. It means so much to everyone and that's why you've never lost until the last frame. I'm not mega-elated for myself but I'm just pleased for the people around me who've stood by me.

'It means so much to my dad. It keeps him going. He said I was totally out of order. He said just to buckle down and to concentrate on playing snooker.'

Ronnie's win created an expectation that he would also beat Peter Ebdon to reach the final but with a 16-14 defeat, his last chance of becoming the youngest ever world champion disappeared.

Trailing 11-6, he started a five-frame winning streak to 11-11 with breaks of 139, 103 and 94, which would have completed what would then have been a unique hat-trick of centuries at the Crucible but for potting the last black at supersonic speed and going in-off.

Although Ronnie never took the lead, he was level at 13-13 and 14-14 but did not pot a ball in frame 29 and in frame 30 missed the last red, which he would normally have potted, to allow Ebdon to clear to the pink for victory, a reverse that Ronnie accepted graciously and perceptively. 'Work and attitude reflect on you in the end. Maybe Peter deserved it more than me because he's more focused. Sometimes I've abused the game and haven't prepared for competitions like I should do, or Peter does.

'I've learned a lot and next year, if I can do it, I'm going to gear up for all the tournaments and maybe pace myself. To win this, you have to do well in a lot of tournaments. I've lost a lot of first rounds this season. I wasn't mentally right.'

It did not occur to him to blame disturbing external events, including his mother's seven months' imprisonment, for any lack of form. Almost uniquely in the snooker world, he seemed to believe that nothing was ever anyone else's fault. It was all his own. Born with a touch of the devil in him, his judgement of the acceptable would frequently continue to waver on a thin line. Capable of pressing the self-destruct button as he was, his admirers hoped that he could retain his spontaneity and peerless ability while keeping the dark forces within him, born of bitter experiences, at bay. He had never before and was never again to show any propensity for violence, so it can only be imagined how tightly he had been strung when he lashed out at Ganley.

While Stephen Hendry was beating Ebdon 18-12 to win his sixth world title, Ronnie was absorbing news he had been given just after his own match with Ebdon. Sally Magnus, who had been his girlfriend for about a year, albeit more casually on his side than hers, was pregnant – just after, according to Ronnie's account, they had broken up as an item.

Like many a lively 20-year-old, Ronnie was interested in girls, lots of them. Girls were interested in him. At the Crucible that year, a young woman working for the BBC alleged that Ronnie had tried to seduce her. The lurid details, as well as those of Ronnie's relationship with his girlfriend, who would later give birth to their daughter, were reported extensively in the tabloid press.

Ronnie, according to her version of events, quoted in the *Daily Star*, 'kept attracting my attention and asked, "are you wearing a G-string under that?"' as a preamble to offering her an interview in his room at the Swallow Hotel. Finally, she alleged, Ronnie invited her to 'come into the toilets and show me your G-string.'

Invited to comment by the *Daily Star*, Sally, 17 at the time, said she 'can't understand why [this young lady] found it offensive. For a start, how did he know she was wearing a G-string? This girl should realise he was just having a joke with her'. She added, optimistically some thought, and in the light of his much later confirmation that he had enjoyed innumerable sexual conquests in adolescence and early manhood: 'Ronnie would never cheat on me'.

Next day, Ronnie told Sasha Jenson of the *Daily Mirror*: 'Sally isn't my woman anymore. I finished with her a long time ago. I don't know why she makes out she's my bird.' This was obviously news to Helen Magnus, Sally's mother: 'He's been saying he's dumped Sally but he's round here quick enough when he wants her. That lad's an idiot. What he needs is a good kick up the arse. I keep telling her I'm going to take her for a brain scan for going out with him but she doesn't listen. I suppose love is blind. That lad's going to get it from me. Even our dogs don't like him now.'

The *Daily Star* reported that 'just hours after crashing out of the World Championship Ronnie was knocking on the door of Sally's home, begging to be forgiven. The couple spent the rest of Saturday in his £750,000 mansion in Chigwell trying to salvage their romance. Sally then left to stay with relatives and ponder her future.'

It seems more likely that Sally's pregnancy was high on the agenda but this kind of reporting confirmed that Ronnie was already stuck in the public goldfish bowl the tabloids maintain for celebrities, an area of journalism not primarily noted for accuracy or balanced, two-sided reporting.

Jensen's *Mirror* feature actually touched on some of the inward issues influencing Ronnie's public behaviour: 'I really want a girlfriend – but there's just no time. I'm always on the road or practising. It's difficult to make it in this business. I've got a lot of pressure on me. I get really ratty and difficult to live with. No one understands what I have to go through. I'd like someone there to look after me but no one will have me. When I'm under pressure I take it out on the ones I love.

'I'm no saint but I don't pretend to be. My dad's done wrong and so have I but I'm trying to make up for it now. I'm sick of people trying to make me into the new Alex Higgins of snooker. I'm not like that.' Ronnie's initial response was one of denial, not only of paternity but of the emotional implications of parenthood. DNA testing after the Child Support Agency had threatened to obtain a court order through which it could have sequestrated one-third of his assets, not only confirmed the obvious but resulted in Sally and her mother co-operating in an aggressive 'love rat' story in the *News of the World*.

This made him look bad but far worse for him was the deadening effect on his emotions of cutting his daughter out of his life, in effect trying to pretend that she had never happened, a decision he came to regret but which he tried to put right when she was four.

Sally was not well disposed towards Ronnie playing any significant part in their daughter's life and Ronnie himself was uncomfortably aware that he was not wanted in that household. Even so, it was to prove beneficial to his emotional wellbeing that he eventually allowed himself loving parental feelings and through the occasions when he did meet his daughter he nourished the hope that when she was older she would understand the background to her birth and early years.

Deep into personal unhappiness, Ronnie was so beset with cares that eating properly and training diligently came low on his list of priorities. Smoking much marijuana and drinking to excess, he overate massively as his weight ballooned to 15 stone.

In the summer of 1996 his mother decided that she could not stand any more of this and threw him out. He moved into a hotel in Docklands, 'living on cheese sandwiches' as he put it. As an easily identifiable celebrity he one night got into a fight in a pub and had to run for his life.

After two weeks of this he returned home and immediately settled into a strict training regime, not least to prove to his mother that he could. However low he was feeling, and however many red lights he went through, Ronnie never completely forgot that he was a great snooker player and always braked at the last. He might have been half in love with self-destruction but never more than half.

As a genius, his natural peers in the sports world were friends like David Beckham, but Ronnie found that he could not endure being around them at times when he was conscious of mediocrity by his own standards. He went to Las Vegas to watch some boxing and had a chance conversation in a hotel with Graeme Souness, a football manager who had become a well-respected pundit. 'Healthy body, healthy mind' was his message, which Ronnie knew already, even if he needed someone at times to emphasise it.

He had slimmed down to 12 stone in time for the first tournament of the 1996/97 season, the Suntory Asian Classic in Bangkok, and duly won it. Fresh and keen, he was prepared to graft even when flu and a chest infection were well upon him by the final day. Although it was to be Ronnie's title, it was to be Brian Morgan's week of a lifetime, in which he beat four members of the top 16, Jimmy White, Stephen Hendry, Tony Drago and Ken Doherty, to reach the final. Morgan twice led by three frames only for Ronnie, at 8-8, to stake everything on an all-or-nothing middle pocket red from which he made a title-winning 71.

Ronnie was full of new-season resolutions: 'I've decided to be more professional. The way I played last season really hurt me. At times there was no effort. I was going through the motions. Being at the business end of tournaments is what I enjoy most and that's why I'm trying to do things properly.'

Of the final, he said, 'I didn't play well. Brian was better in many respects but I always had an inkling that my experience would tell in the end as this was his first taste of something like this.'

Ronnie's 6-2 quarter-final defeat by Peter Ebdon in the Scottish Masters was excusable by Ebdon playing 'the best he's ever played against me', but there were signs that his new-season resolutions were already being compromised when he lost 5-1 in the second round of the Grand Prix to Nick Pearce, who was then the world number 95.

Worse still, Ronnie then lost in the UK Championship to the world number 41 Terry Murphy, who he grossly underestimated. At 3-1 down, Ronnie was to admit, he started to panic and trailed 7-1 overnight. Next day, he found himself hitting the ball beautifully and won six of the session's first seven frames before Murphy potted a difficult key red and made 67 from it to win 9-7.

'All credit to him. That 67 was the best break under pressure anyone has ever made against me,' Ronnie said.

Ronnie knew, though, that he had hit a rich seam of form, his richest for five years as he felt it, and maintained it in winning the German Open in Osnabruck, beating Stephen Hendry, who had just won the UK, 5-2 in the quarter-finals and Nigel Bond 6-1 in a semi-final in which breaks of 101, 121 and 142 featured in a truly stunning display.

The final was not as easy as it promised to be when he led Alain Robidoux 7-3. 'I was cruising, then I was in trouble. It's the most uncomfortable I've felt all week. That's why some of my shots were irrational and why I struggled to get over the line.'

At 7-7, Robidoux led 45-0 but, caught in two minds over positional considerations, he missed an easy ball. Ronnie laid a fiendish snooker on the last red and from the chance that created regained the lead at 8-7.

'As soon as I won that, I knew I was in the driver's seat,' he said after clinching his fourth ranking title with a run of 108.

The Liverpool Victoria Charity Challenge, admittedly not a ranking tournament, although the prize money was real enough, produced an extraordinary final in which Ronnie, 8-2 down to Hendry, played superbly to make it 8-8 before Hendry took the decider with a 147. At the Masters, Ronnie beat Hendry 6-4 in the quarter-finals and Nigel Bond 6-5 in the semis, showing an obstinate will to win by coming through a desperately uncharacteristic and fragmentary deciding frame with a highest break of eight.

He started the final against Steve Davis with back-to-back centuries before the spell was broken by a female streaker. Nevertheless, he led 8-4 only to lose 10-8. 'At 8-4, I thought it was in the bag. Maybe I lost my head. I missed too many chances but Steve stuck in there and put me under pressure. In the last couple of frames, I was a cabbage really. If anyone deserves to win a tournament, it's Steve. Even though I've been beaten, I'm pleased for him because of what he's done for the game. I can't begrudge him after being such an ambassador over the years.' It was to prove the last major title that Davis won.

There were glorious, if brief, spells but Ronnie was starting to fear that he was losing the quintessence of his talent, although to some degree he had felt this way in the five years between his summer of qualifying at Blackpool and briefly regaining it on his way to the German Open title.

For the second time that season, he lost to Terry Murphy, 5-4 in the second round of the Welsh Open, after going 3-0 up in only 33 minutes. 'I didn't fancy winning. I've been struggling really badly here, even in practice, and deep down I knew I wasn't really playing well enough. When I'm playing like this, I'd rather sit at home and watch a video.'

How on earth could Ronnie decide that he was not playing 'well enough' if he was able to go 3-0 up in 33 minutes?

In the quarter-finals of the International Open in Aberdeen, he lost lamely, 5-1 to Ebdon; in the latter stages of his first-round match of the European Open in Malta against Chris Small, he lashed the balls about ferociously, repeatedly attempting outlandish pots, and lost the respect of the crowd, many of whom voted with their feet.

'I'm just playing terrible. I couldn't wait to get out of there. I hate the game. I don't want to play any more. It doesn't make any difference whether I try or I don't try. It's still the same result,' Ronnie said.

What had got him into this state? Was he feeling like this because of his snooker or was something else making him feel bad and affecting his game? When Sally Magnus had given birth to their daughter, Taylor, in January 1997, Ronnie had blocked any emotional reaction and put issues of personal responsibility and acceptable self-image to the back of his mind. In doing so, he deadened other aspects of his emotional functioning.

Nor was guilt in relation to his infant daughter far away and where there is guilt, self-punishment is often not far behind. In Ronnie's case, this often seemed to take the form of abusing his divine talent, the thing which, at heart, he treasured most. His moods swung in the second half of the 1996/97 season but when he was at his most emotionally disconnected, he sank very low indeed.

Ronnie usually managed to lift himself if he was inspired by a setting like Wembley Conference Centre, or if he was opposing one of his peers, like Hendry or Higgins, but otherwise, once he was in a depression, it had to run its course until it lifted, in this case at the Thailand Open, where he played with exceptional self-discipline to beat Davis 5-2 and Stephen Lee 5-3.

'When I say I'm going to pack it in, it's only because I'm annoyed with myself,' said Ronnie, explaining his Malta implosion. 'You've got to take me with a pinch of salt at times.' As if anxious to make up for lost time, he spent most of semi-finals day in Bangkok practising but this proved to be another way of shooting himself in the foot as he looked stale and flat in losing 5-1 to Ebdon that evening.

In peak form, Higgins beat Ronnie 6-2 in the Irish Masters semi-final and after a 5-4 first-round loss to Gerard Greene, the world number 72, at the British Open in Plymouth, it was time for the World Championship again.

'No one has a divine right to win and Gerard was better on the night,' said Ronnie, a gracious loser as ever. 'It's horrible to lose so close to the championship but you've got to be a man and take these things on the chin. I lacked the killer instinct out there. I had enough chances but, at this level, if you don't take them, you end up making life very difficult for yourself.'

So it was that he came to the Crucible after a 1996/97 season that had brought him two world ranking titles, two other major finals and four first-round defeats to players not really in his class. He had continued to demonstrate that while his best was amazing, his worst was abysmal. He was capable of beating anyone – or beating himself. He continued to find it difficult to understand why he could not play to his best standard every day, regardless of what else was going on in his life, as if his snooker could be hermetically sealed off from everything else as soon as he had his cue in his hand. His ongoing concerns bothered him less at some times than others but they were always pecking away at the corners of his consciousness.

Mick Price, his first-round opponent in Sheffield, led him 4-3 before Ronnie came to life to shade their opening session 5-4. 'I made the mistake of going out there not expecting to lose a frame. I've been cueing really well in practice, making eight or ten centuries a day, and maybe I was a bit over-confident. I concentrated a lot harder in the second session.'

In this, Ronnie extended his lead to 8-5 and then produced one of the most extraordinary feats that not only snooker but sport as a whole had ever seen, a 147 break in 5 minutes 20 seconds, easily superseding the previous fastest maximum of 7 minutes 9 seconds by James Wattana in the 1992 British Open.*

At the time, Ronnie's was only the fourth maximum to be made at the Crucible and only the twentieth in professional competition. It earned him a £147,000 bonus and the £18,000 highest break prize. The 36 shots of which it consisted took an average of 8.88 seconds.

So precise was Ronnie's cue ball control that he never once had to pot a difficult ball. The hallmark of the break, as it was to remain of his break building generally for the rest of his career, was his capacity to keep opening the main pack of reds whilst retaining black ball position, a skill in which he and Hendry in particular were in advance of their time.

Even so, Ronnie felt the pressure towards the end. 'My head was shaking and I couldn't keep still on the colours but I knew if I hesitated it'd interrupt my rhythm and I might make a mistake. It was a tremendous buzz out there and an experience you can't describe.'

This was an indelible image of sporting perfection but how to follow it? Ronnie led the determined, methodical Welsh left-hander Darren Morgan 9-7 going into the final session of their second-round match but this ended with Morgan making an 84 break in the decider to win 13-12.

'Something mental didn't click in my head,' said Ronnie. 'I tried my best to dig deep but it was all a bit of an effort. It was a struggle from start to finish. I wasn't scoring heavily enough in the balls. I'm just so inconsistent from one day to the next and that's so frustrating.' He still could not understand why he could not play peak-performance snooker every day.

Most players are snookered out after the World Championship but 1997 was different. The play-offs for the yearly league organised by Barry Hearn's Matchroom had to wait until after the 17 days at the Crucible and the four semi-finalists all wanted to win it.

Hendry had just lost 18-12 to Ken Doherty in the world final but this time beat him 6-3. Ebdon lost 6-2 to Ronnie, who for the first time played most of his shots left-handed.

Ebdon took this amiss. 'I'm disappointed because I've practised hard all week expecting a serious match. Obviously Ronnie didn't fancy that and turned it into something else entirely.'

Ronnie was adamant that the switch was not meant to be provocative. 'I feel really comfortable playing left-handed and it makes my tempo slower. I've practised left-handed for a couple of weeks [the two weeks since losing to Morgan at the Crucible] and I feel at home with it. Certain power shots are a bit awkward but generally I think I'm equally as good from both sides.'

Reducing his left-handed shots to about 25 per cent, Ronnie then beat Hendry 10-8 for a £60,000 first prize, which increased his earnings for the season to £484,105.

What was all this left-handedness about? A new toy to keep him interested? If so, it was a very useful one once he had integrated it into his game rather than using it just because he could. Sometimes, it helped him to maintain concentration when he felt it was slipping and a few seasons later he began breaking off left-handed in the belief that this assisted him to push the cue straight through the right-hand side of the cue ball when, with a right-handed shot, he felt he had a tendency to hit very slightly left to right across it. Playing left-handed, he found he was able to generate more side(spin) and thus whip the cue ball round more sharply off three cushions to leave it tight on the baulk cushion directly behind the green.

However well he was playing, Ronnie never stopped looking for incremental ways to improve.

*An American website, Deadspin.com, established 20 years later that the time from Ronnie's first strike of the cue ball to it coming to rest after potting the last black was 5 minutes, 8 seconds – 12 seconds faster than the accepted time. For 20 years, 5:20 had been extrapolated from the time shown on BBC after Ronnie potted the ninth red, until Deadspin investigated.

Chapter 8

[1997/98]

DURING the summer of 1997, Ronnie switched management camps from Barry Hearn's to that of Ian Doyle, a Scot who had assembled a team of players around Hendry, who always had been and would always remain his primary concern. Immediately, Ronnie made two trips to China for tournaments that Doyle had set up with fields mostly of his own players and locals in this fast-expanding market. Ronnie beat Jimmy White 5-3 to win the first but lost 6-0 in 78 minutes to him in the second.

His early-season form continued to be patchy as he lost 6-2 to John Higgins in the Scottish Masters and 5-2 to the world number 86, John Read, in the Grand Prix at Bournemouth: 'I think that's the worst I've ever played,' said Ronnie.

Nor was he in great form for the UK at Preston but, in the right mood, showed he could be stubborn about losing and grafted his way to the final.

'I've done this just by trying my nuts off. When I'm playing well, I feel I can toy with people but at the moment every match is a battle.'

The disparity between how he – with his prodigious talent – believed he should play and the quality of what he was actually producing ate away at him, even if he was inclined to exaggerate his shortcomings.

'I was so bad, I'm embarrassed that people have paid to watch me play,' he said after beating Gerard Greene 9-6 in their quarter-final. 'My snooker's driving me up the wall. I'm under pressure because I'm playing so awful.'

This was a player so gifted that he aspired to perfection or at least something near it. 'It's not what you do but the quality of what you've done. That's my personal view of life.'

After beating Stephen Lee in the semis, Ronnie conceded that he felt 'a little bit sharper', again undervaluing how well he had played in pulling away from 5-4 to 9-4 in only 44 minutes. There was another inspired burst from 5-5 to 9-5 in beating Hendry 10-6 in the final.

'There wasn't a lot I could do to stop him tonight,' said Hendry, reflecting on that four-frame period in which he did not pot a single ball.

Ronnie finally allowed himself a modicum of self-praise. 'To play so badly at the start of the championship, stick in and come good like this is a triple bonus. Obviously I'm a lot happier with my performance in the final. There's no way you can beat Stephen and play poorly. That just doesn't happen.'

This made it eight wins for Ronnie and eleven for Hendry in their personal head to head, easily better than that of any other player at a time when Hendry was in his prime. It seemed that Ronnie was his natural successor as world number one but there was to be nothing natural about it.

On top of his personal problems, including his ongoing enforced separation from his father, who was still not quite a third of the way through his sentence, a background hum of political unrest was growing louder. It would take a book to describe its roots and the long road, over many years, to its resolution and, in fact, much of my *Black Farce and Cue Ball Wizards* was devoted to this purpose.

In summary, the WPBSA was being run in an amateurish, wasteful way that attracted criticism from progressives like Doyle and myself as the editor of *Snooker Scene*. The incumbent regime responded to criticism largely by trying to get even with the critic. Annual general meetings and extraordinary general meetings developed into intense and often undignified games of 'hunt the proxy'. Few players had the education to grasp the nuances of the situation; some did not know who to believe. The conflict held snooker back because fewer sponsors wanted to be associated with the game and even those that remained could not fail to be aware of the increasingly poisonous backstage atmosphere.

This was not a factor at the Masters because Benson and Hedges, the sponsors, ran the tournament with minimal interference from WPBSA. It has always been one of Ronnie's favourite events, not least because he can commute to it from home without having to hang about with nothing much to do. He relished his quarter-final battle with Davis, to whom he had lost 10-8 from 8-4 up in the previous year's final, but from 3-3 he was again beaten, 6-3.

Davis was 'waiting for a bombardment that never came'; Ronnie was perhaps too preoccupied with wanting to match him tactically. Davis thought that Ronnie was perhaps 'trying too hard'; Ronnie said that he 'didn't play naturally because I wasn't allowed to'.

Just prior to Wembley, Ronnie had lost an entirely different kind of match in the fourth round of the Welsh Open, 5-4 to Anthony Hamilton, who took the last two frames with back-to-back centuries, 113 and 132.

'You won't see any better break building than that,' said Ronnie appreciatively.

Thus, in two different types of game against Davis and Hamilton, Ronnie had played well but lost; in the Scottish Open in Aberdeen, other factors came into play as a forthcoming WPBSA EGM turned the players' lounge into a hotbed of political intrigue.

'I felt terrible all tournament,' said Ronnie despite winning it. 'And a lot of that had to do with what's going on in the game. There was a horrible atmosphere in the players' room. It made you feel like a leper. There are a lot of snidey people who want to stab you in the back. Managers who look after certain players want to grow up and act like adults. I'm certain some people are hanging around tournaments just to cause trouble and stir things up.'

Doyle, Ronnie's manager and the snooker establishment's most vociferous critic, was banned from the venue by the Williams regime, an act as disproportionate as it was ridiculous. At the same time, Hendry was issued with a notice of disciplinary action on a trumped-up charge.

So ill at ease did Ronnie feel that he spent most of his non-playing and practice time holed up in his hotel room. Having led 4-0, he was dependent on a 62 break in the decider to beat Karl Payne, the world number 77, 5-4 and commented, 'I'm just trying to get through the next few months without causing any havoc or headbutting someone. I'm not enjoying the game any more and I've been like it for ages. At the moment, I couldn't care less whether I win or lose.'

Next time out, Ronnie was four times the odd frame behind against Brian Morgan, who nevertheless missed several chances in the decider as Ronnie again survived 5-4.

'My reputation helps. If these guys were just playing solid they'd beat me easy,' said Ronnie.

As these matches showed, though, Ronnie might have been down but not at rock bottom with no survival instinct at the last. Moreover, characteristically, he grew more motivated as the week wore on and a title came into view as he beat Jimmy White 5-3 and Marcus Campbell 5-1, going 4-0 up in 46 minutes with a century and a points tally of 341-18.

'It was better but my position was still poor,' said Ronnie, unable to take any pleasure from his performance. 'I've got a different perspective on the game these days and sometimes I might be too self-critical. That's just the way I think.'

There was more justification for Ronnie's self-deprecation after beating Stephen Lee 6-2 in their semi-final. 'Luckily for me, Stephen didn't perform. Neither of us were up to scratch but I wasn't as bad as him. I've had to rely on people playing poorly to get this far. There's nothing in me. I'm vegetating. I know what I expect from myself out there and it's just not happening.'

For most players, winning is enough because they know there is a chance of playing better in their next match. Geniuses and superstars expect more and, in the latter stages of the final, Ronnie produced it. From 6-5, he beat John Higgins 9-5 to win his seventh ranking title, confirming that 'towards the end that's the best I've felt for ages because I've showed what I can do. I wasn't interested at the start of the week. It just goes to show what a couple of days can do for your attitude.'

At the circuit's next stop, the Liverpool Victoria Challenge at Derby, he reflected that 'the more I win, the more I want to win' and through beating Mark Williams 5-4 on the final black with a 69 clearance and Hendry 6-4, he reached the final, only to be disappointed with his performance in losing 9-8 to Higgins from two up with three to play.

There was an early 5-1 defeat in the Thailand Masters by Alan McManus, who overcame the effects of jetlag by practising most of the night and sleeping most of the day. The veteran Scot admitted that he had 'not played that well in ages' while Ronnie, not expecting such a performance, 'missed too many balls and didn't make enough of my chances. Even when I've been getting results lately, I haven't been anywhere near my peak. People may think I'm being cocky but I don't care what they think. I know, deep down, I'm struggling.'

There was no evidence of this when he beat Hendry for the sixth consecutive time, 6-3 in the Irish Masters. 'At the moment, I feel like I'm ready to start buzzing. For the last week or so, I've been hitting the ball superb in practice.' Having beaten Higgins 6-4 in the semi, he demolished Ken Doherty 9-3 in front of his own Irish supporters to secure his fourth title of the season.

'I was up for this, completely zoned in. When I'm on top of my game I expect to win, no matter who I'm playing. Some people will say I'm big-headed but I always speak from the heart and I know if I play my best stuff it's going to be difficult for anyone to touch me.'

Ronnie had maintained his sublime form despite carousing every night that week with Jimmy White. He drank only modest quantities of Guinness but was persuaded one night to try what he described as 'puff cake'. It never entered his head that he might fall foul of the drugs regulations, even when he was tested after the final. He lost to Williams for the first time, 5-4 in the British Open, admitting that he was 'a bit tired upstairs so at least now I'll have some time off before we go to the Crucible', but once there he was dissatisfied with his performance in beating Joe Swail 10-5.

'My head wasn't there. The form I've been showing on the practice table has been poor. This was even worse. I can't fathom out why I'm so inconsistent. Sometimes I wake up and it's there, sometimes it isn't. And that's frustrating.'

McManus, handicapped by a sore back, did not extend Ronnie beyond 13-4 and White, who had delved back into his prime to beat Hendry and Darren Morgan, sank back into frequent error as Ronnie eliminated him 13-7.

During this quarter-final, Doyle felt bound to inform Ronnie that he had tested positive from the 'puff cake' – marijuana, in fact – he had sampled at the Irish Masters. In accordance with the WPBSA regulations at the time, he was to be stripped of the title and the £61,130 first prize. There is no way that marijuana can be considered performance enhancing but it was on the banned list of drugs, so there could be no argument. This did not cost Ronnie any ranking points because the Irish Masters was a restricted field invitation event. He did not care all that much about the money but it did strike him as unjust that he was stripped, on a technicality, of a title that most people would agree he had won fair and square.

From 4-4, Ronnie lost the second session of his semi-final against Hendry 8-0 and was eventually beaten 17-9. Understandably, once the reason was clear, there was a depressed air about his performance because he knew that a storm would break once his test result came into the public domain: 'I know it's a sad thing to say but I'm not too disappointed. Some defeats hurt but not this. I was never involved in this match. I'm looking forward to going home.'

Chapter 9

[1998/99]

T HERE was another long summer to get through. The game continued to be torn to shreds by political infighting; for Ronnie there was nothing to alleviate the flat, normal life that is foreign to sportsmen accustomed to the stimulus of frequent competition. It rankled that he had achieved something approaching peak performance in winning the Irish Masters only for officialdom to have taken away what he felt was due recognition.

His father still had two-thirds of his sentence to serve and Ronnie was bored, lacking a sense of purpose. He aspired to perfection as a player but as soon as he came near it – or even fleetingly achieved it – something always seemed to happen to send this boulder crashing to the bottom of the hill again.

The ensuing sense of failure amounted at its worst to self-loathing. No matter that his C game, never mind his B, was still good enough to beat most opponents if he applied himself, he feared that he was never going to be as good as his unique talent equipped him to be. Nor did he realise that by too often setting the bar too high, he was setting himself up for failure. In some strange way, he even welcomed failure like an old friend because he knew there was a way back up.

He liked smoking cigarettes and had a weakness for marijuana, which he mostly kept in check, but the more unhappy or bored he was the more he turned to it. At the age of 21, his body could stand a lot and running also helped to keep him in some sort of shape but the lower he sank, the more late nights he had and the less running he did.

It became clear to me that his unhappiness, for various understandable reasons, was turning into full-blown depression. Del Hill, his guide, philosopher and friend at the time, confided to me at breakfast during the Scottish Masters, the first tournament of the 1998/99 season, that Ronnie was becoming a nightmare to be with, miserable and uncommunicative to the point of not saying a word during a 100-mile car journey.

'I just look at the game as a job these days,' Ronnie rationalised after beating Mark Williams 6-5 in his first match. 'I'll just be trying to knock out a few bob and set myself up for retirement. I wish I'd got the recipe for how to enjoy snooker like I used to when I was a lad but I haven't.'

Dashing at times, slapdash at others, he led 5-3 but, as Williams improved and his own standard dipped through impatience, it came to a close decider at 5-5, which Ronnie edged by summoning a high-quality 31 at the death.

'Not many people love their job after 15 years and that's how long I've been playing the game,' said Ronnie as he approached his 22nd birthday. 'Mind you, I'm not going to give it up. Nobody kisses goodbye to 300 or 400 grand a year, do they? I just want to get some cash together to enjoy my summers.'

Next day, a belated resort to disciplined shot selection enabled Ronnie to come from two down with three to play to beat Nigel Bond 6-5 in their semi-final, having squandered sizeable leads in several early frames through pure carelessness and needless risk.

'When I get frustrated, I can't resist forcing the pace,' he said. 'I had no rhythm and couldn't get going. There were times out there when I knew I was playing the wrong shot and couldn't stop myself. It was embarrassing. I'm a nutter, aren't I? Not quite the full ticket.'

Awful as he was feeling, he did not want to be 'buried' in the final but John Higgins, the reigning world champion, did not play to his best standard and with a more conventional approach to shot selection, albeit without producing optimum form, Ronnie managed to beat him 9-7 to take the £61,000 first prize, a virtual reimbursement for his Irish Masters punishment.

He took only grudging pleasure in his success. 'Everything seemed a grind for me all week but I suppose I've come away with something concrete. The only disappointment is that I like to entertain and I didn't do much of it. I didn't show what I was capable of.'

That he was capable of winning a tournament like this in such low gears and low spirits was perhaps one way of showing how good he was but next morning he 'felt like death' and could not bring himself to come down to breakfast. In his paranoia, Ronnie believed that people were secretly laughing at him because he had barely been able to utter a word from the podium at the sponsor's party after the final.

At breakfast, I chatted with Del Hill, who Ronnie had asked to send breakfast to his room. Del was worried about him and so was I because I knew what misery looked like and could see symptoms in Ronnie that reminded me of my own battles with depression. I suggested to Del that he try to get help for Ronnie from Mike Brearley, a distinguished former England cricket captain. Ian Doyle, Ronnie's manager, agreed and Ronnie himself made the necessary phone call to Brearley.

Initially, Brearley was too busy but recommended him to a colleague to whom Ronnie poured his heart out. He always felt better after these sessions, but, on waking up next day, his panic attacks, his sense of alienation and isolation, returned. Instead of realising that there was no quick-fix miracle cure, Ronnie felt, in his all-or-nothing way, that it was all useless. Many days, he could not even bestir himself to get out of the house.

He tried another psychotherapist, then Brearley himself, whom he liked. Again, their sessions usually made him feel better short term and again Ronnie came to feel they were pointless if their benefits were not longer term. Ronnie also came to resent driving from Chigwell to Islington to see him but it was a theory that Brearley tentatively advanced that caused him to lose faith in the process.

Psychoanalysis and psychotherapy invariably focus, to a considerable extent, on the patient's relationship with his parents, so that between Ronnie and Ronnie senior obviously had to be probed.

Ronnie would never allow any blame for his troubles to be attached to his father and empathised with him to a degree in which he even seemed to hope, irrationally, that he could take some of his father's burden on himself. It also seemed unlikely that Ronnie would have found himself adrift in such a turbulent sea of troubles if, ironically, this convicted murderer had been at his side to keep him on the straight and narrow in terms of his career and personal wellbeing.

One day, by Ronnie's account, when he said he was struggling with his cue action and not feeling comfortable round the table, Brearley asked whether his father was right-handed. Ronnie confirmed that he was so they agreed that on the fateful night in Stocks nightclub, Ronnie senior had knifed Bruce Bryan right-handed.

Brearley suggested that by a curious form of empathy this might be affecting Ronnie's right arm, his preferred cue arm, explaining that some soldiers who had been compelled, against their will, to shoot people, in a firing squad for example, had found that years later their trigger arm became paralysed. Could this explain why Ronnie sometimes felt more comfortable playing left-handed or why he always held his knife in his left hand to cut up meat on his plate?

Maybe there was little or nothing in this startling theory. Maybe there was something. Either way, it freaked Ronnie out and he lost faith in Brearley even though he continued seeing him for several more months. Ronnie very much wanted Brearley to like him, so instead of paying him his standard fee of £80 per session he insisted on giving him £90. Ronnie's self-esteem was so low that this was the only way he felt he could achieve this.

Meanwhile, a fortnight after the Scottish Masters, Ronnie was still deep in depression when he arrived at Preston for the Grand Prix.

'I hate the game. I wish I didn't have to play,' he said after beating Mark King 5-2. 'My form is making me feel ill,' he added, not appreciating that it was his illness, his depression, that was affecting his form, not the other way around.

A newcomer to the circuit, Marco Fu, played brilliantly in the last 16 to beat him 5-2, Ronnie making back-to-back breaks of 97 and 134 in the two frames he won. This was enough to show there was still top quality in there somewhere but a few weeks later he was in no state to defend his UK title.

On the first evening of a week's exhibitions in Ireland, Ronnie made a 147 and three more centuries but then spent every day and sometimes all night drinking. If the idea was to blot out his troubles, it only made them worse. On his return home, he flaked out on the sofa and knew that, even if he got the drink out of his system, he was too emotionally and physically exhausted to contemplate competing in the UK Championship a week hence.

When he told Ronnie senior about his week in Ireland, his father was very angry indeed. He was hardly to be blamed for not understanding the roots of the depression that had led to Ronnie's self-destructiveness. All he could see was the externals of Ronnie's behaviour and the week's conversations ended with his disowning him. Everything that Ronnie senior, Maria and Ronnie himself had earned had always been pooled and by this criterion Ronnie was no longer pulling his weight.

With his father in prison, it had been Ronnie who had to buy properties and negotiate mortgages but now, as Ronnie senior perceived it, his son could not even keep himself straight for a snooker tournament.

Ronnie did not come to life until the Welsh Open, where a 1,500 capacity crowd helped sharpen his concentration and will to win as he beat Jimmy White 5-2. 'The reception we got gave me goose pimples. Sometimes, against the lower-ranked players, I have trouble getting motivated.'

Down 3-1 to Alain Robidoux, Ronnie won four of the five remaining frames in exquisite fashion, making breaks of 92, 143, 76 and 78 and impressing everyone except himself. 'It's no good turning it on the second half if you've played bad to start. I've got to learn to gear myself right from the off. I'm lucky to still be here.'

He was certainly sharp from the off next day as breaks of 144 and 147 in the first three frames – thus making three over 140 in under 24 hours – featured in his 5-2 quarter-final win over James Wattana, but he was still far from satisfied.

'Just because I had a maxi doesn't mean I flew out of my skin. If I play well, I'll tell you when it happens.'

It did not happen in his 6-1 semi-final defeat by Mark Williams, in which his inspiration was totally burnt out. Even his arithmetic let him down as he prematurely conceded one frame through misreading the scoreboard. Nor could he regain inspiration, as he often did, for the Masters in which he scrambled past Wattana 6-5 before losing 6-2 to Ken Doherty, playing a large number of shots left-handed in a vain attempt 'to get something going. It just didn't happen for me. I'm practising hard but nothing's going right. This arena's intimidating enough without going in there struggling to begin with.'

Still in low-key form, he tried his utmost against the emerging Paul Hunter in the Scottish Open but lost 5-3; just before the Liverpool Victoria Charity Challenge, Ronnie broke the little finger on his cue hand in a fall at home, although, not for the first time, an extra difficulty to focus on seemed to bring out a stubborn desire to overcome it.

'The bandage was such a big hindrance on certain shots, I couldn't go for too much. I couldn't get my hand wrapped round the cue and some shots, particularly with the rest, were quite painful. I couldn't get any rhythm going and when it came to power shots, I had to put my shoulder into it because my grip was so weak.'

This did not prevent him from beating Alan McManus 5-2 and after his 6-4 win over Jimmy White, he commented how 'great' it was to have his mother supporting him at the venue. 'So many other players always have that,' he added, a touch wistfully.

'I've been practising very hard since Christmas but mentally I haven't been there,' said Ronnie. 'Now I'm reaping the benefits because my head is allowing me to.'

Nevertheless, John Higgins, who had won the Masters and was again in prime form, beat him comfortably, 9-4, in the final. 'You could see Ronnie wasn't 100 per cent out there with the broken finger. Of course he was a sportsman and told me it wasn't bothering him too much, but you could tell on certain shots he was really handicapped.'

Ronnie no longer had this problem for back-to-back tournaments in Bangkok and Shanghai, locations that sound exotic but very often boil down to not much more than a long flight, a hotel, practice, match, practice, match and when defeat comes, a long flight home. A golfer may have the sun on his back, the wind in his hair and a challenging set of variables every week, but for a snooker player it is just the eternal 12 by 6 and a struggle to produce his best in daytime, when his body is telling him it is the middle of the night.

Not really up for it, Ronnie lost 5-4 in the first round of the Thailand Masters to Darren Morgan despite making a fight of it from 4-1 down, and 5-3 in the second round of the China International to Billy Snaddon who, in the best week of his snooker career, also beat Stephen Lee and Hendry before losing to Higgins in the final.

Telling it like it was, Ronnie said that Snaddon had played 'blinding snooker' but that his own game 'wasn't up to scratch'. He added: 'To be honest, I didn't do a lot wrong. I kept waiting for him to make a few mistakes but they never came until it was too late.'

At times, in most of his matches, Ronnie's beautiful best peeked out, as if from behind a curtain, but mostly, by his standards, he struggled, beaten 6-4 by White in the Irish Masters and for the second time that season by Jimmy Michie, 5-3 in the British Open.

'It's the World Championship and I still can't get a buzz out there,' he said after beating Leo Fernandez 10-3 in the opening round at the Crucible. 'I'm just trying to hit a bit of form but it's hard. I've been like this for a couple of years. The way I feel when I'm playing is bad news. If nothing happens in a year or two, then I'll have to rethink what I do with my life. It's no good being in a situation where you're not enjoying yourself.'

He reflected that he would 'have to improve' after comfortably beating Joe Perry 13-8, and did so in leading John Parrott 6-2 after their first session and 11-5 after their second en route to a 13-9 win that was only his third in ten attempts against the 1991 world champion.

'That's as good a result as any I've had in my career because John has always been a bogey player for me and he's given me some drubbings. I knew John would roll up his sleeves and make a fight of it but I was a bit too far in front.'

Parrott enthused, 'Ronnie's scoring was sheer class. He was in the zone and very difficult to stop. They say it's a travesty that Jimmy White has never won the title. Well, it'd be a bigger travesty if Ronnie never won it.'

Not the 1999 title, though. In the semi-finals, he trailed Hendry 6-2 after one session and 9-7 after two before levelling at 10-10. In one of the game's most sustained exhibitions of mutual excellence, consecutive centuries of 101 and 108 from Hendry were followed by 134 and 110 from Ronnie as they adjourned at 12-12. For the first and only time in the match, Ronnie led 13-12 but Hendry played superbly to seize victory without further loss at 17-13.

'The first session was a nightmare for me,' said Ronnie. 'I got the feeling that if I put him under pressure he'd go, but I didn't put him under enough. It was a decent match but I know I can play better than that.' Hendry, who went on to beat Williams 18-11 to win his seventh and last world title, said, 'I can't play much better than that. When the pressure was on in the last session, I didn't think I was going to miss a ball.'

Chapter 10

[1999/2000]

I T was starting to nag at Ronnie that one of his contemporaries, Higgins, had already won the world title, in 1998, and another, Williams, had reached the 1999 final but another year had to elapse before he could do anything about it and another summer yawned before him. He went clubbing a lot, partly to pass the time, partly because he had always believed that this was the way celebrities were meant to behave in the sense that such indulgence was one of the spoils of war. He had some good times but was not a born hellraiser in the Ronnie Wood or even Jimmy White class. In any case, all the hellraising was simply postponing a confrontation with the forces that were inwardly undermining him.

Ronnie's immediate preparation for his first match of the 1999/2000 season was a phenomenal bender in the company of Mick Jagger, Kate Moss and Noel Gallagher, amongst others. He checked into his hotel on the eve of the new Champion of Champions tournament at Croydon at 5pm and slept until 9am the next day prior to starting at 11am against White, who had left the same party a little earlier.

'The worst match ever seen on television,' was Ronnie's verdict, quite widely shared, after his 4-2 victory, but he had a run of 237 unanswered points in beating Fergal O'Brien 4-1 and took only 39 minutes to beat Higgins 4-0.

His 5-4 semi-final defeat by Williams came down to two cruel slices of luck in the decider. 'What happened was out of my control but that's sport, I suppose. The important thing is not to let things get me down.'

In early season his best was excellent, like his recovery from 4-2 down to beat Paul Hunter 5-4 in the third round of the British Open, running through the last three frames with breaks of 100, 52, 55 and 107.

His 6-1 quarter-final win over Higgins was partly attributable to the 1998 world champion having an off day and Hendry's verdict on his tight 6-5 victory over Ronnie in the semi-finals was, 'Neither of us played as well as we can.'

Thus far, Ronnie's fluctuations in form were within the margins that any player might expect but his game and his mental approach were starting to fray at the Scottish Masters when, from 4-2 up, he lost his first match 6-4 to Matthew Stevens, a result influenced more by Ronnie's lack of patience and discipline than by anything Stevens produced. As one positional shot after another went astray, his growing frustration was expressed in several suicidal shot selections.

'You could see that wasn't the real Ronnie out there,' said Stevens, who went on to win the tournament.

At the Grand Prix at Preston, Ronnie temporarily unravelled as he went from 2-0 up to 4-2 down to Andy Hicks but nevertheless scrambled through 5-4, Hicks assisting him by failing to clinch several match-winning chances.

'I'm pleased I didn't let frustration get the better of me, like I have in the past,' said Ronnie. 'The crowd helped. When I was behind, I could see in their faces they were gutted to see me losing, so I tried really hard for them as much as myself.

'In that respect, I'm happy but I much prefer it when I dictate the pace. A few years ago, I went into matches knowing I was going to win and knowing I'd knock people off. Now I'm just hoping to do that.'

Higgins, anxious to avoid losing to Ronnie for the third time in succession, won their quarter-final 5-3, a thumping disappointment that Ronnie took so much to heart that he could hardly get out of the Guild Hall quickly enough.

After coasting through three rounds at the UK Championship at Bournemouth, Ronnie still considered that 'my form is still only 70 per cent but at least I'm here. Last year I wasn't. Twelve months ago, I didn't want to be at tournaments. It was a nightmare, so this is a big improvement.'

The elusiveness of prime form – as he perceived it – did not matter so very much if he was winning comfortably but, in a tight contest against another top player, slackness or lack of intensity was fatal. Ronnie was guilty of both as he lost 9-3 to Stevens in the quarter-finals.

'I set my standards higher than this but I wouldn't be human if I didn't have the odd bad performance,' said Ronnie, attempting to rationalise the defeat. 'Anyway, there's no point in sitting here feeling sorry for myself. You've got to bounce back and make things happen. It's hard to be positive when you're down but you've got to be.'

Buckling down, he won his first title in 16 months, the China Open in Shanghai, but remained dissatisfied with his game. Trailing Shokat Ali 2-1, he switched to playing most of his shots left-handed.

'When I do that, then go back right-handed, the game seems a lot easier,' he said after winning 5-2, the last three frames taking only 27 minutes.

His quarter-final opponent, Paul Sweeny, was very nervous, so Ronnie had to expend little energy in beating him 5-1. 'To be honest, I'd have probably lost if I had come across one of the top players. I still don't feel as though I'm hitting the ball well enough to win a tournament.'

Ronnie's inability to perform as well as he felt he should was compounded in his semi-final, in which he impatiently conceded two frames before the 'snookers required' stage, forfeited another for three consecutive misses from an unsnookered position but still managed to beat Brian Morgan 6-5. Once he was in amongst the balls, he still scored reasonably heavily but, overall, he assessed his form as 'terrible'. He added: 'The way I'm playing, I shouldn't be beating an egg. I didn't enjoy the match one little bit. When you're playing this bad, it's hard going.'

Indeed, Ronnie had been there for the taking but Morgan could not take him. 'I knew that Brian has had two or three chances [actually two 5-4s and a 9-8] to put me away and hasn't done it. That was in the back of my mind.'

Having, as he experienced it, slogged across a desert as far as form was concerned, Ronnie reached the promised land of prime performance in the final, winning the last six frames of the opening session by an aggregate score of 610-93 as he demolished Stephen Lee 9-2. Still, Ronnie did not feel 'totally comfortable' with his form, admitting, 'When you haven't won a title for a long time your confidence suffers, so this is a big boost. Now I can chill out over Christmas and go into the New Year with something to build on.'

He did win 13 of his 15 frames in helping England win the Nations Cup at Reading ('We were in the fortunate position of having a genius in our team,' said John Parrott, the England captain) but fell 5-2 to White in the third round of the Welsh Open and 6-3 to Parrott in the quarter-final of the Masters.

'I can't pin down why I'm brilliant one day and another day I'm not. It's something in my head that's stopping me but I'm working on it, stressing the positive side. Sometimes I think too much about the negatives.

'Other players go back to basics if they're not doing well but I keep playing, going for my shots, waiting for something to happen and at top level you get punished. Some of these people only need one chance and if they get it, their confidence grows and you're on the back foot.

'When I was young, it was a doddle and you find yourself asking "Why was it so easy then and now I'm struggling?" and it's hard to accept. But if you can accept it, you're halfway there. I've found that instead of looking at the past, I should be looking forward.'

The clarity of mind that he had taken for granted in his youth no longer came automatically to him and the higher quality of opposition was also a factor, particularly if he was frustrated by players who, in his heart, he did not believe were in his class. He admitted there were times when he was 'so depressed I didn't really want to play snooker and when you're in the public eye, you can't afford to be as open as I was about my feelings because people were ready to pounce'.

There may have been a chemical component to his depression; undischarged anger probably had a bearing on it. He was able to acknowledge that his father deserved imprisonment for his crime but felt that the 18-year term, not reduced on appeal, was excessively harsh. Through his sense of searing injustice, anger ate away at him and seemed to turn inwards, as undischarged anger commonly does.

In no mood to compete in the Thailand Masters, he was a 5-2 second-round loser to Mark King in a contest of embarrassingly low quality.

'I started to realise his head was going and that put me under pressure,' said King. 'By the end, I couldn't hold my cue. He was smashing the balls everywhere. It really unsettled me. He was throwing his cue at everything and looked like he didn't want to win. When we shook hands, I even asked if he was alright.'

At the Irish Masters, Ronnie was able to harness some of the anger from a sense of injustice arising from another source – being stripped of the 1998 title because of a positive drugs test.

'I know rules are rules but smoking a joint doesn't enhance your performance.

'I still won the tournament. I see all the banners and photographs around the venue with the faces of all the former champions here. I'm not there and I want to be,' he said after his 6-4 win over Stevens, the first time in three attempts he had beaten him that season.

Ronnie lost 6-3 to Higgins in the semi-finals but it seemed that he might have touched the bottom in his own swimming bath of despair and was about to push up to the surface. Moody and magnificent in equal measure, he did so by winning the Scottish Open, four times flirting with defeat but somehow avoiding it.

After his 5-4 win over Dave Finbow, Ronnie made a 147 in only 6 minutes 40 seconds in leading Quinten Hann 4-0 but was still taken the full distance before prevailing 5-4 on the final black. Holding a 4-3 advantage over Marcus Campbell, he conceded the eighth frame when only eight points behind with many reds still on the table but won the ninth-frame decider with no trouble.

'At last, I managed to find a bit of rhythm,' he said after his 5-1 quarter-final win over Dave Harold. 'I like the game to come easy and for most of the tournament it hasn't been because I've been losing control of the cue ball.'

This kind of form slipped away from him like a wet bar of soap next day as he was unable to curb the petulance arising from frustration at his early inadequacies in falling 4-0 behind to Graeme Dott.

'If the interval hadn't come up, I'd have definitely lost 6-0 and been on the road home. Del [Hill] really helped. We had a good talk during the interval about lots of things and that put me back on track.'

Newly focused, Ronnie won 6-4 and after a week of brinkmanship, mood swings and violent fluctuations in form, he overwhelmed Williams 9-1 to win his eighth world ranking title and £62,000.

Again, he paid tribute to Del Hill. 'I couldn't wish for anyone better in my corner. I needed firing up, I suppose, and he's done that.' It was impossible to foresee that only a few years later, they would be bitterly estranged.

Ronnie had played well enough to encourage hopes that he would become the 2000 world champion. Indeed, he maintained this form at the Crucible, making five centuries in his first-round match but still losing 10-9 to one of his frequent sparring partners, David Gray. It was the first time in his life that he had played very near his best and not won.

With breaks of 123, 101 and 115, Ronnie became the first player to make centuries in three consecutive frames in a single session at the Crucible. He was on course for four in four and a maximum but on 96 (12 red/blacks) missed a red to a distant baulk pocket.

This put him 5-1 up but with the last three frames of that session and two of the first three on the resumption, Gray levelled in high-quality fashion at 6-6. Again Ronnie surged to 8-6 with 217 unanswered points, including a total clearance of 136, and at 8-7 made yet another century, 102, to go two up with three to play.

Still Gray did not wilt and as he closed to 9-9, Ronnie showed symptoms of feeling the pressure. Finally, in the decider, he lost some of his discipline, failing at two long pots he need not have attempted. Gray made 39 from the latter and hung on to record the win of his life.

'It's hard to accept any defeat, especially at the Crucible, but this is David's day,' Ronnie said manfully. 'He's obviously improved this season and played a terrific match.'

Exhausted by his great effort, Gray lost 13-1 to Dominic Dale in the next round. Williams, like Higgins, a junior contemporary in the class of '92, beat Stevens in an all-Welsh final. Ronnie had taken over from Jimmy White, the loser of all his six world finals, the unwanted distinction of being regarded as the best player never to have been world champion. At 24, he was feeling his prime years starting to slip away.

Chapter 11

[2000/01]

IT is difficult for many top sportsmen and entertainers to have experiences of extreme emotional intensity in the full glare of public gaze and readjust quickly to what most people think of as normal life. The buzz, the high, often creates a need which has to be satisfied one way or another. The calendar of the snooker circuit imposes a discipline, a pattern of a sort, but life away from it can seem shapeless. There are highs to be had from drink, drugs, women and various other pleasures but there were prices to be paid and the problems of 'real life' cannot be evaded forever. Disappointment at the Crucible and end-of-season emptiness prompted Ronnie's relapse into bad habits.

On 4 June 2000, Ronnie stopped his car at traffic lights in Stratford, east London alongside a sports car containing two young women. For reasons never explained, one was wearing only a bathrobe. When the lights changed, the cars accelerated away. PC Paul Parkinson was to give evidence that they were doing 40–50mph and stated that when Ronnie was stopped 'his eyes were bloodshot and glazed. He seemed agitated and his breath smelled strong.'

Three times, it was to be alleged, Ronnie failed to provide a breath test through a breathalyser and at Plaistow police station told police that he could not give a blood test because of an aversion to needles or, despite drinking six cups of water, a urine sample. During his time at the station, he said that he had trained himself to go for long periods without using the toilet because of the demands of his sport. Since players are free to leave the arena between frames – and exceptionally during – it is difficult to understand why he did this, if he did. He was charged with refusing to give a breath, blood and urine sample but after an 18-month saga, including some farcical moments, he was acquitted.

First, his defence applied for the case to be dismissed because the magistrate had tampered with vital evidence. He had been seen blowing into the mouthpiece of the relevant breathalyser. The prosecution agreed that there should be a retrial but the magistrate, William Rolstone, insisted that the case continue under his jurisdiction.

The next hearing was aborted because Ronnie overlooked the date and when the case eventually resumed, the magistrate was observed winking at a reporter. Ronnie's lawyer, Nick Freeman, not inappropriately known as Mr Loophole in some quarters because of the high profile he had built representing celebrity clients like David Beckham and Sir Alex Ferguson on speeding charges, argued that this was highly prejudicial to Ronnie. But the magistrate responded, 'Why would I wink at anybody? Do you think I'm gay or something?'

Nevertheless, the pressure on him from both defence and prosecution was such that he was forced to withdraw from the case, which then came under District Judge Angus Hamilton, who ordered a retrial that he himself conducted.

The star witness was Dr Stephen Robinson, a police surgeon and sex counsellor, who told the court that Ronnie's inability to produce a urine sample could be attributed to his psychiatric state. 'I am aware of his psychiatric history and know that he was suffering from an anxiety depressive disorder. I also know that he had an obsessive personality. At times, he showed verbal agitation. This psychiatric condition could easily be linked to his inability to pass urine. It could happen to anybody. It is more likely to happen to someone with a psychiatric disorder. We are talking about a stress reaction. Any stressful situations, like being in a police station.'

Dr Robinson explained that when a person felt under pressure the bladder could either be put into a relaxed state, a signal to the brain that there was no need to go, even though it was full, or it could lead to the tightening of the bladder muscle, which would then act like a stopper on a tap. After this evidence, Judge Hamilton halted the trial and declared Ronnie not guilty.

While this fine example of the British legal process was wending its way to this conclusion, Ronnie at last started to deal seriously with his drug problem. He had not long met Bianca Westwood, who was to become a reporter on Sky's *Soccer Saturday*. He liked her very much and did not want to show her how depressed and uneasy he was beneath the veneer he outwardly presented. In particular, he did not want her to realise the extent of his drug usage.

Ronnie still thought that his snooker was his main problem. If he was playing well, his mood was fine; if he was not, he was often so depressed that he simply sat by himself for hours, put in a couple of punishingly hard hours in the gym or yielded to the temptation of drugs and/or drink in company with a friend.

When he rang the National Drugs Helpline, a young woman suggested that he was an addict, an idea he had always resisted. Nevertheless, she persuaded him to spend four weeks in The Priory at Roehampton. Physically, he seemed in good shape but inwardly he was a bundle of neuroses, unable to relax in company and suffering frequent panic attacks of nameless dread. His lack of self-esteem, his sense that people were always looking at him judgementally, amounted to the early stages of paranoia. His drug-taking made this worse. At least he was not hooked on heroin or cocaine but his problems were serious enough and, incidentally, raised questions about the effectiveness of the WPBSA's drug-testing procedures.

By chance, Ronnie had a prison visit booked the day before he went into The Priory. He was apprehensive about his father's reaction but it could not have been more supportive. From his own experience of prison life, Ronnie senior knew inmates who had undertaken the 12-step programme set out by Narcotics Anonymous. One of his fellow inmates, in whose company he sometimes watched Ronnie playing on television, could identify when Ronnie was out of tune and most likely to lose.

Four weeks' residence in The Priory and abstinence not just from drugs but from alcohol – in short anything potentially 'mind altering' – cleaned out Ronnie's physical system and it was also of immense value to him that he talked endlessly to doctors and in collective therapy sessions with the other patients, almost all of whom were so preoccupied with their own problems that they did not know who he was. For the first time in his life, he was in an environment in which his status as a top sportsman was of no account. He was one among many trying to tackle depression and addiction. For his entire adolescence and early manhood, he had been a snooker player to whom the rest of his life was incidental. He was now in the process of becoming a rounded individual who happened to be a snooker player, although he did underestimate the length of that process and the potential for relapse. Drugs and alcohol had not been the problem; they had been short-term palliatives that created problems of their own.

The immediate effect of his sojourn in The Priory was striking. Only towards the end of the summer did he feel like playing but on ten days' practice, five of them on his own, he won the Champions Cup at Brighton, the first event of the 2000/01 season. His concentration, so often wayward, came easily to him throughout a week in which he made only a handful of unforced errors. He was prepared to be patient and there were spells when his clarity of mind allowed his sublime hand/eye co-ordination to express itself in breaks that, though not technically beyond his main rivals, were composed in his own fluently inimitable style.

In his first match, a 5-4 win over John Higgins, Ronnie was a little ring rusty but pleased above all to feel 'as if I've got my life back. I'm much happier because I've realised that snooker's not everything to me. I still love it and the buzz you get going out there, but there are other, more important things. Knowing that is sweet.'

He spoke in similar vein after beating Jimmy White 5-2. 'I'm just happy to be here. I came close to quitting but I've come to realise I couldn't just walk away from the game. It would be something I'd regret somewhere down the line.

'I heard Steve Davis say on television that this is a big season for Ronnie O'Sullivan. It isn't. I'm just determined to enjoy myself and not have any expectations. It's a nice change to feel sweet again. There've been times when I've won a tournament and still been in bits.'

Ronnie had come to appreciate not only that enjoyment was one of the keys to performance but that, for him, intensive practice was, beyond a certain point, counter-productive. 'Hendry, Higgins and Williams are really dedicated but I don't think that works for me. If I over-practise, it spoils my enjoyment of life off table and of snooker itself. That's a trap I won't be falling into again.'

A 5-2 win over Matthew Stevens saw Ronnie undefeated in his round-robin group and by beating Hendry 5-2 and, from 4-1 down, Williams 7-5 he took the £100,000 first prize. 'I'm thinking better now. I've got my life in order and I'm sure the public will see a very different side of me. This one's for everyone who's stuck with me because I must have been a nightmare to be around at times. I'm starting life again at 24. I'm very emotional. I haven't been able to reflect on what I've achieved because in the past I've always been on a treadmill of turmoil.'

Ronnie carried his upbeat mood and disciplined form through the first two rounds of the British Open and led Peter Ebdon 3-1 in their quarter-final. On the verge of leading 4-1, he misjudged a positional cannon and Ebdon, in prime form, did not put a foot wrong in overcoming him 5-3 and going on to win the title. Nevertheless, improving his record for the season to 11 wins out of 12, Ronnie reached the final of the next event, the Grand Prix at Telford, but Williams, the reigning world champion, led 6-2 after their first session and won 9-5.

It should not be inferred that Ronnie would have won every match he ever played if he was in the right frame of mind. Nor should credit be subtracted from the talent and performances of other players. At his best, Williams was among the great players who could beat him on their day and, as Ronnie observed, 'his standard is very good all the time'. All that had happened was that Ronnie had lost a snooker match, albeit a major final on BBC. This entailed natural disappointment but no more than that, no anguished soul searching, nothing to prevent him, two days later, from making three centuries in four frames in beating Jimmy White 5-3 in the Scottish Masters.

The key frame in his quarter-final win over John Higgins was the fourth, which in less happy times he would have conceded but instead fought out to get the two snookers he needed. By stealing that frame on the black, he led 3-1, increased this advantage to 5-1 and held off a late rally to win 6-4.

Playing their eighth match in ten days, both Ronnie and Williams showed unmistakeable symptoms of mental fatigue in their semi-final, 'a funny sort of game', according to Ronnie, a 6-5 winner.

'Neither of us played well. I think we dragged each other down. I felt physically very tired and when you're feeling like that, it's tough to be at your best.'

This did not bode well for Ronnie's chances in the final but, fortunately for him, his semi had been an afternoon match, so this gave him the chance of the early night that refreshed him for his 9-6 win over Hendry. This meant that from the first three tournaments of the 2000/01 season, Ronnie had amassed £209,400 in prize money.

'Of course the trappings are good, you can't deny that, but money is a very minimal part of it. The way I feel at the moment, I'd be happy if I had 10p in my pocket.'

His 2000 UK Championship ended in the semi-finals with a 9-4 loss to Williams, who knew, as others did but could not carry through, how to give himself the best chance of beating Ronnie. 'We were both rubbish, compared with how we can play, but my safety was good. If you keep Ronnie tight, he'll give you chances but if you let him flow he'll steamroller you.'

Even in the last 16, Ronnie's patience and discipline had been fully tested by the cagey approach of Dave Harold, who led him 4-2.

'You've got to bide your time against Dave. He's so solid, so being 4-4 after the first session was a bonus. I carved out a result [a 9-5 win] because I'm learning to accept that winning is the main priority. You've got to grind, grind and grind again.' His quarter-final opponent, Quinten Hann, beaten 9-5, endorsed this. 'Some of the safety Ronnie played in the second session was the best I've ever seen.'

These matches had a cumulative effect. As Ronnie commented after his semi-final defeat, 'I've been to the well a lot this week and sometimes you just don't click, no matter how hard you try. I'm very disappointed. I always am when I lose but I suppose that's part and parcel of being a sportsman.'

After four months free of depression, Ronnie's prolonged exposure to intense competition was starting to peel away his defences against it. Perhaps he also thought that his stay in The Priory had effected a once-and-for-all cure, although susceptibility to depression rarely is cured. The best that can be hoped for, in most cases, is that depressions do not come so often, last so long or go so deep. It is also helpful to identify the onset of depression, so that it can be accommodated rather than denied.

For the next event, the China Open in Shanghai, Ronnie felt low all week but nevertheless won the tournament. It was amazing how effectively he could sometimes play even without his inner wiring fully connected.

Initially, his problems were increased by a pre-match massage that 'cracked' his back and left him 'bruised up' as he managed to beat Dominic Dale 5-2.

'I've never had any trouble like this before,' said Ronnie. 'I was in agony towards the end. I ended up having to get a few shots over and done with very quickly. It's right in the base of my spine.'

Despite experiencing renewed depression in full measure, he beat Paul Hunter 5-4 in the quarter-finals. 'My back is OK now, it's just my head that's screwed up. I'm fed up with the game and need to get away from it.

'I couldn't really lose. If I'd got beat, I'd be going home in the morning. Now I'm in the next round. I'm just not enjoying it – and that's absolutely nothing against China. I felt exactly the same as this in Bournemouth [in his UK semi-final]. I'm frustrated and the game's getting on my nerves again.

'I had a good spell for the first three or four tournaments but now I'm trying to get something going and it's a waste of time. I'm just playing snooker for the sake of it. If I win, I win, if I don't, so what?'

Low as he was feeling, Ronnie applied himself creditably to lead Hendry 5-0 in their semi-final and win 6-3, an outcome from which he did extract some pleasure while continuing to insist that he was 'not enjoying snooker'. He admitted:

'It's good to get through, especially beating Stephen, because that's an achievement in itself. Stephen missed some balls early in the match that normally he'd pot blindfold. That made my life a lot easier.'

As it transpired, so did Williams in the final.

'That first session was right up there with the worst I've ever played,' said Williams, having gone 7-1 down on the way to losing 9-3, but even taking his and Hendry's deficiencies into account, Ronnie still had to pot the balls. Eleven breaks over 60 in the 15 frames he won in these two matches was not bad going for someone who felt he was playing against the grain.

'The way I felt out there, I couldn't believe the balls were going in. It's nice to win but the last ten days or so have been very hard and I just can't wait to get home. I was in a clinic being treated for depression six or seven months ago and getting my life in order is the main priority at the moment.

'For a while, everything was going fine but I've been playing so much snooker lately, and everything's been so hectic, I've been pulled away from my family and the doctors who are helping me. Now I just want to get back and put my cue in the case because I feel drained.

'Obviously it's good to win because, coming here, I didn't feel I had a game to compete.' (This from someone who from four events had won two, lost in the final of one and in the semi-finals of the other.) 'If I could just get to 70–80 per cent I'd be happy, but I'm not there. When things are an effort, and they are at the moment, it's not enjoyable.

'It's baffling to me how I'm winning. I'm not going to say I didn't play well – you've got to if you're going to beat Mark – but the way I was feeling out there, I couldn't believe the balls were going where they were supposed to.'

Pleading back pain, Ronnie withdrew from England's Nations Cup team after its first match but declared this trouble 'OK at the moment' when he recovered from 3-1 down to beat Graeme Dott 5-3 in the opening round of the Welsh Open. He fell at the next hurdle, 5-4 to Joe Swail after forcing a ninth-frame decider from 4-2 down, although his form was nothing like what it had been in early season.

'Ronnie was very nervous towards the end,' said Swail. 'I've never missed so many balls and won.' It was clear – and Ronnie agreed – that he had been more affected by pressure than he ordinarily was.

Nor did he look at ease in losing his opening match in The Masters 6-2 to Jimmy White, who was by then struggling to remain an elite player. On another day and in a different mood, a full-to-the-brim Wembley Conference Centre crowd of 2,374 might have inspired him but this time it simply added to pressure that he was ill-equipped to bear.

Ronnie shot out of his blocks with a break of 101 but, very soon, his body language suggested discontent, agitation, frustration and a troubled state of mind. He did not spare himself. 'I don't want to take anything away from Jimmy but my performance was abysmal. You want to play your best at tournaments like this. It was a blinding atmosphere. I don't think I've ever heard noise like that before but I couldn't enjoy it because I was terrible. I don't know whether I've got the bottle to play this game any more.'

At the Thailand Masters, trying to loosen the blockages in his mind, Ronnie played predominantly left-handed to beat Chris Small, who was 21st in the rankings at the time, 5-1. 'I just fancied a change. I've been practising left-handed for a couple of weeks, so I thought I'd give it a go in a match. I'm here to enjoy myself and I enjoy playing left-handed. But I suppose if I want to win [the tournament], I'll have to play decent right-handed. I'll see what happens.'

What happened was a 5-4 defeat by Shokat Ali, the world number 68. Impatient, prone to error and very quickly irritated by his shortcomings, Ronnie self-punishingly conceded the sixth frame when only 24 behind with six reds still left on the table. His class surfaced in the form of a 129 break to lead 4-3 and at 4-4 he looked a certain winner when he seized control of the decider with a run of 60 that left his opponent needing two snookers.

But somehow Ali was to enjoy the win of his career. Having obtained both necessary sets of penalty points, he added the colours in three visits to tie and flashed in the tiebreak black from distance to reach his first and what was to remain his only world ranking quarter-final.

'I'm happy for Shokat. I can't begrudge him. He clung in there and I know it meant a lot to him,' said Ronnie, relieved at not having to play again that week.

As well as his personal problems, further pressures were being loaded on him through snooker's civil war between a reactionary establishment, the WPBSA, and progressive forces in which the voice of Ian Doyle, the game's most powerful manager, was the loudest. Ronnie's relationship with Doyle, personally and commercially, was sailing on smoothly until the WPBSA, desperate to avert the threat of a rival tour, decided to pay loyalty bonuses to the players it considered most important to its own circuit.

This conflict could and should have been avoided. Doyle's operation, then known as The Sports Network (TSN), had obtained £10m in funding from Warburg Pincus, the City finance house, and wanted to become the WPBSA's internet partners. Incredibly, the WPBSA ignored not only what would have been a very substantial injection of money but the potential of the internet because an important component of TSN's plan was live streaming of major tournaments. The WPBSA stubbornly insisted, even though tobacco sponsorship was about to be banned by government decree, that it did not need any help, leaving TSN, who had to use the funding somehow, to announce a rival tour. It was a doomed gesture because the BBC, as was invariably its practice, was to remain steadfastly loyal to the accredited governing body, however shambolic it might privately consider it to be.

If the WPBSA had offered any sensible compromise, the circuit would have been strengthened financially and the game would have been in on the ground floor of an expansion generated by the internet. Instead, the WPBSA's narrow and personalised objective was simply to defeat Doyle and his supporters.

The WPBSA's offers of loyalty bonuses concentrated on those players whose managers did not much like Doyle. Several were offered 17 days' 'promotional work' at £3,000 a day for three years, a total of £153,000 each. Contracts accepted by Peter Ebdon, Alan McManus, Matthew Stevens and Paul Hunter were believed to be of this order and that for John Higgins slightly more.

Because of his bond with Doyle, Hendry was unapproachable and Williams at that stage was also firmly in the Doyle camp, but Ronnie was the ace for both sides and the WPBSA offered him considerably more, going to him direct rather than his accredited manager, Doyle.

'My understanding is that the offer to Ronnie was slightly more than £1m spread over three years,' Doyle confirmed.

Had such an offer been accepted, Ronnie would have been exposed to action for breach of contract and the WPBSA to one for inducement to breach. Nevertheless, the WPBSA believed that Ronnie was about to sign the contract it had offered and issued a gloating press release, stating that he had 'turned his back on TSN'. However, over the weekend, he talked with his father, mother and friends and next day signed a new contract with TSN.

The ink on it was hardly dry, though, when niggles arose. Ronnie wanted to be managed by Doyle but was unwilling to forego entirely the WPBSA's lucrative inducement. Doyle said that he would be unwilling to manage Ronnie or any other player who had accepted a loyalty bonus from the WPBSA as he believed such payments to be 'unethical, immoral and possibly illegal [and] I would certainly not have taken any management percentage from them.' Ronnie's new contract was torn up, as were those with two logo sponsors that Doyle had negotiated. The WPBSA then stated that their 'loyalty' budget was fully spent up.

This conflict, spread over weeks, was another pressure for Ronnie to cope with, although its resolution, for better or worse, was a relief. There was also good news that Ronnie senior, nine years into his 18-year stretch, had been re-classified from category A to category B, a staging post towards category C, which permits home leave and other privileges.

With his psychological state on an upswing, Ronnie beat Steve Davis 6-3, Peter Ebdon 6-3 and, for the fourth time in four events that season, Stephen Hendry 9-8 to win the Irish Masters.

'If he can keep up that standard and stay composed, it'll take something special to beat him at the World Championship,' said Davis presciently.

'It's been difficult for the last couple of months, splitting with my manager and having to look after myself,' said Ronnie. 'There's been lots of trouble off the table. That's been distracting and I haven't felt right, but this week has been good.'

Ronnie's mind already appeared to be more on the World Championship than on his first match in the Scottish Open in Aberdeen, which he lost 5-1 to Mark Davis, a deceptive 77th in the rankings at the time and, much later, a top 16-player.

It takes a lot of nervous energy to win a ranking tournament and while Ronnie could not be accused of not trying, it was not a time to dig deep with the Crucible's marathon of the mind just around the corner.

Chapter 12

[2001]

IN the few remaining days before the 2001 World Championship, Ronnie's anxiety levels peaked. This was not just another tournament; it was, as it is every year, potentially career defining, life defining even. He felt empty, exhausted before he had even started. His doctor diagnosed depression linked to a fall in his serotonin level and prescribed Prozac for such time as Ronnie felt he needed it.

On arrival in Sheffield, Ronnie was in such a state that he phoned the Samaritans and found it helpful to talk to someone who could understand how he was feeling. Still in a high state of anxiety when he was interviewed on the radio on the first morning of the championship, he intended to utter the usual platitudes but found himself pouring his heart out to the effect that the game was making him ill, that he did not want to play any more and that after the championship it would be three months before he had to face playing again. He felt better for having blurted out how he was really feeling.

Ronnie may have been full of nameless fears but once he was grappling with immediate reality his form was disciplined and solid in beating Andy Hicks 10-2. Inwardly, though, he still felt shaky and started to take Prozac during his 13-6 win over Dave Harold. Initially, there were some side effects but nothing he could not cope with. Not wanting to get carried away, he said that he had 'played quite well in spasms.'

These spasms included breaks of 100 and 92 back to back to start the match and 81, 114 and 106 in the last three frames of the middle session to lead 10-6. Apart from one impatient aberration, when he conceded frame nine while only 22 behind with 35 still on, his general level was very good, much better than Ronnie the perfectionist thought it was.

As he candidly admitted, Prozac had settled him. Indeed, when this came into the public domain, some thought it odd that he should have been stripped of the 2000 Irish Masters title for testing positive for marijuana, which was not performance enhancing, but allowed to take Prozac, which at the least was performance enabling.

If these performances against Hicks and Harold had been good, the second session of his quarter-final against Peter Ebdon was irresistible. From 4-4, Ronnie's genius burst into full flower as he ran through it 8-0.

Between the first and second sessions, Ronnie took his Prozac pill, the immediate effect of which was to make him feel dizzy and a little high, although fortunately he did not have to play until the evening, by which time the effect had worn off.

'Ronnie's the Mozart of snooker. He's a genius. I couldn't help sitting there smiling at times. It was class personified, poetry in motion. Ronnie was awesome. He's got so much artistry and imagination. He was unstoppable,' said Ebdon.

Their brief final session was virtually a formality as Ronnie clinched victory at 13-6. As he was to admit, Prozac had transformed his mood and clarified his thinking. The draw suggested that he would have to play Mark Williams in the semi-finals but the defending champion was a 13-12 second-round loser to Joe Swail, who went on to become Ronnie's last obstacle to a place in his first Crucible final.

In tune and looking ominously comfortable, Ronnie led 6-2 after their opening session and started the second with consecutive centuries, 108 and 119. It was a measure of how well Swail was playing that he was able to split the session 4-4 to limit his arrears to 10-6 at halfway but this became 15-9 to Ronnie after three sessions and a 17-11 win.

'I'm surprised I haven't been in the final before,' said Ronnie matter-of-factly. 'When I was younger, I thought I'd have won it once or twice by now. That's not being big-headed. I'm just being honest because I know how good I was when I was 16 and I know how good I can be now.

'Joe's long potting was superb but he missed a few he should have knocked in at the right time for me. I won quite a few frames from 40 or 50 behind and that made a big difference. You don't get to world finals without working but I always felt pretty much in control, especially after the first session.

'I've managed to make reasonably light work of all my matches here so far, so that's got to be an advantage. You've got to play a lot of snooker to get to the final, so a smooth run obviously helps a lot.'

For Higgins, his semi-final, finishing late in the evening after Ronnie's had ended in the afternoon, was anything but smooth.

'The pressure was so intense I couldn't see the pockets properly,' said Higgins after overcoming Matthew Stevens 17-15.

He was to admit that this protracted struggle took its toll on his performance in the opening session of the final. 'It was a funny feeling. I came out in the first session, after fighting so hard to get to the final, and I just wasn't there.'

Ronnie's 6-2 lead from that session was reduced to 7-5 but in the last four frames of the day he made breaks of 99, 100 and 99 and Higgins one of 107 as play ended with the score at 10-6.

Runs of 81, 139, 85 and 86 featured as Ronnie pulled away to 14-7 but with the loss of the last three frames of the afternoon, this became 14-10. It gave Higgins an outside chance provided he could maintain his momentum and if Ronnie could assist him by wilting, at least to some degree, under the pressure of clinching his lifelong heart's desire, a consummation Jimmy White had failed to achieve from winning positions in 1992 and 1994.

Between sessions, as Ronnie was resting on his bed, Dr Hodges, his GP, phoned, concerned that Ronnie's concentration level appeared to be dropping and advising him to take another Prozac. It would make him feel drowsy initially but by the time the final session started he would feel fine.

'Knowing what happened to Jimmy kept me sharp but it also made me nervous,' Ronnie admitted.

Ronnie lost the first frame but his response to having his lead cut to 14-11 was to freeze Higgins out of the next and make a cool 78 from 0-43 to advance to 16-11.

Higgins gamely reduced this to 16-12 with a clinching 62 but wobbled a red on 60 in the following frame. Fully in control of himself, Ronnie cleared with 68 to go five up with six to play.

With Ronnie in on 45 and leading by 63, his mother and Higgins's parents were embracing in the players' room but Ronnie, finally unable to prevent his thoughts racing ahead, missed an elementary red to the middle when needing only two more basic pots to assure himself of the title.

With a 65 clearance, Higgins exploited the reprieve and if Ronnie had not been at his mentally strongest, he might have collapsed. Even as it was, he imagined the headlines if he were to lose from such an apparently impregnable position. But when Higgins missed a straight red to a corner on 45 in the next frame, Ronnie displayed immense self-control under the pressure, increased by his blunder in the previous frame, by clearing up with 80 for frame, match and title.

Whatever happened now, he would not be remembered as 'the best player who never'.

'It's a blinding feeling, just blinding. I didn't know it was possible to feel as good about anything as this. It's an unbelievable feeling. I know I should have been here before and now I've actually done it.'

Ronnie and his inner core of supporters, his mother, his sister, Del Hill, Bianca, Ronnie Wood and Jimmy White, celebrated far into the night but Ronnie's immediate thought was of his father, still in his prison cell, who kept awake all night so that he could savour, time after time, on the BBC's hourly bulletin, that his boy was world champion at last.

'My dad might not show it but this will mean so much to him. He was the one who helped me when I first got interested in this game. He supported me through thick and thin and we couldn't be closer. I can't wait to go and see him with the trophy. That'll be special.'

The snooker world was pleased for Ronnie. The general feeling was that the world title was his due and was indeed overdue.

Higgins regretted that 'I had good chances to put Ronnie under pressure at 14-11, 16-13 and again at 17-14, but I didn't grab any of them. Ronnie has got so much natural talent and when you add that to great safety play as well, he's certainly one of the greats. He makes the game look so easy.'

Steve Davis, six times world champion in the 80s, said, 'When Ronnie's on song, everybody else looks a carthorse in comparison. It looks as though snooker is what he was put on this planet to do. Alex Higgins and Jimmy White were born to play this game but Ronnie has taken fluency to a different level. It's not just his body that provides co-ordination. Ronnie's got such a quick-thinking snooker brain, it's almost instinctive. I know you can't accurately compare eras in any sport but if you got all the great players over the years and plonked them in front of Ronnie, he's got the ability to blow them all away.'

Ronnie's last public words were to express the hope that 'this will take all that pressure off me when I come back here in the future.' To some degree, in the sense that the biggest difference in a player's number of world titles is between 0 and 1, it did. But he still had battles to fight, many of them with himself, and was to be brought more than once to the brink of despairing retirement. He had enjoyed the rarefied air of snooker's highest summit but there were always going to be problems at ground level.

Chapter 13

[2001/02]

'IT was great to win the world [title] but it's important to live in the present,' said Ronnie after beating Higgins 6-3 and Hendry 9-7 to win the Matchroom League play-offs in Inverness a fortnight later. This took his prize money for the 2000/01 season to £684,130, having won six of the twelve tournaments in which he had competed despite a severe downswing around its halfway mark.

He reflected on the valuable work he had done at The Priory. 'It made me look at what my life was all about. I woke up one day and thought, "I've got to liven up here because if I don't I'm going to lose everything." I'll look back in a few years and think I should have done things differently. My self-esteem and self-worth were pretty low. Being in there made me feel as if I wasn't on my own any more.'

He had not felt so positive immediately. 'After three days, I walked out. It was fucking horrible in there. I felt like an animal. They're all quite well spoken in there, quite well to do – lawyers, a lot of women, a couple of famous people. In I came effing and blinding; I felt like the odd one out. But after a week or so, they all quite liked me.'

Why should he have been surprised? There is no reason for anyone not to find Ronnie likeable and personable or for him to imagine that he would be judged on how successful he was.

Understandably, Ronnie also felt better about himself for recognising his bond with his four-year-old daughter, Taylor-Anne, initially against the wishes of her mother, Sally Magnus, who told him, he said, 'She doesn't know you and I don't want you to mess her head up.' Ronnie's first contact with her in January 2001 had come during his mid-season recession. At first, in his panic, he had been unwilling to accept parentage; then he had simply agreed a financial settlement; but, as time passed, he came to realise that this too was an evasion, a denial even to himself of feelings and responsibilities. 'It was something which was on my mind. I'd stopped going out as much. I realised that I had a little daughter – that she was mine, of my making. I wanted to see her. I was afraid that she'd grow up and think, "Where's my dad? He never came to see me."'

Brought up in a close and loving family himself, Ronnie was unwilling to see himself in such an unfavourable light. To put it another way, it was bad for his sense of self-worth.

As his relationship with his infant daughter developed, it took away a source of the guilt that could cloud his mind:

'She's a lovely, beautiful little girl. I try to spend some time with her at least once a week, which is lovely. It's so nice.

'I was colouring in a picture with her and it was so therapeutic. We didn't speak to each other for two hours, we were so into it. I thought, "Two hours have passed and I haven't thought about anything."'

Recognising his responsibility to Taylor-Anne, with all the feelings that went with it, was a step towards making his life more rounded, not merely a succession of snooker matches with nothing much of value in between. Once the euphoria of winning the world title had worn off, there were plenty of real-life issues to cope with.

Defending himself against the onset of unease or depression, Ronnie's initial impulse had always been to live his life faster only to enact, inevitably, the 'what goes up must come down' syndrome. He is not the only elite sportsman this has happened to after a peak experience. So much adrenalin has been expended that there can be a sort of adrenalin lag or emotional burnout that deepens into depression.

Preoccupation with achieving a lifetime ambition can camouflage issues undealt with. Fulfilling that ambition can have unexpected side effects. The late comedian, Frankie Howerd, was obsessed throughout his career with topping the bill at the London Palladium. As soon as he had done so, he crashed into deep depression. 'I've done it but apart from the initial high it hasn't made any difference to the way I feel,' summarises this sort of reaction and it was one that Ronnie experienced in summer 2001.

At the age of 25, he was reluctantly adjusting to the probability that he would never feel quite the same about snooker as he had when he was very young and that good snooker times with his father would never come round again in the same way.

'When I was ten, I woke up in the morning and couldn't wait to get on the table. Life was purely about snooker. I've tried everything to get that feeling back. I asked my mum about it. I said, "Mum, have I always been like this?" and she said, "No, you were a very happy-go-lucky sort of child." I said, "What's gone wrong then? What's happening to me?"'

It was obviously unrealistic that he should feel quite the same about snooker at 25 as he had at 10, but even so he had a point. Part of the problem was his awesome responsibility to his talent. As the most naturally gifted player ever to pick up a cue, he was well aware of just how good he was and this put him in a position in which anything less than mighty achievement and peak performance counted as failure, certainly in his own mind. Now, having climbed to the summit of his profession, his aspiration was not quite the same. He had to work just as hard and endure just as much simply to stay at the same level.

Ronnie spent much of that summer honing his fitness, joining Dagenham Athletic Club, running several miles a day and signing up for Arsenal's celebrity football team, but his return to competition for his defence of the Champions Cup ended in his four-man group with a 5-3 win over Jimmy

White and defeats by Ken Doherty, 5-4, and Peter Ebdon, 5-1. He felt, he admitted, 'pretty flat'.

He did not feel like playing in the Scottish Masters, partly because his 18-year-old sister, Danielle, and a 22-year-old man, not named, had been arrested on suspicion of possessing drugs with intent to supply. Police had been called because of an argument between Danielle and the man. Their car was searched and the drugs discovered. There was also a significant change in that Ronnie's general factotum, Del Hill, was no longer travelling with him and giving him constant moral and practical support. Ronnie instead pitched up in Motherwell with Frank Adamson, a veteran coach from Bristol.

'Del is like family to me but this was a business decision,' said Ronnie. 'I had to try something different and Del told me that if he'd served his purpose, then I should go to someone else.'

It seemed peculiar to change like this not long after becoming world champion. Del's contribution had been comparatively slight on the coaching side but very considerable in terms of personal support. As for technique, it had been good enough to win a world title but Ronnie said, 'I'm open-minded and Frank has taught me some things that are useful. I haven't found perfection but that's not what I'm after. I want consistency, which is what all top sportsmen need.'

Whether the secret of this lay in his mental equilibrium or some technical tweaking and different practice routines remained to be seen.

Playing 'alright in patches, I suppose', Ronnie beat Matthew Stevens 6-3 but against Marco Fu the negativity returned. 'Even when I was 5-2 up, I kept thinking I was going to lose,' said Ronnie. 'I felt quite nervous and that was horrible.' He closed out the match 6-3 but lost 9-6 to John Higgins in the final, a score that, Ronnie said, 'looks closer than it actually was'.

His volatility of mood was amply illustrated at the British Open in Newcastle. In the last 16, he was 3-0 down to Joe Swail, made back-to-back centuries, 102 and 131, to reduce this to 3-2 then, from 4-2 adrift, ran out a 5-4 winner, taking the penultimate frame with a 143 total clearance and restricting Swail to 29 points in this three-frame spell.

'Even at 4-2, I never thought I was going home,' said Ronnie, who at 5-2 up against Fu could not stop thinking that he was going to lose. 'You've got to have hope and try to fight. There were times in the past when I didn't think it was worth trying hard because I thought I'd struggle in my next match as well. Now, I've got some consistency and feel like I might be close to finding that magic spark.'

Ronnie again played very well in beating Alan McManus 5-1 in the quarter-finals but against Graeme Dott in the semis, a black mood closed over him like a shroud. Although Dott, a top-16 player for the first time that season, made a highest break of only 40 and only two more over 30, he won 6-4 and was 'embarrassed with how badly I played'. Not in seven previous attempts had he come close to beating Ronnie.

Hurried, reckless and careless, Ronnie conceded two frames he was still mathematically able to win without the need for snookers. In his press conference, his eyes were twin pools of despair. He made one brief attempt to treat his defeat as just another snooker match ('the better man won') before confessing, 'I was quite happy to lose. The thought of playing another match like that would have had me hanging off the nearest bridge. It baffles me and it hurts me. You have to accept it, I suppose. I'm 25, I should be at the peak of my career, but I just feel numb. You can't be fantastic all the time and have everything go your way, but that was terrible.'

As if this had never happened, Ronnie again started brilliantly at the LG Cup at Preston, making his fifth 147 in competition in the penultimate frame of the 5-1 win over Drew Henry, which put him in the quarter-finals. At 6 minutes 36 seconds, it was the second fastest on record behind his own 5 minutes 20 seconds. Nor did it affect the discipline of his performance. 'I stayed patient and kept it nip and tuck in the last frame. I'm as pleased with that as I was with my max.'

The following morning, Gordon Burn, the novelist, who intermittently wrote illuminatingly about the snooker world, arrived at Ronnie's hotel for an interview and found him looking 'dog rough' and confessing that he had kept the television on all night, hardly slept and got out of bed believing he could never win another tournament in his life. It was as if, once he had used his supply of what sportsmen call adrenalin, he had no protection from dark, pessimistic thoughts.

Ronnie lost his quarter-final that day, 5-4 to Peter Ebdon. Having gone 3-1 down through Ebdon stealing the fourth frame after needing three snookers, Ronnie recovered to lead 4-3 without his opponent potting a ball in these three frames and was poised to win 5-3 until an elementary positional shot went wrong.

'If you can't drop on a ball in a situation like that, you don't deserve to win, Ronnie said later.

Snookered behind the yellow in the decider, he opted to smash into the pack of reds at pace, fruitlessly hoping to fluke one. A more moderately paced escape might very well have left a red on but, as it was, Ebdon was left with all the reds on a plate and did not give Ronnie another chance. It had been most unlike Ronnie to trust to luck when there was an alternative. 'I'm not looking forward to the drive home. It's 240 miles.'

A 5-4 quarter-final loss to Stephen Hendry in the European Open in Malta meant that the first four months of the 2001/02 season had gone by without Ronnie winning a title. He was not, with the exception of the Dott match, playing poorly but he was not consistently producing his best. He 'wasn't happy' with his standard of play against Hendry, who had not beaten him for 27 months. 'I didn't score heavily enough. I made silly mistakes and I didn't put him under any pressure. It was a very poor match. He just played a better last frame than me. It's as simple as that.'

Ronnie's title drought seemed almost certain to continue when he trailed Ebdon 6-1 in their UK Championship quarter-final at York. In this period, Ebdon had a run of 249 unanswered points and even the frame that Ronnie won was after needing snookers. Down 8-4 in the evening, Ronnie looked out of it but, leading by 40 in what he intended would be the clinching frame, Ebdon jawed a red.

Ronnie was so near to losing that he had resigned himself to it. After Ebdon's mistake, he suddenly had everything to gain. Having cleared up with 74, he outscored Ebdon 373-72 in the remaining four frames, making an apparently carefree 85 break in the decider to win 9-8.

'I just dug in and eventually came alive,' Ronnie explained. 'Peter missed a couple of important balls, the crowd got behind me and it all turned round. It was flowing and I didn't feel any pressure in the last frame.'

Simultaneously, on the other side of the arena, Williams was also coming from four down with five to play to beat Hendry and in the semi-finals gave a performance he described as 'one of the best of my life' even though Ronnie still beat him 9-6.

'I've got electric waves going through me because this is such a good result for me,' said Ronnie. 'Mark is a class act. I've played out of my skin all day. I kept up the gritty match snooker. I hardly missed a ball and he was still difficult to shake off.'

Still brimming with confidence, Ronnie needed only two hours to beat Ken Doherty 10-1 to win his third UK title.

His elusive optimum state of mind disappeared over Christmas. Returning to work, he had to win the last two frames to beat Ian McCulloch 5-4 in his first match at the Welsh Open but then lost 5-4 to Paul Hunter, who went on to win the first ranking title of a career that was to be tragically curtailed by his death from cancer in 2007 at the age of 27.

'With the quality of the younger players around nowadays, you can't keep doing the business. The days when Stephen Hendry won 36 matches on the trot in the top flight are over. If you have an off day, that's usually it,' said Ronnie, who then lost 6-5 from 5-2 up to Jimmy White in the Masters.

This outcome left Ronnie 'angry, very angry', although he declined to reveal why. 'It's something I'm not going to air in the press.' This was to remain a mystery, although, even in the early part of the match, he had not demonstrated his customary authority. As White summarised, 'I played bad and he played bad but I won and the result is the [main] thing.' It might have crossed Ronnie's mind that only Steve Davis, Stephen Hendry and John Higgins had held the world, UK and Masters titles concurrently but pressures like this do not normally affect Ronnie and it may have been, after all, that he never even thought of this.

Ronnie started the China Open well enough, not only making a 109 break in the decider to beat Ali Carter 5-4 but favouring the somewhat bemused Chinese press corps with a rendition of the theme tune from the television series *Happy Days*. He also beat White 5-1 but then lost 5-3 in the quarter-finals to 18-year-old Mark Selby, who was just setting out on a long road that would lead to becoming a three-time world champion.

'To be honest, I don't care. I'm quite happy to get beat,' said Ronnie, who displayed his propensity to self-destruct in frustration after losing the third frame on the pink to go 2-1 down.

'I was no good,' said Ronnie in a judgment that was at variance with his 126 break in the second frame. 'I've just had a stomach full of it.'

Selby could not believe the scale of Ronnie's meltdown. 'I wondered what Ronnie was doing because he played properly in the first three frames.'

Pushing straight on to Bangkok to the Thailand Masters, Ronnie beat a struggling James Wattana 5-2 ('I had empathy for him because I know what it's like when the game gets really difficult and nothing goes right') and played very well in leading Mark King 4-1, although at 4-4 he looked like losing until he summoned a 41 clearance of pure genius to win 5-4 on the final black.

King, like Ebdon and Dott, is one of those opponents Ronnie often found frustrating to play. 'I think snooker is an art and I enjoy it most when I'm flowing, I don't like it when the balls run awkward and everything is messy.'

Ronnie would perhaps, not for the first time, have been happy enough to lose but possibly not to King, a rival since boyhood.

'I know I've got through but I'm still disappointed. There's something going on in my head and I'm puzzled. It's a specialist thing and something that I've got to overcome. It's very frustrating. I'd like to tell you what it is but if I did that, it would be an advantage for anyone I had to play. Let's just say, it's mental.'

His quarter-final opponent, Hendry, invariably motivated him much more and with a tidy 5-3 victory, he arrived in the semi-finals. 'I played decent but not brilliant,' said Ronnie.

That was about it as far as Ronnie was concerned. As if his interest could only be activated when he had a chance to display his break making in all its peerless fluency, he made one of 135 against Mark Williams but still lost 5-2 as the Welsh left-hander, having already won the China Open, went on to complete a Far East double.

'It hurts when I get beat but it doesn't hurt enough to let it really bother me. It doesn't matter whether it's Thailand, China, the World Championship or a pro-am round the corner when I feel like this. I've done what I wanted by winning the World Championship. Now it wouldn't bother me if I never pick up a cue again. Snooker is just a means to an end. It helps me pay my mortgage and with my lifestyle.'

Almost always very open in his press conferences, Ronnie gave two monosyllabic ones after losing his opening matches in the Irish Masters, to Matthew Stevens 6-2, and in the Scottish Open, to Barry Hawkins 5-3. The impression he gave was that he did not care whether he won or lost but he had emerged from the depths of this depression in time for the World Championship and on its opening day progressed from 3-3 to 9-3 and a 10-5 victory over Drew Henry.

'I'm really pleased to finally get stuck into the action. It's terrible to lose early on and watch everyone else on the telly,' he said, mindful of his 10-9 first-round defeat by David Gray two years earlier.

'Before the interval, I wasn't that interested but I told myself to hold my head together. To be honest, I was thinking about what I was going to be doing after the championship. I was half away on a beach somewhere but I got myself bothered afterwards. It bothers me when I'm not bothered.

'I hope I can play myself into form. I did that at the UK. You feel something click. I feel deep down there's something there and although it might sound strange, I'm more confident than I was last year.

'This season, I haven't practised much but since the Irish Masters I've put in four hours a day and that sharpness is coming through. The game can kick you in the teeth if you turn your back on it. To be top of your sport you've got to practise, no matter how much ability you've got. I've been going to tournaments not having picked up a cue for weeks but with this I knew I'd have to knuckle down.'

This was Ronnie at his most mature and sensible. Within days, he was to be at his most immature and irrational. After overwhelming Robert Milkins 13-2, he gave himself a morning off to visit a chiropractor for a 'bad back' that had been troubling him intermittently for about a year and, making him feel 'agitated and irritable', but there was no sign of this problem in his 13-10 quarter-final win over Stephen Lee, who held him to 8-8 after their first two sessions. This became 10-10 but Ronnie went into overdrive with breaks of 83, 102 and 113 to win the three frames he needed in only 29 minutes.

'Stephen kept hanging in there but when it got towards the end I knew I had to step it up a gear and I found some form from somewhere. I felt relaxed and would have done even if it had gone 12-12 because I didn't care about winning or losing. I'm in such a funny mood and it doesn't really matter to me.'

Ronnie was playing well enough to retain the title but needlessly handicapped himself by insulting Hendry on the eve of their semi-final by saying that he had 'no respect' for him. His pretext for this extraordinary remark was an incident during their 1999 semi-final, when the referee awarded a miss that Ronnie felt Hendry should have refused to accept.

No such incident was readily called to mind by Hendry or anyone else and it seemed extraordinary that Ronnie could harbour a grudge for so long simply because a referee had awarded a penalty from which Hendry saw no reason not to take advantage. At the very worst, Hendry was guilty of playing to the referee's decision, which is what all sportsmen are trained to accept.

Like most players on the circuit Hendry has a highly developed sense of fair play, never more strikingly demonstrated than in the deciding frame of his 1994 final against Jimmy White, when he was awarded a free ball but asked the referee to check it because he did not want an incorrect decision, however marginal, to disadvantage his opponent. The referee changed his decision but Hendry still won 18-17.

Ronnie alleged that he had always had to play second fiddle to Hendry when he was in the stable of players managed by Ian Doyle and that Doyle had played 'mind games' during their 1999 semi-final. Doyle rejected this allegation as 'rubbish' but added, 'Stephen has earned a degree of special treatment through the scale of what he has won. He's a very important client not only to us but to the sponsors we represent. Otherwise, all our clients receive equal treatment and our best endeavours.'

Doyle was an acerbic martinet. Rightly or wrongly, things had to be done his way or not at all but in his attention to detail he was a manager who, sometimes literally, never slept.

'I shall miss being phoned up at midnight because Ronnie's in some scrape or other,' Doyle remarked laconically when he parted company with Ronnie in March 2001, two months before the end of his most successful season, in which he won the world title and five others.

'When Ronnie came to me, he had £25,000. When he left three and a half years later, he was a millionaire in assets and cash.' Their parting arose over the WPBSA's loyalty bonuses to several leading players to reduce the power of Doyle, its chief critic, and in particular to hamper any plans his company, TSN (re-named 110sport to avoid confusion with a Canadian broadcaster, The Sports Network), had for a rival tour.

Ronnie, who was politically influenced by his old friend Del Hill, the players' room cheerleader for the WPBSA against 110, wanted to take the money from a loyalty bonus, with Doyle continuing to manage him. Doyle refused.

'[The] WPBSA's money belongs to the membership, including my players, in its totality and should not be distributed to chosen players in this way,' said Doyle.

The reason for these exclusive contracts disappeared when 110 withdrew all plans for a rival tour.

'I'm pleased I got away from all that [Doyle's management] because I've done better since I did my own thing,' said Ronnie, although of the six titles he had won in 2000/01 three had been under Doyle's management and in the 2001/02 season he had thus far won only two in all.

'Hendry isn't my cup of tea. He could do anything in the match and it won't bother me. He could do a moonie in front of me and I'd just say, "get back to your sad little life."'

Hendry responded icily, 'Anything which happens off the table doesn't matter.'

Puzzlement remained over Ronnie's real reasons for raising the emotional temperature, although it was noted that he had been spending so much time with Prince Naseem Hamed and his brother that he had adopted some of the Sheffield boxer's habitual pre-fight trash talk.

In a match of very high quality, Ronnie led 5-3 after their first session, trailed 9-7 after their second, in which Hendry made breaks of 125, 122 and 124, and was level at 12-12 after their third, which produced two centuries from Hendry and one from Ronnie, before Hendry pulled away to win 17-13.

'It's the World Championship and you don't need any greater motivation than that,' said Hendry, who declined to be drawn into a slanging match with an opponent who had injected an unwelcome scent of animosity into the proceedings.

Ronnie acknowledged Hendry's qualities as a player while still defending his earlier attack on his integrity and other disparaging remarks, 'Stephen is a great player. He's proved it time and time again and I wouldn't question him as a snooker player. He puts you under pressure and keeps you there, which is why he's the greatest player that's ever lived.

'I never said that Stephen isn't a great player because he is and he was one of my idols when I was a kid. He's a fantastic competitor, an animal. But I enjoyed making the comments. It made it a great atmosphere and you should buzz it up a bit. There was real tension out there, it was brilliant. What could be better than a grudge match?

'I'd love to have stuck it up him and sent him home, but he's stuck it up me and sent me home.'

Chapter 14

[2002/03]

UNSURPRISINGLY, there was coolness from Hendry's side when he next met Ronnie at the opening tournament of the 2002/03 season, although this did not prevent him from enjoying 'everything except the result' after Ronnie had beaten him 6-3 in the Scottish Masters semi-finals. In fine fettle, Ronnie went on to beat John Higgins 9-4 to win this title for the third time in five years but on sober reflection had come to realise that his trash talking of Hendry and Doyle at the Crucible a few months earlier had been not only unfair but counter-productive.

'Ian was a good manager for me and I like the man,' Ronnie told the final night reception. 'I spent two hours with Naz [Naseem Hamed] at his gym and the boxing talk got in my head. What I said about Stephen and Ian wasn't me. It was like somebody else talking. The worst thing now is that Stephen won't talk to me.'

Ronnie's admission of how Hamed had influenced him showed how he was still, at times, easily led. His attempt to rebuild bridges was welcome, particularly as he had unfairly and publicly held Doyle responsible for many of the game's problems just a few days earlier.

On a lighter note, Ronnie announced a new business enterprise, an underwear shop for women and gay men in London's Soho.

'I don't think snooker players should just rely on snooker for a living,' he said.

On the table, his attitude had been perfect but impatience and a trace of paranoia surfaced at the LG Cup in Preston, where he was contesting a passage to the quarter-final with the talented but volatile Michael Holt, notoriously edgy and, unconsciously, one of the circuit's top face-pullers.

'I was struggling with my game and some of the little mannerisms that Michael has got, like making faces and patting the table, got to me. I thought that he was winding me up but then I realised that's just the way he is,' said Ronnie, who won 5-3 from 3-1 down.

This was the week in which Chris Small, a tall Scot with chronic back problems that were to force him into retirement, emerged from the circuit's chorus to beat John Higgins 5-1, Ronnie 5-1 and, in the final, Alan McManus 9-5 to win the life-changing first prize of £82,500.

Ronnie acknowledged how well Small had played against him but described his own performance as 'unacceptable. My head must be the worst in the world.'

Amen to that—at the time. A perfectionist to an impossible degree, Ronnie scored 355 points without reply, making breaks of 123, 83, 64 and 82, in beating Dominic Dale 5-1 in his first match at the British Open in Telford, yet described his performance as 'not very good'.

'I missed balls early on but that's because I'm not that good. I've watched myself and I'm not really much good. That's a good thing because now I know why I worry about my game.

'I'll keep playing as long as I'm in the top 16 but it wouldn't surprise me if I dropped out because the standard is so high that I'll eventually get overtaken.'

He then lost a high-quality match 5-4 to Paul Hunter, who went on to win the title. Ronnie made two centuries but to listen to him afterwards anyone might have thought he had been struggling to make a 30. 'I'm not disappointed, to be honest.

'I'm happy I got beaten because I half-expected it. I'm not going to say I'll quit the game but I'm not really bothered any more. I'll just keep turning up and try to enjoy it as much as I can.'

Although he made it out to be worse than it was, Ronnie's performance in beating Marco Fu 9-7 in his first match at the UK Championship was flat. He attributed this and other recent victories to 'a combination of playing well in patches and my opponents helping me out', but gave a clue to the wild oscillation of his thought processes when he added, 'Sometimes I'm bang in the balls and wonder if I'll make 20;

another time I'll pot the first red and start thinking about the high break prize.'

His game was just not up to it when Drew Henry, the world number 22, pulled off the win of his career by beating Ronnie 9-4 in the quarter-finals.

'I just didn't get going and I got slaughtered,' said Ronnie, who signalled the end of his title defence by biting the tip off the end of his cue while still seated in the arena. 'I can't put my finger on what went wrong and I don't even want to think about it. I'm very frustrated because my heart is still in the game.

'At the UK in 1994, I lost to Ken [Doherty] and meant it when I said I wanted to retire. It got to me and it's kept getting at me over the years. I don't feel too disappointed but I know it'll hurt tomorrow. It's painful.'

In a more settled frame of mind, Ronnie beat Anthony Hamilton and Tony Drago in the Welsh Open at Cardiff. 'I've played alright even though they've both been 5-4s,' said Ronnie, who then lost 5-3 to Fu.

On the eve of the opening of his new lingerie shop, Ronnie started his Masters campaign with a 6-1 win over Joe Perry that included breaks of 112 (14 red/blacks) 96 and 105, but eventually lost 6-5 to Doherty in the quarters.

Mental turmoil played no part in these reverses, the latter of which was attributable to Doherty's artfully worked 59 break to win the decider from well behind.

'It's very disappointing to lose but Ken deserved it after making a break like that under pressure,' said Ronnie.

These were just two instances of the normal ups and downs of results between leading players, so it did not take a dramatic shift in form or attitude for Ronnie to win the European Open at the Palace Hotel, Torquay.

Not that it was easy. Ronnie nailed Michael Holt 5-3 with a 91 break but admitted, 'I was really nervous. I'm cueing well but getting over the line is difficult. Something is missing from my game and I need to get it back.'

He started with a 121 and finished with a 102 – with a 129 in the middle for good measure – in beating Dave Finbow 5-3 but still commented, 'No job is easy these days.'

A 139 was his parting shot in the 5-2 defeat of Stephen Lee, which put him in a ranking semi-final for the first time since his defeat by Hendry in the 2002 World Championship. His mood could scarcely have been more upbeat. 'The vibes were good and it was a pleasure to play out there. I fancied scoring every time I got the chance.

'I'm keeping my focus all the time now,' said Ronnie blithely, sadly in ignorance that this would not last forever. 'The game plan was just to concentrate on myself and forget who I was playing,' he added, having beaten Peter Ebdon 6-3 to reach his first ranking final for 15 months.

'If players beat me they have to beat Ronnie O'Sullivan the snooker player, not Ronnie O'Sullivan the person. I'm just learning the importance of giving myself the best chance to win every single match.

'With the Crucible coming up, I badly wanted to get to the final here. I want to win two tournaments on the run-in to

Sheffield and the way I've felt I can say that without worrying I'll end up with egg on my face.'

It would have been easy to promote the O'Sullivan/ Hendry final as a grudge match but it was conducted with exemplary professionalism. Ronnie had apologised for his remarks on the eve of the 2002 world semi-final but it took more than this for Hendry to begin to forgive him, although their relationship years later suggested that he finally did.

That week, Hendry spoke about the incident for the first time. 'I don't speak to Ronnie now. It's partly because of his Crucible press conference, saying that he is going to stick it up me and send me up the road.

'Really, talk like that means nothing but to bring up something that happened three or four years before and say that I never gave him a miss call, well, that's tantamount to calling me a cheat, which I'm not.

'I had a miss once against Jimmy White that I never took. It was in a final of a world championship and could have cost me the final. No one could even remember what Ronnie was on about.

'Then he said, "I'll send Stephen back to his sad little life." Well, I suppose that a few people would just love my sad little life. I wouldn't swap it for Ronnie's, that for sure. Ronnie and I used to get on very well but he left our stable [110sport], as did John Higgins.

'I don't think they could handle being number two to me, although they were getting the financial benefits from being involved in the company. In the end, it was like one tournament Ronnie would be your friend and speak to you, the next he wouldn't. It was just so unpredictable and I thought there was no point.

'So I just left it. Now the two of us pass each other in the corridor without anything being said. Och, I dare say it will get to the stage where we say hello and that but it will never be the same again because you'll always wonder when he's going to come out with something.'

The final, one of the finest the game had ever seen, though regrettably not televised, showed how Hendry and – at his most stable – Ronnie could exclude off-table emotions. Ronnie, starting with 140, made three centuries in winning 9-6. Hendry made two. The 15 frames were completed at an average of ten minutes each. 'It might sound strange,' said Hendry, 'but my break-off cost me the match. Every time I left Ronnie a long red and every time but one he knocked it in.' It was, he said, again excluding personal issues, 'a really enjoyable final to play in'.

Ronnie again played superbly all week to win the Irish Masters, converted into a ranking tournament for the first time. 'Snooker is just a game you play with balls and sticks. It's stupid even to be talking about it. I'm just playing for fun. I want to enjoy myself. Winning and losing isn't important.'

These remarks were received with much scepticism. 'Winning and losing don't matter unless you lose' would have been generally regarded as more realistic. Meanwhile, Ronnie came under sustained pressure in a final against John

Higgins comparable in quality to the European Open and exceeding it in drama.

There was an exchange of centuries in the last two frames, 123 by Higgins, 123 by Ronnie to win 10-9. 'It was,' said Higgins, 'the best match I've ever been involved in. Half of me is disappointed I lost, half of me is delighted with how I played. I can't have any complaints because Ronnie's break in the last frame was fantastic.'

Ronnie had proved against both Hendry in Torquay and Higgins in Dublin that his best was better than anyone else's. For once, he seemed to have all his ducks in a row but, compulsively, it appeared, he had to find a way of giving himself a problem. He chose to do this by gratuitously badmouthing Mark Williams.

Promoting his first volume of autobiography, he was reported in a tabloid to have said of Williams, 'I can't think of anyone in the game who likes him. He rubs everyone up the wrong way.' Williams responded with a forthright assessment of Ronnie. 'If you're an arsehole, you'll say stupid things. It'll mean a bit of extra needle next time we meet.'

Ronnie, on hearing this, chose to strike again. 'Mark should be thankful that he's mentioned in my book. Nobody will be writing books about him because he's not interesting. When you're great, people want to know about you but he's just normal. I couldn't care less if he never said hello to me again because I'm a champion in my own life. I've come through a lot of trials and tribulations and I'm a survivor. And I'm sure I'll survive if Mark never speaks to me again.'

O'Sullivan was right, of course, that his own life was more interesting for an autobiography than Williams's would have been, but did this make Williams boring or just somebody who had stayed out of trouble?

In the end, Ronnie attempted a reconciliation of sorts by claiming, after reaching the semi-finals, that he had been misquoted in the coverage of the serialisation.

'Mark confirmed what I believed he thought of me,' said Ronnie. 'But I don't have any bad feelings towards him. If anything, in the book, I've been quite complimentary about him. I was just misinterpreted in the paper. I only said the things I said the other day because he called me an arsehole. It hurt me because I'm a sensitive person. At least I know now where we stand.'

Hugh McIlvanney commented in the *Sunday Times*, 'Defining one player's existence as sad and another's as desperately uninteresting sits uncomfortably with his revelations about his own life. Given that catalogue of problems – and the turbulent family background that presumably contributed to them – his tendency to be patronisingly disparaging about other people's lives makes the mind wince. The trouble with the provocative words that come from O'Sullivan is that, whether or not he really means them, he must expect to take retaliatory fire.'

Ronnie had peaked for the European Open and Irish Masters and did not really want to go to the well again for the Scottish Open, but pitched up nevertheless and lost his second match to Alan McManus 5-1.

'I'm not going to worry about it,' said Ronnie. 'The World Championship is the one everybody wants to win. I'll keep a smile on my face because getting down on myself doesn't make me play any better.

'If I thought that smashing up my cue or driving down the motorway at 200 miles an hour would get rid of my frustration, I'd do it. I know it won't, so why get upset by losing?'

As it happened, Hendry and Williams also lost that day. Like Ronnie, they did not lose on purpose but were mindful that this gave them extra time to rest and prepare for the Crucible. This was to work out well for Williams, who became world champion for the second time, moderately well for Hendry, who lost 13-7 to Williams in the quarter-finals, and not at all well for Ronnie, who lost to Marco Fu in the first round.

Nor could the old snooker adage that a 147 wins only one frame have been better illustrated. Ronnie made one, his second at the Crucible and sixth in all, in the opening session but still trailed 6-3 overnight and was beaten 10-6.

'I've got no excuses. Everybody here is a good player and if you're not firing on all cylinders, they'll take advantage.'

Matthew Syed, a shrewd analyst of the psychology of sport and sportsmen, commented in *The Times* on Ronnie's revealing press conference, 'He was at pains to emphasise that he was happy. When asked about his form, he told us that he was happy. When quizzed about his preparation, he revealed that he was happy. He was even happy about the fact that he was out of the World Championship. After all, it would give him the chance to come back in glory next year. Indeed, he was so very happy about everything that one could begin to glimpse the extent of hurt just beneath the gruff façade of this likeable but troubled young man.

'He is among the most naturally talented sportsmen I have witnessed – in the same bracket as the likes of John McEnroe and Zinedine Zidane; it's as if snooker has been encoded in his DNA. A normal bloke with a traumatic past and an extraordinary talent: not exactly a combination that encourages emotional stability.

'That is why we want him to succeed. We can sense his vulnerability and yearn for him to discover reassurance through victory. But this time at least, it was not to be. The man who is still trying to combat emotional overload came up against an impenetrable wall of ice.'

Chapter 15

[2003/04]

T HE government ban on tobacco sponsorship came into play for the 2003/04 season, so Regal could no longer sponsor the Welsh and Scottish Opens or the Scottish Masters, or Benson and Hedges the Masters at Wembley. Embassy's sponsorship of the World Championship was reprieved until 2005 but the WPBSA's excessive reliance on tobacco support and its non-existent response to the need to prepare for its replacement hit the game hard.

Internally, snooker was riven by political strife; one administration after another failed and was to go on failing until the players turned, albeit by an alarmingly small majority in 2010, to Barry Hearn. The WPBSA remained the governing body but World Snooker, its commercial arm, was privatised and sold to Hearn's Matchroom, who were to make a striking commercial success of it. It was a great pity that so many years were wasted before the game was to leap forward again. Ronnie's father was approaching the end of the eleventh year of his 18-year sentence. There was nothing much Ronnie could do beyond what he had always done to relieve his situation, but he did support a new helpline for the families of prisoners, which had received a lottery grant of £300,000.

'This would have helped me massively,' said Ronnie at the launch of the helpline at Pentonville prison. I remember times when I was on the phone trying to get information, like when I was able to see him and what prison was like for him. The experience of people who know what it's all about would have been invaluable to me at the time. The wider consequences of what happened were that I went off my head a little bit. At times, I didn't know who to trust and felt I had to do it all on my own. I didn't know if I was coming or going and was trying to make everyone happy. I ended up exhausting myself and leaving nothing to myself.'

Searching for at least a partial solution to his own problems, Ronnie inadvertently almost converted to Islam because of his misunderstanding of a ceremony in which he took part in the Islamic Multicultural Centre in Regents Park, London.

'I went along to a mosque because I'm interested in Islam but I didn't know anybody would be interested in converting me,' said Ronnie. 'Even when they called me to the front of the mosque, I didn't know what was happening.

'They were very friendly and in my ignorance I thought it was just a social thing, their way of welcoming a stranger. I felt a bit overawed by all the people around me, especially because they were talking all the time. I'm the kind of person who doesn't want to offend and I just thought I'd keep everyone happy and then politely leave. Now I know differently.'

Ronnie's mother was quoted in the *Sunday Times* as saying, 'Ronnie is a lot better in himself since he converted. I hope it will steady him.' However, Ronnie senior was reported to have been much less sanguine about his supposed conversion.

Quoting a source within Swaleside prison, the *Daily Mirror* claimed that Ronnie senior had been so angry that he trashed his cell and was 'shouting and screaming. An inmate tried to calm him down and he beat his head in. Three officers held him to the floor and carted him off to solitary.'

Ronnie himself described accounts of this incident as 'a load of bollocks' and claimed that his father was being punished unfairly by being moved from Swaleside, a category C prison from which he might have been looking forward to home visits and other privileges, to the top-security category A prison Belmarsh.

Subsequently, he was moved to Long Lartin, another category A prison for those serving long sentences. Recategorisations of this nature have clear implications in terms of loss of remission and eligibility for parole.

Ronnie claimed that his father had been victimised and even suggested that 'if I hadn't been a snooker player then maybe he wouldn't have had all this grief'.

His filial loyalty, as ever, was entirely admirable but objectivity is not always easy to come by in regard to family matters. Whether a prisoner is liked or not by prison personnel and administrators, there are procedures to be followed and Ronnie senior's recategorisation could not have happened for no reason whatsoever. Nor was it productive for Ronnie to blame the press en masse. 'That's what you're paid to do – write stories. If you'd written the truth, it wouldn't have been that interesting,' he told the snooker writers, not one of whom wished him ill or would ever falsify a story to his or for that matter anyone else's detriment – not a claim that could be made for all journalists.

It may not have been all that surprising that Ronnie should turn to religion, which gives some people a greater sense of inner repose or a new sense of focus or purpose, but which is used by others as some sort of compensation fantasy for a life they find unsatisfactory.

The O'Sullivans are a Roman Catholic family but it was Maria O'Sullivan's impression that Prince Naseem Hamed had been instrumental in Ronnie's supposed conversion and introduced him to Khalid Yassin, a high-profile Muslim preacher who was involved in trying to set up an Islamic satellite television station.

'I'm privileged with the friendship of Muslims who have been there for me and I value as true friends. I'm interested in Islam but I'm also interested in Buddhism and Christianity. Perhaps I've been naive and given people the wrong impression and if I have, I'm sorry.'

However low Ronnie's sense of self-worth sank, it did not extend to his finances. Having won Barry Hearn's

Premier League three times, he declined to participate in the 2003/04 event because he deemed the prize money, including £45,000 for the winner and £500 for every frame won in the seven-man round-robin stage prior to the semi-finals, to be insufficient. Even to win it would have required only eight one-night appearances.

In any case, it was not entirely a question of money. The circuit was beset by toxic internal conflicts and Ronnie did not always act upon the best advice or form the most objective view on what was best for the sport and, therefore, in a way, for him.

Yet, as he generally did, Ronnie started the new campaign well: 'I'm in the unknown. You know your own ability is good but you sometimes feel you might have lost your game in the summer.'

There was no sign of this as he brushed aside Dave Harold 5-0 in the opening round of the LG Cup only to lose 5-0 to Matthew Stevens, aggregating only 30 points.

'I did well to get nil,' said Ronnie, generous in his praise for the performance of Stevens, whose claim to be the best player never to win the world championship rivals that of Jimmy White. Twice runner-up at the Crucible and three times a losing semi-finalist – all in close matches – as well as a Masters, a UK and a Scottish Masters title offered support for that claim, which might well have been even stronger if his father, Morrell, his strongest supporter, had not died suddenly and unexpectedly in 2001, a year after his son's Masters triumph.

A coating of Stevens whitewash finally shook Ronnie into active mode. He had turned down three overseas invitation events in the summer as well as Hearn's league and had even contemplated withdrawing from the LG Cup, which was won by Williams, who thus became the first player to hold the titles of the four tournaments that the BBC then covered annually.

At the British Open in Brighton, Ronnie spoke in detail of his personal life and in particular of his 'sabotaging behaviour'. Four-day benders, 'seedy gaffs' and his ongoing love/hate relationship with snooker all featured in his press conference after his 5-3 victory over Stephen Maguire.

'I set the foundations by winning the European Open and the Irish Masters and built up a lot of confidence, but I sabotaged it before the Scottish Open by doing a lot of things I shouldn't have been doing. That spilled over into the World Championship and after I lost in the first round, I just decided to go ballistic.

'I can't just go out for a couple of halves of lager. I have to go out for four days. I turn my phone off and nobody can get hold of me. I ended up in all sorts of places, some real seedy gaffs. I just have to accept that I can't do this any more.

'I didn't go down to the club and play the good players who make you sharp. A few weeks ago, after the LG Cup, Ali Carter beat me 18-2 in practice and it hurt. The kids were on half term coming down to the club and laughing because I was just picking the balls out. I had to decide whether to commit to the game or not and whether or not I even wanted to turn up.'

Further wins over Quinten Hann, 5-1, and Gerard Greene, 5-4, took Ronnie into the British Open quarter-finals but after beating Stephen Lee 6-2 he commented, 'I'm not feeling confident. I'm just grinding it out. This isn't like Torquay or Dublin, where I was blitzing everyone in sight. I'm proud because I've been full of doubt and full of fear. It's been a battle but I'm up for a battle. Stephen missed a hell of a lot of balls. I kept thinking what would I do if I lost with him playing so bad. I'm really surprised I'm in the final. I only came here to get a couple of results but Ronnie O'Sullivan has enjoyed himself.'

Why would he suddenly start speaking of himself in the third person?

Bringing the best out of each other, as they so often did, Ronnie and Hendry made five centuries in five consecutive frames in the first session of the final. Ronnie ended this with a 5-3 lead but Hendry swept past him in the evening by taking six frames out of seven to win 9-6, only his ninth defeat in 37 finals and his first in seven against Hendry.

Hendry was elated. 'It was getting silly out there. We were making the game look easy and under that kind of pressure it certainly isn't.'

Ronnie was downcast, entirely unconsoled by having played very well only for Hendry to play better. 'I'm trying to be positive but my natural reaction is to be negative. I'm hurting at the moment, really hurting. I just hope I feel better in the morning because it's difficult to be upbeat when something hurts you so much. Stephen's a great champion and he proved that again here. There was nothing I could do. Everything I did wasn't good enough. He was too strong for me.'

Winning might have muffled some of the pressure Ronnie was feeling but there was a lot more to it than that. By any standards except the impossible ones he imposed on himself, he played superbly in beating Alan McManus to reach the quarter-finals of the UK Championship in York. Yet despite making five centuries and unleashing an unanswerable sequence of four frames in 44 minutes from 5-5 to 9-5, Ronnie would only say, 'I suppose it looked great to everyone but I'm struggling to keep myself together. I'm hurting like you wouldn't believe.'

He admitted after beating Quinten Hann 9-3 to reach the semis that at the interval of his match against McManus, he had spent 20 minutes 'crying in the bath'.

'There's so much going on emotionally that I haven't dealt with. I don't feel comfortable at the table or around the tournaments. I'll see how things go after this. It may be good for me to take some time out.

'I've not fallen out with snooker but there are other things I can't handle and it's crippling me. Inside, there's a lot of pain and anger I'm carrying round like a rucksack and it's weighing me down.

'It may be that I go to the powers that be and see if they can do some sort of deal because I wouldn't want to go back to qualifying. If the board aren't willing to make a deal, it's a bigger decision I've got to make.'

Ronnie felt better for 'letting it all out' but was well beaten, 9-4, in the semi-finals by Hendry who, in prime form, was then expected to take the title but in fact lost 10-8 to Stevens.

Uneventfully, if such a thing is ever possible where Ronnie is concerned, he reached the final of the Welsh Open in Cardiff for the loss of only five frames in four matches. Steve Davis, at the age of 46, came through the other half to appear in what was to prove the last ranking final of his career and almost delivered the victory that the wide sentimental support for him desired.

'It was an unbelievable game to be involved in and I can't believe I've won,' said Ronnie, who had to come from three down with four to play to do so, 9-8. 'Steve made it hard to get into any sort of rhythm.'

Davis led 4-1 and almost 5-1 before Ronnie closed the opening session at 4-4 with consecutive centuries, 125 and 139. In the evening, Davis led 6-4 and 8-5, Ronnie impulsively conceding the thirteenth frame after missing a blue when only five behind with the colours remaining. Though probable, it was not certain that Davis would have made the necessary clearance to pink but Ronnie admitted: 'I was just angry. I decided to give him that one and then come back and attack.'

His flying 118 launched the recovery that continued with a frame-winner of 77 from 36 behind, a 48 clearance from 29 behind and finally the capture of the deciding frame in bits and pieces. Ronnie had conclusively proved that he was much more than a frontrunner. In the right mood, he had displayed battling qualities in reacting to adversity with everything from canny shot selection to death-or-glory bravery and sublime break-making skill.

A fortnight later, Ronnie seemed certain to win the Masters as well when he led Paul Hunter 7-2 in the final only to lose 10-9. As inspirational players sometimes can, Hunter got on a roll while Ronnie, clearly feeling the pressure of having a reasonably anticipated victory snatched away, made a few mistakes to help him on his way.

'You've got to take your hat off to Paul,' said Ronnie. 'He came back really well and showed a lot of character. I'm not going to let this get me down. I'm happy. That's the main thing. Life goes on. It's only a snooker match. I could be in Iraq.'

Although he struggled with full commitment for 3 hours 32 minutes, the longest best-of-nine he had ever played, Ronnie still lost 5-4 to Stephen Lee in the European Open quarter-finals in Malta.

'It was shocking, very, very poor. In a way, I'm relieved it's all over because it was like pulling teeth. It just wasn't me. I can win playing badly, I know that, but the juices don't flow around my body when I'm grinding.

'I can't believe what I've managed to do in the last few tournaments considering the way I've been playing. I've put together one good session [the first of the Masters final] and the rest has been terrible.

'I've toughed it out but that's not the way I like to play the game. It's been too much hard work. I want to win playing Ronnie style but my rhythm's just not been there.'

What was causing this snooker version of writer's block? Ronnie had no idea but simply endured it as some malign visitation.

Chapter 16

[2004]

ALTHOUGH Ronnie was to become the 2004 world champion, it was an odd season: one event in October, two in November, none in December, two in January and another four crammed into March and April. Hendry and Williams both confessed that their motivation for practice and competition was not what it had been. Ronnie spoke even more forthrightly at the Irish Masters. 'My goal is to play good at the Crucible.

'To be honest, I don't want to be here. I'm fed up at being at tournaments at the moment. I enjoy life so much when I'm at home that when I come away, I wonder if this is really what I want to do.'

The backstage atmosphere at tournaments, reeking with interpersonal and political factionalism, was not inviting and there was also an underlying feeling that, as the circuit contracted, the game was going nowhere.

Virtually on autopilot, Ronnie went through two rounds in Dublin but lost 6-2 in the quarter-finals to Ebdon, conceding the fourth frame at 0-30 with no fewer than 11 reds remaining.

'I expected Peter to clear up,' said Ronnie. 'There was always the chance he could have missed but we'll never know now.'

It was as if Ronnie was trying to control the future in both a good and a bad way. If he could not win by performing in his desired manner, he wanted to impose what he felt was a deserved punishment on himself rather than waiting for an opponent to do it. Years later, the WPBSA was to clamp down on players conceding frames they could arithmetically still win without the aid of snookers. However obvious it might be that a player might clinch the frame, it was owed to the spectators that the drama was properly enacted. Most playgoers know that Hamlet dies in the end but this would never justify the actors departing for the pub at the end of act four.

Ronnie was also a quarter-finalist in the new Players Championship (replacing the Scottish Open) in Glasgow but was defeated 5-2 by Hunter, losing his discipline in the fifth frame by throwing his cue at several shots and openly defying the authority of the referee, Colin Brinded.

When Ronnie's failed attempt to escape from a snooker scattered the balls hither and yon, he thought it helpful to pick up a red and replace it in its original position only for the referee to inform him that he had given away four points for doing so. Not appreciating that he was at fault, Ronnie defiantly replaced another, giving away another four points.

The experienced, mild-mannered Brinded said, 'Please Ronnie, this is going out on live television. Don't touch any more balls.' Ronnie, his shortest fuse blown and his instinctive reaction to an authority figure now in play, replied aggressively, 'What are you going to do about it?' Brinded ignored this and the game moved on but the incident showed just how tightly wired Ronnie was.

On the face of it, none of this boded well for Ronnie's chances in the 2004 World Championship. As it turned out, he won it as comfortably as this would ever be possible, albeit not without incident.

On the way to his 10-6 opening-round defeat of Stephen Maguire, he gave three causes for complaint.

Leading 6-4 but trailing 61-0, he cleared to the pink with 73 and celebrated by powering both black and cue ball off the table, an act that would in tennis have constituted an unacceptable abuse of the game's equipment.

At 8-4, he left a doubled red just short of a middle pocket and obscenely gestured at it with his middle finger.

'They can fine me if they want to, I've got plenty of money,' he commented unapologetically.

At 9-5, he was only 31 behind with six reds left when his failed red left Maguire in prime position. Oblivious to his obligation to the spectators, television viewers and the conventions of the game to play each frame to a proper conclusion, Ronnie conceded forthwith.

'In my eyes, it was like asking a golf pro to hole a one-foot putt in match play. I just wanted to get on with the next frame,' Ronnie explained unsatisfactorily.

Ronnie's toughest match was against Andy Hicks, whom he trailed 10-9 but beat 13-11. In fact, on each of the three occasions Hicks went a frame in front, Ronnie responded with a century. He made five in all but let himself down by prematurely conceding a frame, as Hicks also did, by deliberately powering a black off the table, as he had in his opening match, and by making an unmistakable masturbatory gesture in the last frame of the second session that attracted several e-mails to the BBC.

After all this, Ronnie made himself into the victim. 'I keep coming back despite what you've tried to do to me over the years,' he told an extremely brief press conference.

However, Ray Reardon, six times world champion in the 70s, newly engaged by Ronnie as his mentor, did not want to be associated with such behaviour, 'I don't condone his actions. I deplore them.'

Through his influence, Ronnie toned it down and there was nothing to criticise as he beat Anthony Hamilton 13-3 in the quarter-finals and afterwards acknowledged the benefit of having Reardon in his corner. 'He's giving me a different kind of support to what I had before. It's nice to share with someone on the same level.'

As well as Ronnie had played, no one expected that he would beat Hendry by the massive margin of 17-4 in the semi-finals.

'It's nice to be able to do it against someone of Stephen's quality,' said Ronnie. 'It's not that I played hideously badly,' said Hendry. 'I just didn't get going quickly enough and he ran all over me. Ronnie played great all the way through and I didn't. You beat Ronnie by putting him under pressure. If you do that, he can go but what chances I had I didn't take.'

Graeme Dott, who had never reached a professional final, was not considered – even by himself – to have even a remote chance against Ronnie but briefly, when he led 5-0, this unanimous judgement acquired a scintilla of doubt.

It came to be suggested that Ronnie's composure might have been disturbed by Del Hill, now in Dott's corner after years in Ronnie's, poking his head round his dressing room door a few minutes before the match. It seems improbable that this was done with any ill intent but it did not take much to stir Ronnie's paranoia.

Ronnie did make a few mistakes in those early frames but the main component of Dott's 5-0 lead was his excellence, including a spell of 343 points without reply.

'I wasn't getting carried away at all,' Dott was to say. 'I might have done if it had been first to six.'

Ronnie kept his discipline, getting off the mark with a 100 break in the sixth frame just as if he was leading, not trailing, 5-0 and ending the first session only 5-3 adrift. Dott was to win only three more frames. After two sessions, Ronnie led 9-7 and after three 16-8, leaving an anti-climactic final session of only 24 minutes as Ronnie passed the winning post at 18-8.

Dott afterwards described Ronnie as a 'phenomenal player, I didn't do much wrong but he was unbelievably good. For two sessions I managed to give him a game but his safety was incredible. Everybody talks about his potting and the breaks he makes but every time I came to the table the white was on the bottom rail and I was left with a horrible shot I didn't want to play. I was quite happy with the way I played. It just wasn't good enough. When Ronnie's zoned in like this, it's hard to imagine how he could possibly get beaten.'

Although the Welsh Open was his only other title of the 2003/04 campaign, Ronnie reached the quarter-finals or better in seven of the eight ranking events and finished top of the end-of-season rankings by the proverbial mile. By some convoluted process, he had managed to peak when it most mattered.

He described Reardon's input as 'huge', adding, 'I'm actually more excited about working with Ray than I am about winning this. We've developed a plan B. At times during the fortnight I didn't cue as well as I wanted, but I've got a new dimension to my game.

'I never thought I was going to lose. In fact, I thought I was going to win it before I came here. I've rehearsed this in my mind I was so convinced about what would happen. I always knew I could sustain consistency over a long period of time but I still think there's room for improvement. I know I can play better. Perfection isn't possible but I want to hit the balls sweeter and make them talk.'

There was, at that moment, only one cloud in his sky. His father was in Long Lartin prison, still not quite two-thirds into his 18-year sentence. In tears, Ronnie said, 'This one's for you, dad.'

Chapter 17

[2004/05]

A
S DOMINANT as Ronnie had been in the 2004 World Championship, few expected him to establish a hegemony akin to Steve Davis's in the 80s or Stephen Hendry's in the 90s. His temperament was too volatile and a five-month summer away from the discipline of tournament play offered maximum scope for him to go off the rails.

Whether he did so privately in the summer of 2004 is not known but he was certainly on track for the 2004/05 season's opening tournament, the Totesport Grand Prix in Preston. Never coming under serious pressure in any match, he acquired his sixteenth ranking title in his twenty-first final by beating Ian McCulloch, a solid left-hander on the fringe of the top 16, 9-5.

There were, during the week, passages of play that demonstrated his best but mostly he showed the high quality of his second best. With his artistic temperament, he wanted 'to play a beautiful game and caress the balls around' but no one, not even Ronnie, plays at his peak all the time and the overriding essential is to win.

'I've been really struggling this week,' he said, oblivious to how it must have felt to the opponents he was still beating so comfortably. 'But my matchplay was solid and I relied on my safety. In days gone by, I would probably have thrown the towel in but I got through on my B game and by rolling my sleeves up.' And by having Reardon in his corner.

Reardon rated Ronnie's ability so highly that he bet £100 at 150-1 that he would win all eight ranking events that season, only to discover that Ronnie did not intend to travel to the Malta Cup or the China Open.

In any case, it was too good to last. Only a few weeks later, Ronnie described his performance in beating John Parrott 5-2 in the second round of the British Open at Brighton as 'fucking awful'.

An aversion to overseas travel had also surfaced. 'Unless I'm on top of the world, I don't think I'd be able to bear a fortnight there,' he said of China.

'I'm not the full ticket. They'll have to call the nuthouse to collect me if things go on like this. There's no rush but I'm going to have to sit down with my dad, my mother and Ray to work things out and see if there's a solution.' He then suggested that he might 'play enough to stay in the top 16' then 'have another go' when his father was eventually released from prison, a date still about six years distant.

Next day at Brighton, in apparent perversity, he brushed aside Stephen Lee 5-0 in only 83 minutes, two centuries featuring in a performance of pure class. 'Momentum does help,' he said of his thirteenth consecutive win. 'I felt at one with myself. You know you've got to stay in the groove and not look too far forward. If you do that, you miss what's happening in the present and that's the place you need to be.'

He gave himself a 'high mark' for his 5-1 quarter-final defeat of Andy Hicks before his winning streak stopped at 14 with a 6-1 defeat by the fast-rising Stephen Maguire, who had won his maiden ranking title, the European Open, eight months earlier.

'Snooker's got a gem with Stephen. I think he'll do big things,' said Ronnie, having sat out two centuries and two 71s.

Although Maguire lost 9-6 to John Higgins in that final, his next great moment was only a few days away, another victory over Ronnie on the first televised day of the UK Championship.

Ronnie made three centuries and Maguire two as their opening session was split 4-4. After Maguire had taken five of the seven evening frames, Ronnie told him that he could 'rule snooker for the next ten years'. He took the title with a frames tally of 55-19 from his six matches and was to establish himself as a leading player, though not the dominant one that Ronnie had predicted.

The other side of Christmas 2004, Ronnie retained the Welsh Open title, responding to pressure as one might expect from a world champion in a series of tight finishes. Level at 3-3 with Anthony Hamilton, he produced a pair of centuries to go through 5-3. At 4-4, he edged the decider against Neil Robertson, who he accurately predicted 'is going to be a future world champion'. Ronnie then seized a 6-4 semi-final win over Barry Hawkins with a break of 146. Down 7-5 to Hendry in the final, he prevailed 9-8, making an exceptional 67 break in the decider when, initially, neither blue, pink or black were available.

Only a genius could have been so difficult to please with these performances. 'My cueing has been awful all week but I found something extra when I needed to.' From 7-5 down to 8-7 up in a period in which Hendry did not pot a ball, Ronnie played a high percentage of shots left-handed: 'I knew I wasn't cueing well, so that was the game plan.'

By what impossible standards was Ronnie measuring himself?

He did not want to compete in the Malta Cup but travelled anyway and lost 5-0 to Dott in only 57 minutes. He potted only one ball in the first two frames and inexcusably conceded the third when leading by 25 with ten reds remaining. Dott went 4-0 up with 114 and after completing his hollow victory said that he 'had the impression Ronnie wasn't up for it before we went out'. Given that he had two titles and a semi to show from the season's first four ranking events, it was bizarre for Ronnie to conclude, 'I haven't played well for a while and it's difficult to motivate yourself when you're not comfortable with your game. I've managed to pull myself together for a couple of tournaments this season but you can't keep doing it. I'm not surprised with this. It's been coming for a while.'

This may have been a manifestation of the separation anxiety Ronnie was to continue to suffer on trips to overseas tournaments. He had, after all, been in Thailand when he had received news of his father's arrest, just the sort of happening that might develop in his subconscious into a fear that something terrible could or would happen if he was a long way from home, particularly on a small, claustrophobic island like Malta.

Back home, there was no sign of any malaise at Wembley, where his stunning mixture of deadly break making and precise tactical play gave him his second Masters title. Dismissive of his defeat by Dott in Malta — 'Stevie Wonder would have beaten me in the frame of mind I was in' — he reached the final with a frames tally of 18-6 and trounced Higgins 10-3 for the title.

'Ronnie's playing to a standard I don't think we've seen before. It's up to the rest of us to catch up,' said Higgins candidly.

Against both Maguire and Barry Hawkins in the Irish Masters, he was held to 3-3 but won 5-3 and 5-4 respectively and made four centuries in beating Gerard Greene 6-4 in the quarter-finals.

There was nothing wrong with his game but he seemed intent on making it into a problem as if to overlay the one that was not susceptible to solution – his father's continuing incarceration.

It did not help that he was suffering from a heavy cold that confined him to his room for long periods. Perhaps more pertinently than he realised, he said, 'It's like being in prison, like solitary confinement.'

Not wishing to burn him out, Ronnie did not have the 71-year-old Reardon with him to keep his spirits up and give him a sense of perspective. Easily bored, it must have been easy for him to view home as an alluring prospect. Indeed, after beating Greene, he said, 'There were times when there were just rubbish things going through my head. I wanted to lose and go home and take next year off. I don't know what's wrong with my head. If I'd lost, I'd have woken up in the morning and been gutted. I gave Gerard a load of chances but he didn't take them. I deliberately played some shots knowing they could go wrong but I'd have been pig-sick to lose.'

He was looking forward to 'testing my game' against Williams in the semi-finals but this proved, in Ronnie's words, 'not much of a match to watch' as he won 9-5. A final, knowing that next day he would be going home, win or lose, cleared Ronnie's head, as it usually did. When he led Matthew Stevens 6-1 an early night beckoned but this became 6-6. Ronnie never fell behind but was again level at 8-8 before he made 59 from around level pegging to go one up with two to play.

The contest seemed certain to go the full distance when Stevens opened the scoring in the next with 68 but from his missed red to middle, Ronnie cleared with an exquisitely executed 69 to clinch frame and title.

This excited everyone except Ronnie. 'All the balls were there, so it was just a case of controlling the cue ball. I'm delighted to have won but there are still things to work on. Winning titles is great but I want to play in a beautiful way and I didn't do that. I found it hard to motivate myself. I didn't enjoy it and I felt despondent at times but you have to dig in and find a way of winning.'

If he was like this after such a dramatic win, what would Ronnie have been like if he had lost?

As threatened, Ronnie did not travel to Beijing for the China Open. He did not fancy 17 hours flying, there and back, particularly to play such a dangerous first-round opponent as Maguire. A first prize of only £30,000 did not incentivise him and it was also a fair point that with the World Championship coming up immediately afterwards he did not want to deplete his resources, even though all the other top players were prepared to accept this. Perhaps, though, these were rationalisations rather than reasons. The plain fact was that he did not want to be so far from home.

In Ronnie's absence, the tournament was significant in two ways. Paul Hunter was diagnosed with cancer of the colon, which proved to be terminal; as a wild card, Ding Junhui became China's first ranking title winner at the age of 18 years 2 days by beating Hendry 9-5 in the final.

If Ding's success was surprising, Shaun Murphy's capture of the world title as a 150-1 qualifier was astounding. Ronnie had started as a short-priced favourite and once he had rallied from the brink of defeat to beat Maguire 10-9 on the opening day, some assumed that the worst might have passed and that no one could beat him over either three or four sessions, a view that was to be exploded in an extraordinary quarter-final.

Maguire led Ronnie 9-7 and was in with 54, 19 in front, when he jawed a quarter-ball black from its spot. That pot and two more would have been enough but Ronnie creditably launched a 34 clearance with a do-or-die long red down a side cushion and momentum irresistibly shifted.

'That black was a twitch,' Maguire admitted. 'After that, I never got a chance.'

It was a defeat that was to leave scar tissue on his mind for future challenges at the Crucible.

'I've been struggling all season with my game,' said Ronnie, who had won four titles in retaining top place in the world rankings and the money list. It was as if nothing was enough to alleviate his central, burning hurt. 'My heart isn't in it, to be honest. All the way through the day, I was thinking it wouldn't be all that bad if I went home tonight. At the moment, I'm not really interested. I'm pleased to get through but if I'd lost it would have been OK. I don't know what to say but I'm not going to try and make things up just to sound positive. I was suffering out there but I kept battling and stayed professional.'

Ronnie then beat Ali Carter 13-7 without any great alarms but again emphasised the negative. 'I know I've won tournaments this season but I can't take much more of the way I've been playing. I'm close to a breakdown. I want to be coming here for the next 10 or 12 years but if I carry on like this I don't think it's possible.

'I'm not looking for perfection, I just want to get my game to somewhere half decent. At the moment, I'm not enjoying it but I love snooker. If I pack the game in, I'd be gutted but I want a family and I don't want my kids coming home and seeing me depressed. I've been going through the pain barrier and I don't want people around me to suffer because I'm suffering.'

Ronnie seemed to believe that snooker was the problem but it was far more likely that his difficulties arose from his personal life and complex psyche, with snooker as the proverbial straw to break the camel's back.

For all Ronnie's mental convolutions, he seemed a certain semi-finalist when he led Ebdon 8-2 but with his opponent already proceeding at a snail's pace and Ronnie adjusting to a new tip, the pendulum swung. Ronnie did manage to win the last frame of their middle session to carry a 10-6 advantage into the evening but Ebdon knew that his only chance lay in disrupting Ronnie's rhythm with a funereal pace of play. If Ronnie was, as Ebdon had previously described him, Mozart, then Ebdon himself was Salieri in undermining him by stretching the rules to the limit.

As the sole judge of fair or unfair play, the referee, Colin Brinded, was to attract considerable criticism for not intervening as Ebdon should have at least been warned for 'taking an abnormal amount of time over a stroke or selection of a stroke' and thus unfairly distracting his opponent.

Even after two sessions, Ebdon was averaging 31 seconds per shot. By the end of the bizarre final session, from which Ebdon emerged a 13-11 winner, it had risen to 37, which meant that his final-session average would have been significantly in excess of 40. This slowness was unanimously condemned. John Parrott, the 1991 world champion, working for BBC, said, 'I've never seen anyone play that slow. If it had been me, I'd have asked the referee if he was within the rules to play like that and I'd have said it loud enough for other people to hear me.'

Some shots do require considerable thought. Such was the position that Ebdon pondered for 3 minutes 5 seconds but the more questionable instances included 1 minute 40 seconds for one routine safety shot, 90 seconds for another and 5 minutes 30 seconds for a break of 12.

Hugh McIlvanney of the *Sunday Times*, winner of innumerable journalistic awards, described Ebdon's approach as 'outlandishly laborious'. To Matthew Syed of *The Times*, these tactics were 'shameless'.

Ronnie, not the sort to complain to an authority figure, made no protest, although he broke the skin on his forehead with a scratch of frustration. At one point, he feigned sleep; at another he asked a spectator the time and even grinned openly in Ebdon's face as he returned to his chair from some tortuously slow contribution. His concentration and rhythm were utterly destroyed.

Ebdon won six consecutive frames in this fashion to lead 12-10. With his highest break of the session a paltry

42, Ronnie broke the sequence but his game was in tatters. Needing the last four colours to force a twenty-fifth frame decider, he wobbled the brown and left it where Ebdon could not fail to pot it.

Anger could justifiably have been directed not only at Ebdon but principally at the referee for allowing such a travesty. But Ronnie, more generously than was deserved, understood his opponent's point of view. 'Peter's got to do what he's got to do. He's got a wife and four kids to feed, so I can't criticise him. He's there to stop me playing.'

Had he not been – unfairly – prevented from playing his normal game, Ronnie would probably have won his third world title. As it was, Murphy beat Ebdon 17-12 and Stevens 18-16 to become, at 22 years 9 months, second only to Hendry as the youngest ever world champion.

Ronnie, who had been undone by his opponent's excruciatingly slow play, had also been an initial critic of the 25 seconds per shot time limit introduced to the Premier League, but soon found that he could cope with it better than any other player. At the Manchester Evening News Arena, ten days after the Ebdon debacle, Ronnie played superbly to beat Hendry 5-0 and Williams 6-0 to win the Premier League for the fourth time, his fifth title of the season.

'There've been no slow frames with people falling asleep,' he said pointedly.

Chapter 18

[2005/06]

I T gradually sank in to the sceptics, some too proud to admit it, that they had backed the wrong horse in a vote between Altium, a company introduced by 110sport and backed by Warburg Pincus, the City finance house, who were prepared to guarantee a nine-event world ranking circuit with £6m in prize money in 2002/03, and World Snooker Enterprises (WSE), who guaranteed nothing but were backed by the incumbent WPBSA board.

In the first three seasons of the projected deal, Altium were guaranteeing £16.4m plus inflation against the £13.021m that the WPBSA promised through WSE. The Altium deal had also guaranteed two further years at £5.5m plus inflation.

The comparison of the deals was a no-brainer but unfortunately too many players did not demonstrate much brain power, only prejudices fed to them by managers and hangers on who did not like Ian Doyle, manager of Hendry and others, who had brought the deal to the table.

The players, with those near the top the most vocal, feared their potential earnings were going to be much lower than they had hoped or indeed had been only a few years earlier. Embassy's sponsorship of the 2005 World Championship was the last of snooker's tobacco support and replacement sponsors were hard to come by, particularly those who could put up anything like the same money. Already, the circuit's total prize money had declined from £5.189m in 2002/03 to £4.885m in 2003/04 to £2.952m in 2004/05.

Some players started to explore other sources of income and Ronnie was among those who eyed a new American 8-ball pool circuit originated by Kevin Trudeau, described by the *Wall Street Journal* as 'a master of modern marketing' but later jailed for ten years for multiple misrepresentation and fraud.

Ronnie said that he would give events on this pool circuit priority over snooker's Welsh Open and Irish Masters and that he would not compete in the China Open anyway but, perhaps predictably, the new pool circuit soon experienced problems and Ronnie played in only one of its events.

Invariably conscious of his own worth and status, Ronnie was and remained resentful of anything he sensed smacked of exploitation in terms of competing for low prize money.

'I love snooker. If there was suddenly heaps of tournaments for proper money that'd be different, but I'm not going to hang around and wait. We've all been told to be patient and we have been for three or four years, but nothing much has happened.'

Better late than never, Ronnie admitted that 'greed got the better of me' when he accepted a £500,000 loyalty bonus from the WPBSA during snooker's civil war with Altium.

'I'm sorry for that,' he told a press conference when he rejoined 110sport after a four-and-a-half-year absence. 'It's not just me that's lost out, it's every other snooker player and I do shoulder some of the responsibility.'

Against this uncertain background, Ronnie's form, if not his mind, was in good order as he reached the semi-finals of the Grand Prix in Preston with minimum difficulty. Connoisseurs of his press conferences knew enough to realise that more serious notice needed to be taken of what he did rather than what he said since his sporadic threats to retire seemed to arise from a yearning for relief from the pressure of fulfilling his own expectations, not so much in results but in terms of prime performance. Perpetually restless and emotionally volatile, he was easily bored, not so much by snooker as by what went with it. In Preston, he played the first match of the tournament and the last, so there was a lot of spare time hanging heavily on his hands.

During the summer of 2005, his interest in running had deepened. He had always taken satisfaction from it and was well aware of its value, but it was now well on the way to becoming an obsession. During that summer, he finished eighth in 37 minutes 12 seconds in a 10,000m race at High Ongar and eleventh in 37 minutes 18 seconds in a field of 425 in another 10k at Felsted. 'Running gives me endorphins and helps me manage my snooker,' he was to say.

At Preston, though, he was carrying an ankle ligament injury, so even running was denied him. By the time he played Barry Hawkins in the semi-finals, his instinctive competitive reflexes, demonstrated by responding to every impending crisis with a substantial break and taking the deciding eleventh frame with one of 117, were in conflict with a wish to be away from it all.

'I'd rather be at home in the garden, planting a few shrubs,' he said. 'Barry's trying his nuts off trying to get to his first final and I don't care whether I win or lose. Now I've won and he's lost. It's not right.'

Usually, with the prospect of going home that night or the next day, Ronnie raised himself for a final but this time John Higgins did not give him a chance to do so, setting two records for the circuit, four centuries in four frames and 494 unanswered points, in trouncing him 9-2.

As usual, Ronnie gave due recognition to quality when he saw it. 'He destroyed me but it was a pleasure to watch. It was amazing. I've never seen anything like that before. You just have to sit in your chair and feel like an idiot. I'm delighted for John. He's a lovely guy and a top-drawer player.'

For the top players there was no tournament action in November 2006, ordinarily a prime competitive month, except for the one-night stands of the Premier League, in which Ronnie won 27 frames at £1,000 each and made ten centuries, also at £1,000 each, before overwhelming Hendry

6-0 in the play-offs final to take his earnings from this independently promoted event to £87,000, a sum greater than the winner's cheque for any ranking event that season except the World Championship.

His 6-3 semi-final win over Steve Davis had included a run of 341 unanswered points and not only four centuries but a match-clinching 85, jawing a red along a cushion when within four pots of a fifth.

Ronnie was playing about as well as anyone had ever played but it was still not enough. If he could have used his form as a kind of currency to alleviate his ongoing problems or his father's imprisonment, he would have done but this was, of course, impossible.

It therefore seemed as if he needed to give his game an avoidable difficulty, one that could be solved rather than his intractable personal problems.

The mentorship of Ray Reardon had paid immense dividends, not so much technically but in terms of psychological support, but Ronnie felt that he was to some extent compromising his instincts. He wanted to do it his way, on his own. His way of saying this in his opening match in the UK Championship against Mark King was to play some shots that he knew were wrong. Reardon realised what this meant and left during the match. Their professional relationship had ended.

At 5-5 against King, Ronnie conceded the eleventh frame when 29 behind but with 51 remaining and two reds under cushions. For much of the rest of the match, he chose to drape a towel over his face while King was at the table. From 8-6 down, Ronnie levelled at 8-8 but King, whose determination often compensates for an ungainliness in style, won the decider.

Ronnie afterwards told him that he was alright but was fed up with snooker and also skipped his mandatory press conference. Perhaps this was just a symptom of a downswing in his established manic depressive cycle, but it was bizarre even by Ronnie's standards.

A month later, he brought everything from exemplary patience to his highest level of skill to the Masters. Characteristically, Ronnie buckled down when he felt he had some misbehaviour to make up for. Sporting an 'I love snooker' logo on his waistcoat, his attitude and performance counteracted the impression he had generated by repeatedly stating how bored he was with the game.

His 6-2 quarter-final win over Ebdon included a frame of 59 minutes, the longest Ronnie has ever played. After 44, he heeded a call of nature and was absent for seven minutes, and also made backstage visits between each subsequent frame. Although he claimed this had nothing to do with the circumstances of his Crucible quarter-final defeat by Ebdon nine months earlier, it did seem that he was making a point by keeping him waiting.

Stephen Lee also gave Ronnie some Ebdon treatment by frustrating him in their semi-final. At 3-0 down, Ronnie felt that he was 'being totally out-safetied, I felt so isolated. I was being buried but not with big breaks.' It was a testament to his resolve that he got in front at 4-3 and 5-4 and at 5-5 summoned enough fluency to make 74 for victory. 'It's good that I've found a way to beat the players who are trying to keep me quiet and taking their time.'

Ronnie had the form and, even more pertinently, the attitude to win the title but was denied by a phenomenal last-gasp effort from Higgins. At 9-9, Ronnie opened the scoring with 60 before missing a tricky cutback that was effectively match ball. Several balls appeared to be safe but Higgins developed all these into pottable positions and completed a magnificent 64 clearance to win 10-9.

'It was a great clearance,' Ronnie acknowledged. 'It was a tough game all day. It was difficult to keep any momentum going because I wasn't being left any easy chances.'

Ronnie's defence of the Welsh Open title did not survive his opening match against Ian McCulloch, whose 5-1 win was his first over him in six attempts. Wearing strapping on his right wrist, Ronnie missed several balls he would normally have potted and McCulloch made three major clearances. Ronnie told him during the intermission that he had hurt his wrist while boxing in the gym but declined to confirm this in his press conference, not wanting to risk accusations of making excuses.

Contrary to his expressed intention not to travel to the China Open, Ronnie did only to lose 5-0 to the Thai veteran James Wattana. Present in body but not mind, Ronnie was outscored 419-68. His highest break was 25. He did not attend the mandatory press conference.

There was no dramatic reversal of this at the Crucible, where he tried his best but without inspiration. He did beat Dave Harold 10-4 and Ryan Day 13-10, bouncing back from 9-7 down going into the final session.

'I just had to hope the occasion would get to him,' said Ronnie. 'He had his chances and wasn't able to finish me off. This place is very intimidating and gets to everybody. It can play tricks with your mind.'

Ronnie seemed to be gathering momentum as he beat Mark Williams 13-11, having been 11-11, from 10-6 up. 'Mark's the hardest opponent I've ever faced. He's one of the greatest players I've ever seen, up there with Hendry and Higgins,' said Ronnie, who after the match took the opportunity to apologise for any past derogatory comments he had made about him. For Williams, 'it was a fantastic match. He played really well. So did I and I could have had him in the end.' Of Ronnie's tide-turning 90 break from 0-37 in the penultimate frame, he said, 'It was just excellent. No matter how much pressure you put him under, he doesn't look like missing in amongst the balls.'

Despite everything, it seemed that Ronnie might yet become champion for the third time but the Williams match drained what little remained in his tank and his psychological collapse against Graeme Dott in the semi-finals was painful to watch.

Had only the pressures of a world championship been involved, Ronnie's challenge would surely not have capsized as it did but snooker pressures, on top of all the others with which he struggled, did for him utterly. He led 5-3 after one session and was level at 8-8 after two, but as he lost all eight frames in the third he was clearly in the grip of a condition that deadened his emotions, impeded his exceptional hand-eye co-ordination and shattered his self-belief. Until he became resigned to his fate, Ronnie did try to hold on when there was nothing in him but as that awful third session proceeded he could hardly string three pots together and missed some absurdly easy balls.

Dott's two wins over Ronnie in 12 attempts, in the 2002 British Open in Newcastle and the 2005 Malta Cup, had revealed that Ronnie's mind, will and game could unravel, but this was shocking in its totality. The chief symptom of Ronnie's irrational but ultimately disabling insecurities was his search for a tip with which he could be entirely satisfied. It was as if he had convinced himself that if he could find the perfect tip, everything would be alright. He made it seem that it would have been easier to find the holy grail. Defying the bounds of reason, he tried about 20 as a way, it seemed, of externalising his anxieties.

From 16-8 down, Ronnie duly lost 17-11 and immediately called a young lad forward from the audience to present him with his cue. Ronnie admitted that 'there was nothing wrong with it' but that he 'felt like a new start'. A psychiatrist might have said that Ronnie was acting out a desire for a different kind of new start, perhaps a whole career with his father by his side, as he had been until he was 16, rather than being wrenched away from him as he was.

But there are really no new starts in life. No one can change the past and sometimes aspects of the present cannot be changed either. The best anyone can do is to deal with them in a different way and it was clear that Ronnie needed help to do this.

Chapter 19

[2006/07]

THE central event of Ronnie's 2006/07 season was his abrupt retirement from his best-of-17 frame quarter-final in the UK Championship when he was trailing Stephen Hendry 4-1. With no injury issue involved, this was unprecedented. It came, he was to reveal much later, against a background of domestic turmoil.

Since 2001, he had been with Jo Langley, who he had met at a Narcotics Anonymous meeting. They had two children, Lily and Ronnie III. Ronnie loved fatherhood but stated that it was unrealistic for any top sportsman to share domestic responsibilities equally with his wife or partner, who had to accept that most of the burden of looking after children would rest with them. It was, said Ronnie, 'not ideal but life's not ideal'.

Champions have to be selfish. They have to travel, compete, spend a lot of time away from home. When they are at home they need to practise, keep in shape – by running in Ronnie's case – to empty their minds out so that they can give everything to snooker and, at all times, do what is best for them. The last thing they need is domestic stress.

It was also at the back of Ronnie's mind that he was not making as much money as he considered appropriate in what should have been his prime earning years. There was widespread dissatisfaction with the WPBSA of the day and there were not enough earning opportunities for the players. There were only two ranking tournaments prior to the UK Championship in late November.

Having given his cue away at the Crucible, Ronnie did not find it difficult to get used to a new one. In this first tournament of the new season, the Northern Ireland Trophy, he played sublimely to beat Dominic Dale 6-0 in 53 minutes in the semi-finals, the quickest best-of-11 on record.

'I play like that all the time in practice and exhibitions. The only time I don't is when I get bogged down and people are trying to spoil my rhythm,' said Ronnie, overlooking one of sport's enduring truths: that if player B cannot reach the standard of player A, he will try to bring him down to his own level.

Not that this happened in the final, in which Ronnie's 9-6 defeat by Ding Junhui provided the 19-year-old Chinese with his third ranking title. Ronnie led 3-1 but went from cruising to crisis and from unstoppable to powerless as he failed to pot a ball in the remaining four frames of the afternoon. He levelled at 6-6 in the evening but that was as far as he got.

Another rising star, Neil Robertson ('He was on fire,' said Ronnie), beat him 5-1 in the quarter-finals of the Grand Prix in Aberdeen, so Ronnie was alive to the reality that there were, in addition to his long-standing rivals, players younger than him who were now capable of beating him.

At the UK Championship, he had to go the distance to beat Ricky Walden 9-8 with a typically smooth 108 in the decider and even when Hendry, who had not beaten him in his previous six attempts, took a 4-0 lead, reduced to 4-1, in their quarter-final there was plenty of time to turn the match round.

However, leading 24-0 in the sixth, Ronnie missed a tricky red, walked over to shake Hendry's hand and left the arena to a stunned silence.

Backstage, Hendry asked Ronnie what was wrong. Ronnie told him that he was just fed up. Spectators who had paid £24 for a ticket were not that cheerful, either. Nor was the BBC, the host broadcaster.

Three hours later, Ronnie issued a widely derided statement through his PR company. 'Anyone who knows me knows I'm a perfectionist when it comes to my game. I got annoyed, lost my patience and walked away from a match that, with hindsight, I should have continued. At this moment in time, I'm feeling very disappointed with myself. I'm hurt and numb but I'm a fighter and I'll be back fighting stronger and harder than ever very soon.'

So if he was hurt, who had hurt him except himself? And if he was such a fighter, why had he conceded at only 4-1 down? More to the point, perhaps, what had lodged in his psyche to make him do this?

Astonishingly, he was to reveal in his second book that he had been on the brink of walking out two weeks earlier in both his semi-final of the Premier League, in which he beat Steve Davis 5-2, and the final.

He remembered on both occasions missing a ball, going to shake hands, stopping himself and sitting down. He remembered his 4-0 lead over Jimmy White in the final becoming 4-2 in this way, although in fact he won 7-0 in 71 minutes.

What did this show, apart from a faulty memory? Maybe that Ronnie felt the need of a grand gesture either to show how little snooker meant to him or to show his contempt for the WPBSA.

'There was something in me that wouldn't be satisfied until I'd done it,' he said. 'It was just a matter of time before I got into flight mode. It did cross my mind to get to the final and just not turn up. Part of me wanted to have a go at World Snooker. I also had people revving me up in the background. Friends were telling me they couldn't get into the players' lounge and they couldn't get into matches and they were encouraging me to have a pop at World Snooker.'

It did not emerge until a couple of months later that, on top of all his familiar problems, Ronnie had been in a state of high anxiety over whether his father would be granted early release from his recommended sentence of 18 years. He was to be told that he had to serve the full term and that the best he could hope for was a category upgrade, although even this was considered to be in doubt as his behaviour in prison had not been impeccable. Ronnie spared no expense on legal fees and was devastated that his father's release date of November 2010 remained unchanged. It must have been difficult in such circumstances to convince himself that a snooker match mattered all that much.

It is not uncommon for someone harbouring intense resentment to imagine dramatic ways of evening the score, but carrying them through usually amounts to no more than a futile self-injury from a doomed charge against the battlements. It was fair enough to describe the WPBSA/World Snooker as 'a load of tossers', but he had put himself in the wrong and it was to cost him £20,000 in disciplinary fines.

In one strange way, Ronnie's walkout at the UK did help him. When he has something to prove or, rather, something from which he has to redeem himself, it often brings out the best of him. So it did at the 2007 Masters as his seventh final yielded his third title.

He made two centuries in beating Ali Carter 6-1 and another in the deciding eleventh frame against Ken Doherty. His 6-4 semi-final win over Stephen Maguire was poor on both sides in the main, although Ronnie still rose above mediocrity with frame-winners of 76, 88, 130 and 69. Against Ding in the final, he was simply irresistible. At 9-3, having lost six frames in succession and been outscored 639-92, Ding tried to shake hands, although the scoreboard clearly showed that the contest was best of 19, not 17.

Compassionately, Ronnie put his arm round Ding's shoulders as they left the arena at the intermission, with Ding about to give way to tears.

'I told him: let's go and have a cup of tea.'

Ding's problem was not only Ronnie's excellence but some ill-mannered heckling: 'It's different from playing in China. In this country, I feel I'm playing alone.'

It was a trouncing that appeared to affect Ding's mental approach to future matches with Ronnie.

Still, Ronnie was hard to please: 'The balls were going in the holes but I wasn't in control. I'm not knocking the way I played but I felt as if I had to put a lot of effort into that.'

Truly, geniuses have different standards from the rest of us. Imperfections unnoticed by others niggle at them. Like a tenor with a sore throat, Ronnie often does not really want to play if he does not feel capable of his best.

In headline terms, there were now four categories of player on the circuit: (1) the Steve Davis/Jimmy White generation, whose title-winning days were behind them; (2) the Hendry generation, to which Doherty and Ebdon could sometimes be attached; (3) the O'Sullivan/Higgins/Williams class of 92; and (4) the new wave of Ding/Robertson/Murphy and, sporadically, Maguire. As always, it was to be fascinating to observe how long one generation could hold off the next.

Murphy won the Malta Cup in which Ronnie, showing very little interest and issuing only a 'no comment' at his press conference, lost 5-3 to Michael Holt; Robertson, beating Ronnie 5-4 in the quarter-finals, won the Welsh Open.

Ronnie said that he had, every day at Newport, 'been working on things and broadening the boundaries of my game' and promised also to do this in China before 'the one that really matters' in Sheffield.

However, none of this came to pass. Ronnie did win a non-ranking event in Kilkenny, making a 147 on a table with generous pockets, and despite complaining of jetlag beat Ali Carter 5-4 in the second round in Beijing, making 63 in the decider at absurdly breakneck speed, pulling the trigger on several shots only a split second after the referee had replaced the colour on its spot.

'In the last frame I was trying to play quickly rather than think about anything,' said Ronnie, who thus became a quarter-finalist for the fifth time in the season's six ranking events.

He then beat Marco Fu 5-3, winning the last three frames with breaks of 63, 87, 55 and 79, a sequence that would surely have pleased anyone except Ronnie. 'I don't enjoy snooker enough any more. I'm proud of what I've achieved but I've already decided when I'm going to stop. In my mind, I've already retired. It's strange. I'm winning and playing so poorly.'

This was not at all how Fu saw it. 'Ronnie is the best player in the world and he was superb towards the end.'

There was no shifting Ronnie's malaise, though. Depressed and demotivated when he lost 17-11 to Dott in their Crucible semi-final 11 months earlier, Ronnie grew progressively more self-destructive in his shot choices as he lost to him again, 6-2 in their semi-final in Beijing.

Dott stole the first two frames from losing positions and from 4-0 behind Ronnie had no appetite for the fight as he refused to temper a 'go for everything' policy. 'I baffle myself sometimes with the way I play. It's a relief the match is over. I feel good now. I've got more important things to look forward to when I get home.'

This defeat meant that Ronnie had gone two years and 14 events without winning a ranking title. He had won the Premier League (one-night stands), the Masters (for which he could live at home) and the Kilkenny Masters (for which he had to be away for only three days). Otherwise, away from home, he was restless and uneasy.

His repeated contemplation of retirement seemed to amount to a yearning to be released from the pressure inside his head, some of which arose from knowing just how good he was and the frustration that he could not play to the standard he expected of himself. In terms of enjoyment, it was clear he would rather play exhibitions. He made two maximums in one of these at Kidderminster but he could not get away from the fact that places in the pantheon of greatness mostly depend on what a player has won.

Ronnie simply did not have it in him to sustain a world title challenge at the Crucible, although he started well enough, trouncing Ding 10-2 much as he had drubbed him 10-3 in the final of the Masters four months earlier.

'How people will see it and how I felt will probably be different but I got the result,' said Ronnie, who then led Robertson 8-3 but was within a ball of going 11-10 down before winning 13-10. I wasn't that comfortable,' said Ronnie. 'My long potting wasn't that good, my safety was average and with anything from six feet or more I was miles out. When you're not potting long balls, it's like losing your serve in tennis because you have to work harder to get chances. I was aware of that, so when I was in amongst the balls I made the most of it because it was difficult for me.'

Long potting was again his most obvious problem in his quarter-final against John Higgins, although he did score heavily enough when he was in to split their opening session 4-4.

Next morning, though, he imploded, not as starkly as he had against Dott a year earlier but enough to lose seven of the eight frames, missing pots and losing position with baffling frequency.

Ronnie did not accept his fate as passively as he sometimes did and won four of the first five frames of the final session before the axe fell at 13-9.

Higgins went on to win the title. Ronnie reflected, 'I didn't pot any long balls, I missed a lot from middle distance and my safety wasn't competitive either. I was fighting my game all the way.'

Most of all, he was fighting his own internal demons, difficult to define but deadly in their effects. He topped the 2006/07 money list with £307,595, taking his career prize money beyond £5m, but money, as many have acknowledged, is not everything.

Chapter 20

[2007/08]

PLEADING a bad back, as he had for the 2005 China Open, Ronnie withdrew from the Shanghai Masters at the start of the 2007/08 season, so his first tournament action was the Grand Prix in Aberdeen in late October. Fresh and rested, he reached the final, beating Shaun Murphy 6-5 from two down with three to play in the semi-finals, but was beaten 9-6 by Marco Fu, who made eight breaks of 60 or more in the nine frames he won. Apart from an unexpected miss when he looked like drawing level at 7-7, there was nothing much to criticise in Ronnie's performance but much to praise in that of Fu, whose maiden ranking title extended Ronnie's drought in this category to 31 months.

Nor was this sequence ended in Belfast, where he was a 5-2 quarter-final loser to Fergal O'Brien, the day after he had set a record of five centuries – 108, 122, 107, 147 and 129 – in a best-of-nine in beating Ali Carter 5-2.

This exceptional performance did not make Ronnie happy. 'I just got lucky today and Ali made it easy for me by missing a few. I can't face practising because I'm playing so badly.' After losing to O'Brien, he was again harshly self-critical and not at his most talkative. 'You should be disappointed when you play like that. I found it tough. That's snooker. Good luck to Fergal, he deserves his chance.'

Perhaps Ronnie was unconsciously seeking a way to put across how depressed he was feeling.

'No matter what happens I feel like a failure,' Ronnie told Matthew Syed of *The Times*. 'I feel lucky to have won two world titles but I feel robbed because that's all I've won.'

By what did he feel robbed? His opponents? Not really. A feeling of detachment from his core self-belief? More likely. Did he see this as some inexplicable affliction or did it have origins and causes such as his father's imprisonment? It was not his game that was the problem, it was him.

'I threw away two titles because I wasn't strong enough in myself [2005, 2006] because I couldn't take it. I knew I was capable of challenging Hendry's record [of seven world titles] but I haven't produced. How can I be anything other than a failure?'

It was as if he was grieving for blowing his chance of becoming the statistically confirmed greatest ever player, already putting his career mostly in the past tense with relentlessly lacerating self-blame quite divorced from any small satisfactions he could salvage from having done the best he could at the time. It was as if he was no longer competing for first prize and could not see any attraction in second.

'A lot of the time, I'm in pieces and I still don't know why,' said Ronnie, doomed to repeat the past because he could not understand it. He needed to consult, if not Mike Brearley, then someone of that ilk that he could trust in order to get to the roots of his manic depressive cycles, dealing with the sources of the guilt, self-loathing and at times paranoia that were often making his life a misery, all the more so because he had to live it out in public. He was eventually to find that person, Dr Steve Peters, albeit not for a few years yet, so in the meantime his moods continued to fluctuate.

On an upswing, Ronnie won the Premier League for the fourth time in succession and seventh in all – with £83,000 to go with it – and then his fourth UK title, although there was still a melancholic air undermining any satisfaction he felt.

He attributed his first two victories in the UK in considerable part to the shortcomings of his opponents. Having beaten him 9-6 from 6-5 down, he noted that Michael Holt 'got faster and faster in important situations'; Mark King, who he beat 9-1, 'usually makes you work hard for everything' but 'left me in the balls time and time again'. He was much more pleased with his 9-2 win over Jamie Cope, commenting, 'My break building has been pretty good this season and for whatever reason my long potting came together today, so I ended up sustaining the pressure on him. I've stumbled on to something and I'm quite optimistic. That reminded me of how I played when I was 15 or 16.' In other words, it was how he felt before his sense of certainty was shattered by his father being sent to prison.

Mark Selby, a much less open sort of player than Cope, did not allow Ronnie so many chances in their semi-final and forced him to play against the grain for most of the day. In fact, Ronnie trailed 3-0, 4-1, 6-3 and 7-5 before producing a grandstand finish at 8-8 in the form of a 147 to settle the issue.

Even this only marginally alleviated the gloom. 'It was alright but I'd rather have played a solid game and won 9-3 with no unforced errors,' said Ronnie, who then revealed his novel way of staying focused throughout a long day.

'At times my head was going, so I had to find a way to keep concentrating. They won't let me put a towel over my head any more – which worked by the way – so when he was at the table I started counting the dots on a spoon I'd taken into the arena. My thanks go to the spoon.'

Like Bernard Malamud's baseball-playing protagonist in his novel, *The Natural*, the purity of Ronnie's extraordinary talent could be and often was blighted by the confusing forces of real life, but Ronnie's decisive maximum was like Malamud's Roy Hobbs smiting a match-winning homer deep into the bleachers.

Ronnie's relentless 10-2 trouncing of Stephen Maguire in the final put him only one below Hendry's five UK titles and two shy of Davis's six, but he admitted that matching their overall records 'will be very difficult now'. He took consolation in comparing himself with Mike Tyson, pointing out, 'Whenever he was in the ring, [he] brought excitement to people and that's as important to me as records. Tyson was explosive, on the edge and with an edge. There was always something going on and at his best no one could live with him.'

At the age of 32, Ronnie was reflecting wistfully that he was unlikely to prove statistically that he was the best player of all time, hence his identification with Tyson, another towering figure in sport whose greatness was flawed.

'I wish I could tell people who suffer depression how to control it but there's no cure. It's about finding a way to deal with it.'

Ronnie found it helpful to immerse himself in running. He liked the camaraderie of being with other runners, one of the lads with nothing awesome to prove but capable of giving him a sense of enjoyment not available from a sport 'you're doing for a living'.

He took a modest pride in finishing 28th in the Essex cross-country championship and developed an ambition of making the Essex team, but his devotion to training did not improve his relationship at home with Jo. Taking second place to snooker she could accept. Taking third place to running was not so easy and it was not long before their relationship was in trouble.

Unusually, he did not shine at the Masters, falling at the first fence 6-5 to Maguire, who observed that 'the luck you need is to catch him when he's not in peak form'.

From 0-51 in the decider, Ronnie was on 47 and apparently clearing up to win until he missed a routine blue with the rest.

Selby won the tournament to establish himself as a rising force and emphasised it by beating Ronnie 9-8 from three down with four to play in the final of the Welsh Open.

From this result, it was clear that Ronnie had another major rival to contend with, one moreover with a method of play that he found frustrating. As with many rivalries, it was the clash of styles that, over the next few years, was to prove so fascinating.

As Selby saw it, 'I didn't think I had much hope at 8-5. I wasn't cueing well but I knew if I dug deep and made things scrappy, it wasn't over.'

Ronnie considered that he 'had a chance in every one of those last four frames and didn't take any of them', revealing how irritating he found Selby to play. Certainly, a series of turgid, slow-moving frames was not his idea of fun.

'With Mark, everything is so deliberate, slow actually. There's no rhythm in the game and it's hard to concentrate. I don't know if he's talented. He never takes on a ball if he's going to leave it. He's a bit like Dott or Ebdon in that respect. It's more like an endurance test but you've got to try and find a way of coming through and getting the better of these players.'

Ronnie was seen to mouth the words 'I'm bored' to spectators but Selby's approach, measured, considered and not dissimilar to that of Steve Davis in his prime, was well within the parameters of fair play and simply demonstrated that there was more than one way to win a snooker match.

For the next few seasons, Ronnie could not get it out of his head that he 'ought' to be beating the much less talented Selby without too much trouble. In fact, Selby was not without talent and made up for any shortfall in this department with total dedication to improving his game. The proof of the pudding was in the eating or, in Selby's case, the ability – as conclusively demonstrated in their 2014 world final – to add heavy scoring to grindingly effective tactical play.

The China Open, the only other ranking event prior to the World Championship, was distinguished not so much by Ronnie's 5-4 first-round defeat by Marco Fu as by his lewd comments into what he may not have realised was a bank of live microphones at his press conference.

Throughout the match, he had played extremely quickly, hardly giving the referee time to re-spot the colours, but at 50-0 in the decider was a hot favourite to progress until he unexpectedly missed a brown.

Fu recovered to lead 57-50 with just the last three colours remaining, whereupon Ronnie launched two very high-risk attempts at the blue, the second of which gave Fu a simple match-clinching chance. Ronnie had looked a million dollars in amongst the balls so why, at the end, had he apparently not cared whether he won or lost?

One theory was that, at this time, Ronnie could take only a limited amount of pressure. Was it a frailty of nerve that had caused him to miss the final blue in the decider of his 6-5 defeat by Maguire at the Masters? Why, in the decider against Selby in the Welsh Open final, having failed to dislodge the last red in potting a black, had he as good as fallen on his sword by attempting a suicidally high-risk cross double?

'I knew it wasn't the right shot, but in for a penny, in for a pound. You've got to have a giggle,' he explained unsatisfactorily.

Why have you? Yes, his immediate wish to develop the last red had not been gratified but would it not have been better, and given him more satisfaction, having been trying so hard to make a successful defence of the title, to swallow his disappointment and play a more considered shot rather than belatedly pretend that the outcome meant nothing more than 'a giggle'?

There was some immaturity in all this, wanting to win but when this wish was not gratified in the desired way, pretending it did not matter. So it was with the concluding shots of his defeat by Fu, although the match was almost forgotten in the light of his press conference, audio and video of which was quickly posted on the internet.

Ronnie's boredom threshold is notoriously low and losing does not make it any higher. He soon grew restless because of the time taken to translate Chinese questions and his own replies, and resorted to a series of indecent references to his manhood. 'While his first answer was being translated, he was seen pointing to his penis and asking, 'Do you want to suck that? Do you want to come and suck that later? Anyone want to give me a nosh? Suck my dick?'

What on earth lay behind this display of infantile vulgarity? Was it, unconsciously, an expression of aggression arising from a deep-rooted anger that he was unable to discharge against its true target? Perhaps he really did not want to go to China at all and did so only because of lucrative personal sponsorships for Chinese products and this was his way of saying, 'OK, I've played. You've had your money's worth, I'm off home now.' Whatever the explanation, it was astonishing that, once he was there, he did not give winning his highest priority.

Again, Ronnie had needlessly landed himself in trouble, although the WPBSA, weak as it was at the time and not wishing to kill the golden goose that they conceived him to be, had no appetite for suspending him and in the light of his profuse apologies limited their disciplinary action to the forfeiture of prize money and ranking points from that event.

He could have done without the ensuing furore but there was little sign that it had distracted him at the Crucible, where he rounded off his 13-7 second-round defeat of Mark Williams with his third maximum in that arena and ninth in all, thus overtaking Hendry's record.

This was followed by a 13-7 second-round quarter-final win over Liang Wenbo ('It wasn't special but it was OK') and from 4-1 down a 17-6 semi-final drubbing of Hendry, who described Ronnie's performance as 'the best snooker and safety I've ever seen. I've never been so completely outplayed in my career. The way Ronnie was hitting the ball was as close to perfection as you can get.' Ali Carter reached the final from the other half of the draw but did not have all that much left in his tank and Ronnie, in any case, was too consistent and too good. 'It was', he said, after beating Carter 18-8, 'a professional performance because a job needed to be done and I did it.'

Few world championships had been won with such absence of drama, although it was not, of course, Ronnie's responsibility to supply this. Jo and the infant Ronnie III shared his moment of triumph in the arena, but only a few weeks later it was reported that Ronnie's relationship with Jo had ended, although she was still living in Ronnie's house.

Ronnie, Williams and Maguire left the 110sport management agency, a formidable force under Ian Doyle but much less so under his son, Lee. Players were growing increasingly dissatisfied with the WPBSA, under the chairmanship of Sir Rodney Walker, and how its board was increasing its own pay. There were match-fixing scandals, none of them involving Ronnie, just around the corner. Snooker was starting to struggle, not because there was anything wrong with the game or the entertainment it provided but because of how it was being run. Ronnie, as its top attraction, had earned £638,850 in prize money alone from the 2007/08 season but the middle and lower- ranking players on the circuit were beginning to feel the pinch.

Chapter 21

[2008–2010]

RONNIE'S longings for 'new starts' were frequently enacted by flying starts to new seasons. So it was in the 2008/09 campaign, which he began by winning the Northern Ireland Trophy. He had to win the last three frames to beat Ken Doherty and also survived two more 5-4s against Barry Hawkins and Ali Carter before beating Dave Harold 9-3 in the final. If not consistently in overdrive, he was still in his higher gears most of the time. If he had serious off-table cares, they were not reflected in his performances.

'A couple of years ago, I would have got fed up with a match like that and wanted to go home,' he said midweek. 'But I've got more confidence in my game now. Even if I'm not playing well, I want to be in the next round because I know I could find something tomorrow.'

All very sensible. Ronnie noted that 'it's great to blow the cobwebs away this early in the season'. Harold was left in awe of the quality of a 76 clearance Ronnie made in the last frame of their afternoon session, in which he had to develop four reds that were under a cushion and prise the brown away from the pink. 'That clearance was 50-1. He's the only one in the world who could have done that. He mesmerises you sometimes.'

Ronnie was also fully focused on becoming the first player for 15 years to win three ranking titles in succession but came up just short, losing 10-8 to Ricky Walden in the final of the Shanghai Masters. Again, some of his performances were touched by genius, notably his 145 break in the eleventh-frame decider of his semi-final against Maguire. Williams, beaten 5-3 in their quarter-final, thought Ronnie 'probably the best player ever. He makes breaks from nowhere.'

Still, Ronnie was not judging himself on results but against his highest standards. After beating Marco Fu 5-1 to reach the Grand Prix quarter-finals in Glasgow, he said: 'I'm just trying to make the best of a scrappy spell. My bad level isn't as bad as it was a couple of years ago. It's keeping me semi-competitive but I'm still not pleased. Most people haven't been world number one, world champion or at the top of a sport, so they can't relate to what I'm saying. Most don't know what it takes and the emotions you go through. Probably only about 20 people on the planet can understand.'

The rest of his early-season form burnt out with a 5-4 quarter-final loss to Judd Trump, for whom, at the age of 19, this was a major breakthrough. Trump made only one half century but Ronnie said he 'just ran dry, very dry. I can't seem to pot a ball over six feet.'

Citing his 'hectic playing and promotional schedule', which caused him to feel 'very run down', he could not face going to Bahrain for the next tournament. With a 7-2 win over Selby, Ronnie won the Premier League play-offs for the fifth time in succession but his inward disarray surfaced when he lost his second match in the UK Championship 9-5 to Joe Perry.

Ronnie made three centuries in building a 5-3 overnight lead but the next day was plagued by wild inconsistency. A perfectionist often unable to deal with his own shortcomings, he lost the first three frames of the second session. At 6-5 down and trailing 23-0 in the twelfth frame, but with nine reds still remaining, Ronnie missed a tricky red and impatiently conceded, sweeping his cue across the table and stomping to the mid-session interval.

'I wanted to get out of there and have a cup of tea,' said Ronnie after he had lost 9-5. 'This is just a little £250 fine and a letter through the post. It's no big deal.' He gave Perry due credit and observed that inconsistency was just something he had to live with, although the reality was probably that this arose, at least in part, from off-table factors connected to the end of his relationship with Jo. This said, several months later, the possibility of a reconciliation was mooted.

Interviewed by Gabby Logan for the BBC, Ronnie said, 'It would be fantastic if we could live together and bring up our family together. I'm probably a difficult person to be with. It's difficult for a wife to be married to a sportsman who's trying to stay at the top of their game.'

With his father's release date now just under two years away, Ronnie admitted to apprehension about how their relationship would work. 'My last memory of dad was when he was out on bail, driving me to a snooker tournament when I was 15. I didn't know if he was going to go away or not, so it's as if 18 years have gone. I have no memories other than a telephone conversation and a visit every two months, so you can't make up for that. It's going to be a different relationship now. I'm 33. I've got two [sic] kids and I've had my career.'

His father's situation was always bubbling on the back burner throughout his career and there were more immediate concerns, including the state of the game. Though never prone to bragging or boasting, Ronnie did want to ply his trade in a context fit for heroes.

'I love the game but I'm at a stage where I don't care whether I play or not and I don't want to go through the rest of my life like that,' he said on the eve of the Masters. He was hoping that snooker tournaments would again be lively and stimulating places to be instead of taking place in an atmosphere of disaffection between players and the governing body. It seemed to have been forgotten that the WPBSA board and officials were supposed to be working for the players rather than vice-versa.

'The people who are running snooker just seem to be going backwards. I just think that the people making the decisions are killing the sport. It's on a real downward spiral. It's quite uninspiring coming to tournaments, to be honest.'

A combination of private and professional frustrations plunged Ronnie into impulsive and dramatic action. Two days before his opening match against Perry in the Masters, he smashed the cue with which he had won his third world title, a surprisingly cathartic experience as it proved.

'It was like a detox. I feel like I've been cleansed,' said Ronnie. With the replacement, he made two centuries in beating Perry 6-5 despite being unsure of how it would react on certain shots and having difficulty with long pots and thin safeties.

In an odd way, Ronnie found it stimulating to deal with a new problem. 'I get excited by having a new cue and a new challenge.' He rose to it amazingly well, concluding his 6-2 win over Carter with breaks of 128, 115 and 91 in the last three frames, making another two centuries in crushing Maguire 6-1 and taking the title with a 10-8 win over Selby from 7-5 down.

Wise old heads were amazed at the standard – including eight centuries in the tournament – to which Ronnie had played with an unfamiliar cue. John Virgo summed up this feeling: 'People who don't play snooker at a reasonable level can't comprehend what Ronnie has done this week. It's unbelievable.'

Once again, spectacular success had followed a crisis. His 2007 Masters triumph had come only a month after walking out of his UK quarter-final against Hendry; his

2008 world title had immediately followed the unacceptable vulgarities of his China Open press conference. Now he had handicapped himself by having to use a new cue – and still won the £150,000 first prize.

Ronnie's adrenalin had responded to an unusual challenge and a special atmosphere that the Masters invariably generates, but the Welsh Open did not supply the same stimulus. Beaten 5-3 in the second round by Fu, he said, 'For a while, I've known there's something wrong with my game I've got to sort out, but until now I haven't bothered. Now I know it's a problem I've got to solve quickly. If I don't, I've no chance at the World Championship.'

Whether because of this problem or not, Ronnie's season petered out with a 5-4 quarter-final defeat by Higgins in the China Open, a match whose standard Higgins described as 'really bad', and a 13-11 second-round loss to Mark Allen at the Crucible, in which his main problems, apart from Allen's fine performance, were his long potting and apparent lack of conviction on 50/50 balls to which he had to commit.

It had not been a busy season for Ronnie, particularly after Christmas 2009/10, with ranking events reduced from eight to six and total prize money falling by £435,000 to £3,063,600.

True to precedent, Ronnie started the new campaign very well. He won the Shanghai Masters, with 5-3 the best score against him, and started the Premier League with a hat-trick of centuries. In the Grand Prix, for which seeding was abandoned, the luck of the draw pitted him against Higgins early on. He led 4-3 and by 50 late in the eighth frame only to miss a simple close-range red when within a few pots of victory. Inevitably rattled, he soon missed another, though more difficult, match-clinching opportunity and ended up losing 5-4.

'I just messed it up,' said Ronnie gloomily. 'If it hadn't been that shot, it would have probably been another. I had the game in my hand but I made a lot of mistakes. I suppose I was semi-competitive but my long potting was really poor.'

As there was no more ranking event activity for another two months, Ronnie had plenty of scope to indulge his passion for running, although his decision to compete in the Norwich half marathon on the morning of his Premier League final against Shaun Murphy may have been carrying his enthusiasm too far and could have contributed to his 7-3 defeat.

'I wanted to test myself,' Ronnie explained.

Maybe Ronnie felt that he needed to make up for this. Certainly he played with exemplary discipline, if only fleetingly with inspiration, in recording a trio of 9-3 wins over Matthew Stevens, Peter Ebdon and Mark Selby in the UK Championship in Telford and from 8-2 down to Higgins in the semi-finals almost pulled off a miraculous win, sustaining something approaching his best as he won six consecutive frames to equalise at 8-8 before missing an early chance in the decider. This allowed Higgins, under enormous pressure, to hold his technique and his nerve together to make a match-winning 56.

'When Ronnie's coming back at you with full flow, that's a frightening thing,' said Higgins. 'Even when it was 8-2, I wasn't taking anything for granted. As every frame slips by, you start to get more worried about losing. At 8-8, though, the pressure went back on Ronnie.'

Ronnie masked his disappointment in self-criticism: 'To get to 8-8 flattered me. A fair score was probably 9-4. At the start of the season, I made a pact with myself not to get too excited if I win or too disappointed if I lose. Otherwise, I'd get frustrated and annoyed and I don't want to spend the rest of my career feeling like that. I'm trying to be philosophical.'

It was not so much losing that he feared but the feelings it would bring. Unpleasant as these can be, particularly if a chance to win has been squandered, they are part of the package for any professional sportsman.

Disappointment also lay in wait at the Masters, which he was also within a frame of winning despite emitting a depressed negativity after each of his four matches.

Down 3-0 to Neil Robertson he won 6-4, manoeuvring, coaxing and cajoling the cue ball through breaks of 106 and 76 in the last two frames.

'The last time I played a good tournament from start to finish was in Torquay years ago [2003 European Open]. In practice, I'm awful but playing in front of a big crowd makes you want to salvage some pride.'

Ronnie completed his 6-3 win over Ebdon with a run of 103 but lamented, 'There were only three or four shots that seemed effortless and out of the middle of the bat.'

Ronnie and John
Higgins at the 1995
Masters

Young Ronnie at the
World Championship,
2002

*Ronnie at the funeral
of Paul Hunter, Leeds,
October 2006*

*Ronnie kisses daughter
Lily after winning
the 2008 World
Championship*

Ronnie with his great rival, John Higgins, at the 2011 World Championship.

Ronnie sits it out during the 2017 World Championship.

Ronnie with Ronnie Jr after winning the 2012 World Championship

Ronnie checks whether the pink is just pottable. 2012

Ronnie with girlfriend Laila Rouass, 2013

Ronnie with the 2013 World Championship trophy

Ronnie with his great friend, Jimmy White

Thinking out a shot, 2014

Ronnie breaking off left-handed, as he invariably does. Brendan Moore was the referee. World Championship, 2014

Ronnie shakes hands with Barry Hearn after losing the 2014 World Championship final

Ronnie in action against Stuart Bingham in their 2015 World Championship semi-final. Terry Camilleri was the referee.

Ronnie makes his entrance at the 2016 Masters

Ronnie watches his opponent's shot on one of the arena television screens. Champion of Champions event, Coventry, 2016

Ronnie hugs Ding Junhui after quarter-final defeat, World Championship, 2017

Ebdon saw it differently. 'The last twice I've played him he's been almost perfect for long stretches. I think he is playing a fantastic brand of snooker.' This opinion was echoed by Williams, who he edged 6-5 in the semi-finals. 'The way I played, only Ronnie could have beaten me.' Ronnie said, 'I was just willing the balls in. I'm petrified going out there. I feel I'm going to miss anything and everything.'

What lay behind these excessively downbeat remarks? Was he subconsciously trying to deny himself pleasure and satisfaction? Was he seeking a shield against disappointment by pitching his expectations low? Such pronouncements did not seem likely to stop him winning the tournament when he stood three up with four to play in the final, but Selby resisted resolutely and Ronnie could not nail him.

Ronnie had two chances to win 10-8 but could not convert either of them and did not pot a ball in the decider. He claimed he was 'not too disappointed' but his demeanour suggested otherwise. 'I'm surprised I even got this far playing like I did.'

This lacked all sense of proportion. Ronnie had not played as well as he was capable of playing but how many times a year does any player do that? 'For the last 17 years [i.e. since his father went to prison], I've been playing like a plum. It's got nothing to do with my demons or problems, but blowing hot and cold makes me depressed. I have to fight these feelings all the time when I'm playing.'

Yes, but *why* was he blowing 'hot and cold'? Surely he was fighting certain feelings that affected his play rather than the other way round. It seemed that what Ronnie wanted most was immunity from emotional hurt.

'Defeats like this used to hurt a lot more. Now it's just about seeing out my career and filling up my life with something more important.'

Like what?

Perhaps realising that some of his remarks in his press conferences were not making much sense to 'normal' people, Ronnie resorted to stock responses as he reached the Welsh Open semi-finals with a frames tally of 15-3 before losing, for the fourth time in five matches that season, 6-4 to Higgins. The odd mistake, the odd slice of bad luck and a high level of consistency from Higgins accounted for the difference between winning and losing.

It was to emerge that for much of the 2009/10 season, Ronnie had two important issues on his mind. His father was within months of reaching the due date of his release in November 2010 and his split from Jo was bringing into play serious and expensive conflict of a legal and financial nature. There was maintenance to pay and child access to discuss. He had been granted five hours on Saturdays and two on Wednesdays, but if he was restricted to these times he could not play in tournaments.

In fact, his father had been on limited release for a while, working in a charity shop and spotted in an unobtrusive place in the crowd at the Welsh Open. The terms of his weekend release allowed him to be in Sheffield for the World Championship as long as his presence was low key and unreported, but Ronnie was uncertain how all this would affect him.

In his early days, Ronnie hated playing in front of his father because he was so critical. 'It stopped when I was 12. When he stopped coming to see me, I started winning.'

Maybe the legacy of this was Ronnie's propensity to criticise himself, often in absurdly judgmental terms, before anyone else could. He loved his father but was it going to be all good news to have him around on a daily or regular basis? Ronnie was not 15 any more. He was 33.

He did not want to travel to Beijing for the China Open but was talked into it by his then manager, Django Fung. He was given the best suite in the hotel but 'just sat there, crying my eyes out, I felt so lost'. He knew he was in no fit state to play and felt even worse in the arena. He just wanted to go home.

Since he made breaks of 93, 77, 59, 61 and 62, he did not play badly once he got into a break or by any standards other than his own but, having missed frame ball in two frames, found himself 4-3 down to Tian Pengfei.

Clearing the colours in the eighth, Ronnie seemed certain to level at 4-4 but chose to roll the elementary black from its spot at dead weight rather than pot it firmly, as he normally would have done. The black finished on the brink of the pocket.

Some observers thought that Ronnie had missed on purpose. Others believed that he had simply given himself the best chance of missing it. 'I was shocked by Ronnie's final shot,' said Tian.

There was no suggestion that this was a case of match fixing. Rather was it explicable by a feeling he characterised in his second book: 'I felt lost, lonely in myself and I just gave up [in some] matches. I never threw matches but I did give up. There's a big difference. One is planned, illegal, the other is unplanned, unconscious.'

All this took place against the background of a situation that always upset him: enforced separation from his loved ones. It had been so when his father and, more briefly, his mother, had gone to jail. Now it was limited access to his children that was pressing on this emotional nerve.

Ronnie's publicly expressed opinion that he was not playing well enough to win the world title became a self-fulfilling prophecy at the Crucible. Initially, he was playing well enough but other pressures weighed upon him and, not for the first time, he lacked the necessary mental staying power.

On the opening day, he made two centuries in taking a 7-2 overnight lead over Liang Wenbo. His 9-3 lead was reduced to 9-7 but a quickfire 73 ended the contest when 'the pressure was getting to me a bit'.

Neither did Ronnie's title chances have cause to be downplayed when he produced his best session of the season in progressing from 9-9 to a 13-10 win over Williams. After Ronnie had made breaks of 104, 75, 111 and 106 in four of the closing five frames, Williams asked, 'How can you not be impressed by that? In my opinion, the only player that could stop Ronnie winning this is Ronnie. I don't think there's another player in the game that can do what he does or make the game look so easy. You've got to take your hat off to him. He pots crazy balls and gets in even when you've put him in trouble.'

All this at an average shot time of 15 seconds, although Ronnie refused 'to let myself get too excited. That [performance] was better for a change but I still didn't flow. I had to give every shot a lot of thought. I've thrown in too many bad displays at the Crucible over the years to allow myself to feel confident.'

Selby's stubborn, at times grinding, style was just what Ronnie liked least. Having come from three down with four to play to beat him in the 2008 Welsh Open and 2010 Masters final, Selby trailed 9-5 but again prevailed 13-11.

The longer the match wore on, the more vulnerable to error Ronnie became. He led 11-9 but grew increasingly ragged, did not win another frame and afterwards gave the impression that he had reached the end of his tether.

He still thought his game was the trouble rather than the factors that were undermining it, although he did say, 'I can't keep coming here moaning to you lot [the press] and expect you to understand what's going on in my little world. I've tried not to fight it but the competitive side of me makes it hurt when I lose.'

In other words, he could convince himself that it did not matter if he lost to Tian Pengfei in the China Open, but not if he lost at the Crucible.

'I haven't felt comfortable or confident for 17–18 years. It's my bad game that taken me this far. It's a shame but I can't play as well as I used to.' Actually, he could but not with the same feeling of not having a care in the world. When he was asked whether he would return for the 2010/11 season, Ronnie replied: 'I hope so.' He loved the game but hated what it did to him. It could be argued that he had done incredibly well to win three world titles considering all the emotional turmoil he had endured. How many would he have won with an uncluttered mind?

No sportsman can feel happy if he knows in his heart that he has not delivered a full return on his talent. Defeat at the Crucible that year, or any year, guaranteed the pain of accepting that one more fruitless season had gone by, albeit with the small consolation that this had given him some relief from what had become a terrible struggle.

No amount of rationalisation could lastingly resolve the conflict between his responsibility to his own talent and his longing for respite from pressure. 'It's a job, innit? This year, I took the attitude that I don't expect anything, just go out and play and if you win, great, if you lose, so what, enjoy your little life away from the table. If I can keep on playing for the next five, six years, it's irrelevant whether I win tournaments or not.'

He added, more disturbingly, 'If I stop playing, what am I going to do with my time? Even if I'm not enjoying the snooker, it still fills the time up. It's all about filling your day up.'

How unutterably sad was this? Little life? Filling his day up? Where was the joy? The pursuit of glory? It was tragic that he had come to feel like this about his snooker.

Chapter 22

[2010–2012]

RONNIE senior's 18-year sentence, seemingly interminable, eventually ended with his release in November 2010, nine days before the Premier League play-offs. Ronnie had long gone past imagining that their relationship would pick up exactly where it had left off; Ronnie senior's last few years inside had been spent more quietly and with a stronger sense of acceptance than his first few. In the last couple of years, he had gained quite a bit of weight.

We shook hands backstage at the play-offs. He thanked me for sending him *Snooker Scene* each month and he had also become a loyal reader of *The Times*, for whom Phil Yates was able to write at greater length than other newspapers allowed for snooker. It was all very cordial and Ronnie duly delivered the desired result, beating Neil Robertson 5-1 and Shaun Murphy 7-1 to win the title for the sixth time in seven years.

'For the last three to four weeks, I've been playing a lot better in practice and generally my form has been a lot better than for the last couple of years,' said Ronnie, not making the explicit connection that many of us did with this improvement coinciding with his father's release.

Ronnie had certainly not been so upbeat when he withdrew from the Shanghai Masters two months earlier 'for personal reasons' and again after losing 5-1 to Robertson in the final of the World Open (in reality a re-branding of the Grand Prix) in Glasgow. 'To be honest, I've gone,' he had said with considerable but not unfamiliar exaggeration.

This was the tournament in which he was in play with a break of 140 but at first, in protest against the absence of a prize for a maximum, declined to pot the black for a 147 until persuaded to do so for the crowd's benefit by the referee, Jan Verhaas.

Nor did the euphoria arising from his father's release last very long. 'It's going to need a lot of adjustment for both of them,' Django Fung predicted. Immediately after the play-offs, he lost his opening match in the UK Championship 9-6 to Stuart Bingham after leading 6-4.

'At 6-6, I could see he was annoyed with himself and he started throwing his cue at some shots. I knew it was my chance to beat him,' said Bingham.

The previous few months had been a period of dramatic and favourable development within the game as the 2 December 2009 WPBSA annual general meeting had ended the chairmanship of Sir Rodney Walker together with two boardroom supporters and shortly afterwards the remainder.

Barry Hearn, who as chairman of the Professional Darts Council had been able to increase its circuit's total prize money from £500,000 to £5m and also add considerable value to low-profile sports like 9-ball pool, match angling and tenpin, had indicated he might ride to snooker's rescue under a new arrangement whereby the WPBSA's commercial arm, World Snooker, would be privatised, with his own company, Matchroom, taking a 51 per cent holding, and the WPBSA confining itself to a rules and regulatory role. After several meetings and stiff resistance from supporters of the *ancien régime*, this process was completed on 2 June 2010 and very soon, after years in the doldrums, snooker was again on the up.

Hearn, who Ronnie described as 'the Ronaldhino of promoters', wanted to use him as a 'flag bearer' but Ronnie was locked in conflict with Jo over a financial settlement and access to their two children and had no hunger for competition. One of Hearn's major innovations was the Players Tour Championship (PTC), a series of 12 new events with comparatively low prize money followed by a 24-man grand finals. But, financially, taking a whole weekend to win a £10,000 first prize in a PTC did not make as much sense as £10,000 for a one-night exhibition, particularly as weekends were the only feasible time he could spend whole days with his children. He played in only two of the twelve events in this series and of his ten withdrawals several were without prior notice. Meanwhile, Ronnie's rivals were accruing an advantage in competitive sharpness through regular matchplay. Certainly, he made more unforced errors than Mark Allen did in losing to him 6-4 in the first round of the Masters.

Some of his shot selections suggested a certain indifference to the result. Ronnie himself told *The Times*, 'When you get beat, it's kind of a burden off your shoulders.' His interviewer, Tom Dart, found it odd that he was 'rationalising defeat instead of raging against it' and wondered if a true champion's necessary 'fury' was still there.

Conflict between Ronnie and Hearn escalated when he withdrew on the very eve of the German Masters, a new ranking event in the impressive setting of Berlin's Tempodrom.

'I don't care if Ronnie doesn't play but what he can't do is enter and pull out at the last minute without very good reason,' said Hearn. 'It's his face on all the posters in Germany. It's a very important tournament for us as we try to develop the European market and an awful lot of people are going to be disappointed he's not there. This can't go on. Ronnie's very likeable when he wants to be but he should start considering his future in the game and his responsibilities to it.'

Ronnie produced a medical certificate but whatever the problem may have been it had not prevented him from making six centuries in eight frames against Jimmy White in a sell-out online exhibition in Blackburn the evening before he was due to fly out to Berlin.

In short, 10 withdrawals out of 12 in the PTCs, plus others from the Shanghai Masters, when he would have been defending champion, and the German Masters, was not the level of commitment Hearn was keen to see. Ronnie lost his first match to Ryan Day, both in the Welsh Open, 4-2, and the China Open, 5-2, appearing to lack all conviction, particularly in broken play.

When the settlement with Jo was finally agreed, it was based on his very successful 2007/08 season, in which he had won both the UK and world titles. His attempt to save legal fees by representing himself misfired and he ultimately paid lawyers in excess of £200,000 anyway. By not entering tournaments, he had no prize money coming in and could not indefinitely afford this level of expenditure. On the other hand, his head was so crammed with these issues that he could not face playing.

He was at such a low ebb that a few days before the World Championship, he phoned World Snooker to say that he would be withdrawing, terminating his membership and thus retiring. After he had been told that he would need to put this in writing, Ronnie phoned back next day to say he had changed his mind.

Perhaps he would have competed at the Crucible anyway but what ensured that he would reach the starting line was that Django Fung, after three years of urging, had persuaded him to consult Dr Steve Peters, a Sheffield psychiatrist who had made his name in the sports world through his role with Great Britain's highly successful cycling squad in the 2008 Olympic Games, in which Victoria Pendleton and Chris Hoy were gold medallists.

Four days before the championship, Ronnie met him for the first time and a relationship was formed that not only prevented Ronnie's career from imploding but promoted, subject to a few setbacks, a happier and more settled approach to life.

After his series of no-shows and early exits, less was expected of him than usual but these low expectations were confounded when he beat Dominic Dale 10-2, compiling three centuries and even enjoying the match 'as much as I did the first time I played at the Crucible. I didn't want it to end. I've never felt like that before.'

He did not play quite as well in beating Shaun Murphy 13-10, noting that 'there were frames when I needed three or four chances and that shouldn't be good enough', and in the quarter-finals could not summon quite the required level of consistency to defeat John Higgins, although he led 7-4 and 8-5.

Beaten 13-10, Ronnie said that Dr Peters had already given him a different way of looking at things. 'It was still substandard snooker but I wasn't smashing myself to pieces. I felt like I wanted to but I've worked on a couple of things which have made me not get too involved and I'm just trying to be objective about it.'

Ronnie had sometimes arrived at the Crucible with the game but not the attitude. This time, he had the attitude but not the game.

Over the whole season, his commitment to practice had been insufficient and he was not match-sharp, but he could at last see a way forward. 'If I do play next year, my main goal is to sort my head out.'

Those who have never suffered from depression tend to be unsympathetic, believing that it can be conquered through sheer will. This can help, particularly in the short term, but unless root causes are addressed the real problems remain. The past cannot be changed but it is often useful to gain insight into it, enough anyway for Ronnie to mitigate his habitually harsh self-criticism. He left the Crucible hoping through his involvement with Dr Peters 'to find a way not to beat myself up and ask, "what's the point?"'

It fell nicely for Ronnie that Dr Peters worked in Sheffield. In pursuit of his frequent need for repose, Ronnie lived a quiet life on a friend's houseboat, the Double Kiss, when he was there and most of the English events in the PTC series took place at the WPBSA facility at the nearby English Institute of Sport.

Only seven weeks after the end of the 2010/11 season, a new one began with PTC 1 and Ronnie won it. 'My game wasn't too bad. I'm just having a go and doing my best. This is a big season for me. I'm giving myself one more year, or possibly two, to see if I can improve. It's a work in progress but I do feel some optimism. I'm still seeing Steve Peters. I still need help but I feel a lot better.'

He entered the inaugural Australian Goldfields Open in July 2011, obviously fully intending to play, but after flying to Bangkok, about halfway to Melbourne, he declined to travel onwards when the airline could not provide him with an on-board bed to ease some neck pain. An 11-hour Bangkok to Melbourne flight may not have been the best treatment for a painful neck, but he would not have had to play until three days after arrival and it is not as if Australia has no physiotherapists.

One of the theories for his withdrawal was that, notwithstanding the progress he was making with Dr Peters, Ronnie was still suffering from acute separation anxiety based on an irrational fear that something dreadful might happen if he was a long way from home for an extended period of time. Supporting this theory was the fact that since winning the Shanghai Masters in September 2009, he had withdrawn from or lost early in every event that had required a long-haul flight. It was a withdrawal that invited comparison with the retirement of Marcus Trescothick from Test cricket because he suffered from acute depression on overseas tours, while continuing to accumulate heaps of runs in domestic cricket. Meanwhile, this incident did nothing to improve Ronnie's relationship with Barry Hearn and World Snooker.

He lost 4-3 to Fergal O'Brien in the quarter-finals of PTC 2, 4-1 to Graeme Dott in the second round of PTC 3 and 4-3, from 3-1 up, to Mark Selby in the semi-finals of the Paul Hunter Classic, PTC 4, in Furth, where he made a 147. Anthony Hamilton, with an exceptional second-round performance, beat him 5-3 in the Shanghai Masters (Ronnie having set aside any excessive anxieties about travel to faraway places), although even this did not affect his predominantly upbeat mood. 'I'm enjoying playing. It would be nice to be back near the top but I don't expect it. I'll just enjoy whatever's left of my career. I've got nothing left to prove and I'm not young any more.'

He did not enter PTCs 5 and 6 but beat Selby 4-2 to win PTC 7 in Gloucester. He followed his 4-1 second-round loss to Xiao Guodong, a rising young Chinese, in PTC 8 in Killarney and reached the final of PTC 9 in Antwerp, where he lost an exceptionally fine and fast-flowing match 4-3 to Judd Trump.

After overwhelming Ding Junhui 7-1 to win the Premier League for the tenth time, Ronnie was so enthusiastic that it was tempting to believe that his most serious troubles were over. 'That was brilliant. Last year, I wasn't going to play any more but I got my head right and I was able to play on. Now I want to play. I'm enjoying it and that's the most positive I've felt.'

It was too good to last. Beaten 6-5 by Trump in the second round of the UK Championship, Ronnie sang an all-too-familiar song. 'I feel I'm in a good place and I don't want to take the shine off Judd, but I seriously can't see me playing much longer. Even though I'm in a good frame of mind, I don't want to feel how I feel when I play.

'My game isn't up to scratch where I'd like it to be or where it used to be. It's not even playing, it's how I feel between matches and tournaments. It leaves me feeling quite nervy and anxious and I feel like I've had enough of the anxious moments. I want to enjoy my life. I feel like I've had a good go. I'm 36 and I'd like to meet somebody and share my life with someone. I still want to work. I don't want to wake up with nothing to do but I don't want to be living on my own and being anxious and lonely.

'I'm not an easy person to get along with when I'm playing snooker because I'm in my own little world. It's not fair to someone you want to be with to put them through that. For me to be the real Ronnie, I need to get away from what's causing the problem.'

Of course there was more to life than snooker but without it he knew in his heart that there would be less to life. This was his dilemma and his composure started to crack.

He had already said that he felt 'blackmailed' by World Snooker in the person of Hearn to play in the PTCs for modest prize money in the interest of his ranking and now complained on Twitter that the travelling was tiring him out. 'Fuck the PTCs,' he tweeted.

Motivated by a capacity crowd of 1,500 for the Masters at Alexandra Palace, Ronnie beat Ding 6-4 on his first appearance after Christmas and made a break of 141 against Trump in a quarter-final of mutually high standard that Trump won 6-2. However, mostly through his no-shows at 12 events carrying ranking points of various tariffs in the previous season, a crisis had developed in terms of securing the place in the top 16 that would exempt him from having to qualify for the Crucible. Hearn had instituted a rolling two-year system to replace the long- established one whereby end-of-season rankings stood for the whole of the following campaign.

Ronnie reckoned that he needed to win either the German Masters or the Welsh Open and do well in the other to avoid this but was lucky not to lose in the first round in Berlin. Andrew Higginson led him 4-0 and at 4-1 potted a black from its spot to bring his break to 63, running the cue ball off the side cushion towards his next red, which lay diagonally between the green on its spot and its own pocket. Anything other than a full ball contact on the green would have given Higginson the easiest of chances to pot the one ball he needed to clinch the win of his life, but this was the fate that befell him.

Ronnie cleared with 67 to steal the frame, won the match 5-4 and kept winning until he recovered from 6-3 down to beat Stephen Maguire 9-7 in the final. It was his first ranking title for 28 months.

He was exhausted but laid himself open to disciplinary action by not carrying out the traditional autograph-signing session. This added to his sense of persecution, although what was intended was simply that the same rules should apply equally to all players. He argued that he was suffering from the aftermath of glandular fever, although it would have been better if he had made this clear beforehand. Even at the Welsh Open, which followed immediately afterwards, he said that he was feeling lingering effects. 'I went for a 20-minute walk this morning because in the last three or four weeks I felt my body getting stiffer, but then I had to go back to bed and rest for two hours. The doctors have told me to be careful and monitor myself so I'm trying not to stress myself.'

None of this stopped him from making a century and four half centuries in beating Marco Fu 4-1, another century in eliminating Mark Williams 4-1 and another two in beating Trump 5-3. Back-to-back titles looked a possibility but, perhaps unwisely, Ronnie admitted that he was not looking forward to a semi-final against Selby, whose pace of play he described as 'painful'. Williams tweeted that 'Selby has the knack of getting under Ronnie's skin' and so he did in winning 6-2. 'If I tried to play as fast as Ronnie, I'd probably never win a match,' said Selby.

The lingering effects of glandular fever and the burnout from playing two high-pressure tournaments in succession prompted Ronnie's withdrawal from the Haikou World Open, although this was insubstantial in comparison with failing to take up his entitlement to compete in the 24-man PTC play-offs in Galway.

On the morning of his match, Ronnie boarded the plane for Ireland but felt faint and wanted to sit with a friend. When this request was refused, he left the plane and went home, the plane's departure having being delayed by an hour while his luggage was taken off.

Ronnie did travel – against medical advice, he insisted – to Beijing for the China Open only to insult the intelligence of anyone who understood the game with several illogical and uncaring shot choices as he fell 3-0 behind to Marcus Campbell. Playing more sensibly after the mid-session interval, he emerged a 5-4 winner through a 77 break of absurd nonchalance in the decider. Next day, treating the match and his opponent with due respect, he beat Williams 5-1 but lost 5-4 to Maguire in an excellent quarter-final through the Scot fluking the final black, an outcome Ronnie greeted with a philosophical 'it's just the way it goes'.

Virtually every player welcomed the vastly increased number of earning opportunities World Snooker was able to offer under the Hearn regime. Perversely, Ronnie saw this as 'World Snooker squeezing you at every opportunity' even though no one had demonstrated better than he had that no player was compelled to compete in any tournament if he did not want to. On the other hand, once a player had entered an event, he was automatically fined under the terms of the standard World Snooker players' contract if he did not turn up, unless he could offer a very good reason for withdrawal.

Some tabloids, thriving on conflict, were keen to portray Ronnie as the exploited star and Hearn as a ruthless slave driver. Since some of Ronnie's reasons for withdrawal had seemed flimsy, he was perceived in some quarters as the boy who cried wolf and therefore did not receive all that much sympathy even when his reason was genuine.

In less than two seasons he had accumulated 14 late withdrawals, all carrying fines. Not wanting to incur another, he had played, it was to emerge, against his better judgement in PTC 10 in Sheffield on the day following the Premier League final.

'I felt terrible after a run of travelling and late nights. I felt like I was on a treadmill. I didn't feel right but I went. I collapsed in my hotel room.'

He lost 4-2 in the first round to Sam Baird. 'I was so ill, I had to get home. I shouldn't have driven. I should have got the train but I wanted to get home. When I got home, my mum looked after me for three days. I slept, got to the UK and played alright after a week's rest [although he lost 6-5 to Trump in the second round]. 'They [World Snooker] want to keep pushing me and pushing me but when you're ill you need support.'

Ronnie admitted that he had withdrawn from some tournaments simply because he did not want to travel, sometimes due to preoccupation with matters arising from his separation from Jo. So, without a very close relationship, how could World Snooker tell the difference between an authentic reason and a convenient excuse? Sicknotes were, of course, provided but some of these were regarded with suspicion. Nor was Ronnie justified in describing the World Snooker players' contract as a restraint of trade simply because it restricted his right to play in non-World Snooker events.

Hearn's role was to do the best he could for the circuit and if that conflicted at times with Ronnie's wishes, that was just too bad. Hearn, disappointed that Ronnie had not played in the One Frame Shoot-out, recognised his prerogative not to do so. Django Fung, Ronnie's agent, was entitled to point out that this was not a ranking event and that Ronnie wanted to avoid the dangers of burnout, a concept that Hearn dismissed too easily. It was rather more suggestive of a power struggle when Fung said that a more selective policy in entering events might mean that Ronnie would not compete in the Premier

League, which was promoted not by World Snooker but by Hearn's company, Matchroom.

This conflict remained on the back burner through the annual 17 days at the Crucible when Ronnie proved that, at his best, he was simply the best by winning his fourth world title. Nobody came close to beating him. He was held to 9-8 by Neil Robertson but two centuries in winning the next three frames put him within one of the finishing tape, which he duly reached at 13-10.

Ebdon, his 10-4 first-round victim, said that 'even though Ronnie didn't play his best there were four or five occasions of sheer brilliance'. Williams, not having beaten Ronnie for ten years, lost 13-6 and commented, 'At his best, he's just so far in front of everyone else it's frightening.' Ronnie permitted himself some satisfaction from the way in which he won the first six frames of their second session. 'In another 50 years they might show some of those shots on YouTube or when I'm dead and gone and they'll say, "Look at this player, see what he did." It's just one of those for the memory bank.'

For Ronnie, there was a difference between how his 17-10 semi-final win over Mark Selby looked and how it felt. To the spectator, he never looked in the slightest danger. To himself, it was different. 'You could never call that comfortable, not in my eyes anyway. I didn't find this easy but Dr Peters has really helped me manage my expectations. There are so many sessions you come to realise that it's impossible to pot them off the lampshades all the time. I've learned to control my emotions a lot better. I try to go on a roll when it's going good and limit the damage when it's not. Seventeen days up here feels like two months. It seems a lot longer than it did when I was 21, that's for sure.'

The final was a similar story. Poised, implacably determined and emotionally stable, he drew steadily away to an 18-11 win over Ali Carter, an action replay in many respects of the 18-8 margin by which Ronnie had won their 2008 final.

'The man is a genius,' said Carter. 'And when he puts his mind to it, like he did there, he's awesome. When his head's on, he's the best player in the world by a mile and his all-round ability is unbelievable.'

The defining aspect of his supremacy, Carter felt, was not even his potting and scoring but his safety. 'Time and time again, he put me under pressure. It was fantastic from start to finish.'

For Ronnie to have Ronnie III there made a huge impact on him. He admitted, 'I was more emotional after I've won a tournament than ever before. Even before the end of the match, when I looked up and saw him and heard him cheering, I was emotional.'

Chapter 23

[2012/13]

BECAUSE he had missed so many tournaments in 2011/12, Ronnie was ranked only ninth at the start of the new season but he had topped the money list with £457,827 and everyone knew who was king. However, Ronnie's attempt to exploit that status off table, orchestrated by his agent, Fung, was fiercely resisted by Hearn on behalf of World Snooker.

It was fair enough, because of the travelling involved, that Ronnie did not enter the first two ranking events of 2012/13, the Wuxi Classic and the Australian Goldfields Open, but there seemed to be something personal, if ultimately self-defeating, in not entering the Premier League, which had always been very much Hearn's baby.

Fung attributed Ronnie's refusal to sign the standard World Snooker players' contract to a matter of principle, describing its terms as 'too onerous' and imposing 'too many obligations'. Ronnie was the only refusenik of the tour's 98 players.

'If there had been money on the table, other things might have been easier to swallow,' Fung added. Hearn was even more forthright. 'This is all about money. Django put a letter in front of me that Ronnie had signed saying that he wanted no further direct contact with us and that everything had to go through Django. I would have preferred to sit down with both Ronnie and Django but I've had no contact with Ronnie himself on this.

'The players' contract is virtually identical with the one that has been in operation for years. The only thing that's new is that if someone wins a tournament, he has to give that sponsor three days of his time over the next year.' (Such appearances generally lasted about four hours, with the player receiving expenses but no fee.)

'The contract is a red herring,' said Hearn. 'Django said to me, "Give him a few quid and he'll sign the contract." This is not going to happen with Ronnie or any other player. If anyone has told Ronnie that because he's world champion he's got us by the balls, they're wrong.

'Django said, "This can be a private deal" but there aren't going to be any private deals. Everything is going to be transparent.

'If Ronnie or his representatives approach a sponsor or promoter for appearance money, I couldn't stop them but I don't think they would get anywhere because everyone would realise this would be the start of a slippery slope. As soon as Ronnie got appearance money, the next world champion would want it and so on.

'It's been put about in some quarters that I'm making Ronnie play in tournaments he doesn't want to, but he's free to pick and choose as much as he likes. It's just that if he doesn't play, he doesn't get any prize money or ranking points. There's no [individual] sport that's any different.'

Fung stated that he had never asked for appearance money but had argued that if ancillary or promotional activities were required, then he should be paid for them. 'Ronnie just wants to turn up and play,' he summarised.

Most players might have expressed a similar preference but some realised that some ancillary activity was justified in the common interest of the circuit. Perhaps it had rankled that Ronnie had been fined £800 for not signing autographs after the 2012 German Masters.

This conflict took place against a background of unresolved disciplinary business arising from a sliding scale of penalties for no-shows: £250 for a first offence, £500 for a second, £1,000 for a third (in the same season) £5,000 for a fourth, £10,000 for a fifth, suspension from the next three ranking events for a sixth and a six-month suspension from all events for a seventh. Ronnie had missed ten PTCs and three ranking events, 13 in all.

By the time Ronnie signed the World Snooker contract, identical in every respect to the one the other players had signed, the closing date for entries to many events had passed. It was Hearn's impression that Ronnie himself had never read the contract until he went through it with him. 'I explained a few things that Ronnie hadn't understood before. It was all very amicable.'

This might have been the end of a paragraph but it was not the end of the chapter. Ronnie entered the China International in Chengdu but on the eve of his departure, after playing an exhibition in Liverpool, declared himself unfit to travel.

Jason Francis, the promoter of this and other subsequent Ronnie exhibitions, suggested that 'the truth was that he was scared about the flight and what the pressure of his comeback and playing again would do to him'.

Inevitable speculation that he was messing people about for no good reason was emphatically quashed by the WPBSA chairman, Jason Ferguson: 'I've spoken to Ronnie at length and I've ended up feeling very concerned about him. He clearly has problems. He offered to resign his membership but this isn't the way to go. A month ago, he was really looking forward to playing again. There's no way he would have entered if he hadn't been fully intending to play.'

Ronnie withdrew from all events he had entered and indicated that he did not intend to defend his world title.

'He has some personal issues that he needs to resolve and we wish him all the best for the future,' said Hearn. 'I've known him since he was 12 and I'd like to see him back to the bubbly character he used to be. He needs total time away from the game. It's a good decision he's made.'

For years, Ronnie had been torn between a desire for repose (or relief from pressure) and his need for excellence through snooker. He came to see the game as a demanding master rather than a source of joy. To say, as he did of his career, 'I've got through it' made it seem like an endurance test not of body but of mind.

Ronnie therefore looked like sitting out the rest of the season. To combat boredom he worked as a farm labourer, giving *The Sun* a chance to have some fun by inventing names for his rivals like John Piggins and Mark Swilliams. Ultimately, though, he found unlimited leisure boring and three days before the closing date submitted his World Championship entry form.

'I had a lot of fun and I needed the rest. I just thought it was time to get back to doing what I've done for a lot of my life. I have a different perspective on it now. I worried about the pressures and not playing well, but I thought two or three months ago, "I'd take that back like a shot now". Hopefully, I won't be as hard on myself. Hopefully, I'll enjoy it more.'

It had become obvious that Ronnie was, and was likely to remain, too highly strung to grind it out on the circuit week after week and it was understandable that he should often have seen retirement in terms of a blessed relief from pressure but, on the other hand, there were some satisfactions open to him only through snooker.

There were also practical considerations to be borne in mind. Ronnie had assets, notably in property, but his cash flow could not be fully serviced by a few exhibitions. It was

Francis who came up with the deal that was to make his return financially attractive.

Francis had arrived in the snooker world to promote a series of Legends events featuring retired former world champions and other leading players approaching the end of their careers, a new departure for his company, Premier Stage Productions Ltd, which specialised in tours of such children's shows as *Thomas the Tank Engine* and *Bob the Builder*. After learning during a chance meeting with Ronnie that Ronnie III particularly liked *Thomas the Tank Engine*, tickets were arranged and they became firm friends. Indeed, in several ways, aside from exhibitions, Francis helped Ronnie more than many of his managers did.

The deal that Francis set up was with the ROK group, based in Los Angeles, whose interests embraced everything from oil and water to energy drinks, beer and publishing. At the time, they were promoting their new Oval vodka brand and it was agreed that Ronnie would wear their logo at the 2013 World Championship and for ten tournaments in the 2013/14 season. His comeback was under way.

He had been away from the circuit for almost a full season but was never one of those players who needed to prove his quality to himself virtually every day. His class would always be there and he would go to Sheffield as fresh as a daisy, but would his extreme lack of matches be an insurmountable handicap?

To the casual eye, it made no difference at all. After beating Marcus Campbell 10-4 on the first day, he said, 'I was not as slick or as tight as usual but you've got to expect that if you've not played for a long time. You can only get that through playing matches. It's like trying to get fit for a marathon the day before.'

Ali Carter, who had never beaten Ronnie in 12 attempts, held him to 7-7 but after losing 13-8 predicted that he would win the title 'unless his head falls off.'

Engaging overdrive, he accelerated passed Stuart Bingham 13-4 in the quarter-finals, dissatisfied only that he had not earned himself an evening off by converting a match ball at 12-3 in the last frame of the morning.

'In the first session, he was just unbelievable,' said Bingham, reflecting on how Ronnie had taken a 7-1 lead with the aid of two centuries and five more breaks between 54 and 87.

At 12-1, Ronnie was poised to record the first-ever 13-1 result in a Crucible quarter-final, but Bingham, in his professional way, never gave up and was able to burden Ronnie with the inconvenience of a third session, albeit one of only 11 minutes' duration.

This most minor of setbacks put him into a disproportionately black mood. Directly contradicting what he had told the media in preparation for and earlier in the tournament, he said, 'I had that year out and I never really missed the game.

'I missed having something to do and I was struggling for money. I've not paid the kids' school fees for the last two or three months.

'I've had two months preparing for this and I didn't really know what was going to happen. I've made a little bit of money but I don't think snooker is for me. This could be my last major event.'

Why this sudden downbeat mood? Could it have been that he felt that he had fallen short of the goal he had set himself, not simply winning but winning with a session to spare? He certainly did not utter these sentiments after going on to win the title.

'I might play in a few PTCs if I get really bored but as far as top competitive snooker and putting my heart into it goes, I don't think that's what I want to do. I think it's about time I looked for something else. Having that year out bought me some time to realise I didn't need snooker.'

What might have been nearer the truth was that he did not need – indeed could not take – snooker every day. To perform to the standards he demanded of himself, he needed frequent recharging of his batteries. And as for looking for something else, what was there that was not snooker related and probably dependent to some extent on keeping himself in the public eye?

As the press conference continued, he approached the nub of it, 'The game is a great buzz but I just don't deal with the pressure. I've worked hard with [Dr] Steve [Peters] and he's helped me but I still find it hard and I just don't want to put myself through it now. I have no intentions to come back.'

Once he settled into his semi-final against Trump, though, he felt more positive: 'Once you start to get involved, you start to get a bit of confidence and self-belief but if you'd told me at the start of the championship that I'd be in the final, I'd have agreed it was one of my best-ever achievements.'

In other words, contemplating a future challenge of daunting or of indefinite length is one thing, actually experiencing it and immersing himself in it day by day quite another.

In beating Trump, Ronnie was not at his most fluent. His highest break was 93, so ending a sequence of 18 matches at the Crucible in which he had made at least one century. At the same time, his pot success rate was 93 per cent, including most of the key balls he had to attempt in various frames. Ronnie did not believe that either he or Trump had played to his best and correctly identified some of the sources of extra tension: a derby feel because both practised at The Grove in Romford and a clash of generations between 'someone who's been around a long time' and 'the future of the game'.

When Ronnie's 4-1 lead became 4-4 at the first interval, there was a suspicion that he might have missed the boat but he led 9-7 after two sessions, 14-10 after three and clinched victory at 17-11.

'As soon as Ronnie gets in front, he's so hard to peg back,' said Trump. 'Over the last couple of weeks, he's missed fewer easy balls than the rest of us. He's so much better than most of the other players that having no match practice didn't really come into it.'

Ronnie was expected to beat Barry Hawkins in the final with something to spare and eventually he did, although Hawkins did himself justice and was still in it at 7-7.

No one is more conscious than Ronnie of the desirability of a good start. For his thirteenth consecutive session at the Crucible, he won the opening frame and also the second but fell behind 3-2, the only time he was in arrears in the whole championship, before running through the remaining frames of the afternoon with 76, 113 and 100.

With a break of 133, Hawkins levelled at 7-7 but again Ronnie went two clear with 103 and 106 back to back to lead 9-7, although it was a disjointed 33-minute frame that he won on the black which gave him a three-frame overnight lead at 10-7 instead of an advantage of just one that it could have easily been.

At 11-8, Ronnie delivered the hammer blow of a 55 clearance to win on the black and lead 12-8.

Sitting in his chair, Hawkins had reasonable cause to hope that he would return to the table as the four remaining reds were not promisingly located, but two exceptional pots and some exceptionally precise positional play kept Ronnie going for the clearance that put him ahead by four instead of two.

Ronnie made two more centuries, 133 and 124, in securing a 15-10 lead after the third session and despite frame-winners of 127 and 66 from Hawkins in the first two frames of the evening, everyone knew it was not the result but only the score that remained at issue. Finishing with 77, 88 and 86, Ronnie passed the post at 18-12 and declared, 'This is one of the most amazing things I've ever done. This is Harry Potter stuff.

'In the final, I had everything to lose and nothing to gain in many respects. I know how good Barry is. To the outside world, they think I should never lose but on the snooker circuit everybody knows how good Barry is. To beat him, I had to be really sharp.

'Two decades ago, I started to overanalyse my game and got my knickers in a twist. Now, though, I can stay patient more easily and the negative stuff is like water off a stone. Steve [Peters] has helped me realise I can't be strong all the time. I've got to keep going, keep chipping away and when I hit a good spell I've got to overpower opponents. That's why I'm a lot better equipped to win titles.'

Ronnie also remarked, 'It was never my intention to take a year out. I always wanted to carry on playing but I was advised not to. If I had sat down with Barry [Hearn] immediately, I would have started playing from the first day of the season. There are a lot of regrets because I put myself in not a great position and at this stage of my career, I've probably not got that many years left.'

Even in triumph, there was a hint of melancholy.

Chapter 24

[2013/14]

FIVE times world champion, Ronnie had nothing left to prove, particularly after winning his fifth in such extraordinary, indeed unique, circumstances. He would never have been able to do it without the input of Dr Peters, with whom he had formed a bond of friendship that underpinned their ongoing work.

'Going to see Steve is probably the best thing I've done in my life. He's helped me deal with the difficult emotions that were holding me back,' said Ronnie.

The central idea behind Dr Peters's work is that the brain has a number of different parts. The frontal part, which he calls 'the human', is responsible for rationality; the limbic is the emotional part that Peters calls 'the chimp'.

When we are calm and rational, so this theory runs, blood flows to the frontal area; when we are angry, or otherwise emotional, it flows to the chimp.

The extent to which this blood flow actually happens is still a matter for debate among neuroscientists, some of whom maintain that the brain always functions as an integrated unit. At the very least, though, this is a useful 'believable myth', as one American psychiatrist put it.

Another believable myth had been propounded a few years earlier by Professor David Collins. This was based on alpha brainwaves controlling motor function, with beta waves controlling the thinking function.

If the beta waves (e.g. thinking about the outcome of the shot rather than just playing it) impinged on the alpha waves, like one wire touching another, this could often explain, so the theory went, why a key shot, well within a player's normal ability, could be missed.

Physiologically, two wires do not actually cross like this but the way in which key, relatively easy, shots are sometimes missed illustrates that the effect is much the same. Some years earlier, Dr Timothy Gallwey wrote along the same lines in *The Inner Game*, relating it chiefly to tennis.

What all these theories demonstrate is that emotional and inappropriate thinking can damage motor function and the less a player is thinking – almost to the point of playing automatically – the better he is likely to perform.

At root, this is another name for intense concentration, being 'in the zone', fully focused on the shot rather than anything beyond it.

There is only one question to ask of any theory of this nature or any attempt a sportsman may make to understand how his mind works or to change destructive habits of thinking away from competition. This is: is it effective?

Victoria Pendleton was in such a terrible emotional state before she became a patient of Dr Peters that she was self-harming. Another Olympic cycling gold medallist, Sir Chris Hoy, was, said Peters, 'very robust emotionally'. Of Hoy, Peters observed, 'There was no dysfunction that I had to sort out. I was just adding to what he already had.'

Dr Peters did not make Ronnie a better snooker player but by assisting him to gain insights into his habits of thinking and behaviour on and off the table, he made him better able to produce the standard of performance that had always lain within him.

'He's helped me turn my life around,' said Ronnie. 'It's taken a lot of practice but I've learned to manage my chimp.'

In cheery mood, Ronnie started his 2013/14 campaign by winning the Paul Hunter Classic in Furth, beating Gerard Greene 4-0 in only 44 minutes in the final.

'I just enjoy playing, whatever the tournament,' said Ronnie in notable contrast to some of his pronouncements over the years. 'These events suit me because you play three or four matches in a day and I don't like hanging around.'

The major story around at the time was, for once, not Ronnie but Stephen Lee's 12-year ban for score fixing. Ronnie took to Twitter to share his thoughts and, because of his high degree of celebrity, unwittingly became the story himself.

'I've heard there's many more players who throw snooker matches. I suppose Steve Lee was just caught out,' he tweeted.

'No need to worry if you got nothing to hide. But plenty of people have got loads to hide. That's why there is no free speech. They're hiding.

'They will prob (sic) fine me for talking about it. They don't like you doing that. Like to keep things under the carpet.'

While it was true that some WPBSA administrations had not been as vigilant or active over apparent match fixing as they should have been, this was not the current situation and the WPBSA and World Snooker considered it deeply unhelpful for Ronnie to imply that it was.

The WPBSA chairman, Jason Ferguson, said that it was 'very disappointing that Ronnie has said we like to brush things under the carpet. The Lee case has shown exactly the opposite'.

Nor did the WPBSA or World Snooker, in contrast to previous regimes, frown on free speech, provided what was said was either true or fair comment.

Immediately, there was a furore. Two days later, Ronnie issued a clarification that he was referring to 'rumours of many years ago when there were only a few tournaments on the circuit,' and added that the circuit 'has undoubtedly been cleaned up since World Snooker has been taken over by Barry Hearn'.

He did not want his comments to leave a damaging mark on the game and said he understood that if he was aware of match fixing, it would be up to him to report any fears to the association.

Of course, Ronnie did not want to damage the game but the incident did illustrate how a spur-of-the-moment tweet could have unintended repercussions. As one tweeter colourfully put it: 'Twitter is like giving a monkey a machine gun.'

In early PTCs, Ronnie lost 4-2 in the second round to Ben Woollaston in Mulheim; 4-3, from 3-1 up, to Mark Selby in the Antwerp final and 4-2 in the third round to Neil Robertson in Gloucester. Then came a 6-4 defeat by Liang Wenbo, who had previously never beaten him in five attempts, in the third round of China's International Championship in Chengdu.

Considering that he had won the world title a few months previously without match practice, it sounded a little odd that Ronnie should attribute this defeat, in part, to lack of matchplay.

'This is only my fifth tournament in 18 months so I'm a bit rusty,' said Ronnie, who had made breaks of 120 and 121 in leading 3-0 before a few mistakes started to creep in. He thought it was about time he won another event and put everything into the inaugural Champion of Champions at the Ricoh Arena, Coventry, a new event for ITV. Down 3-0, 4-2 and 5-3 to Ding Junhui, he eventually got home 6-5 on the final blue. In the semi-finals, he again had to go the full distance to beat Neil Robertson 6-5, making a spellbinding 119 in the decider.

Yet again, Ronnie showed a formidable will to win in beating Stuart Bingham 10-8 for the £100,000 first prize from 7-6 down. He had certainly won the title the hard way.

'It was ebb and flow all the way. At one stage, I didn't think I was going to win it because I thought Stuart was playing freer snooker, but I managed to hold it together in the end.

'I think sometimes when you get near the winning line, you have to make it happen. I learned my lesson years ago against Stephen Hendry where I maybe played a couple of negative shots in the latter stages of a match and he didn't.'

Six days later, Ronnie started a run to the quarter-finals of the UK Championship but on his 38th birthday lost 6-4 to Bingham, who again emphasised what a force he had become.

'Stuart is in form and a seasoned player now,' said Ronnie with his habitual grace when defeat came only because his opponent had played slightly better in a high-standard match.

Having been so disciplined and patient throughout the Champion of Champions and the UK Championship, Ronnie elected to play completely differently in the German Masters. This was the season in which, for all tournaments in which it was practicable, the old qualifying system was abandoned so that the seeds started in the round of 128, the same as everyone else. For some tournaments, including the German Masters, the first round had to be played in advance at a preliminary venue, which is how Ronnie's title defence ended in Barnsley.

Perhaps considering this beneath his dignity, Ronnie attempted to play his first-round match against Thepchaiya Un-Nooh, the 2008 world amateur champion from Thailand, with utter scorn of safety play and lost 5-4. Ronnie potted some eye-catching low percentage balls but inevitably left too many chances. The longest frame took 11 minutes, while the average was eight. In Barnsley, he was also given a £1,000 fine for refusing the match referee's request to tuck his shirt in (in line with the dress code) and abusing the head referee when this request was repeated. Ronnie pleaded in mitigation the poor conditions at the venue and that he was feeling unwell, but underneath he seemed unwilling to recognise that regulations applied to him as much as they did to anyone else.

Nor was the WPBSA enchanted by a passage in his second book, in which he alleged that the cloth had been changed after the semi-finals and before his 2013 world final against Barry Hawkins 'to stop me winning it'. He seemed to believe that a slower and heavier cloth had been fitted to give Hawkins, with his heavier, punchier style, a better chance but produced no evidence whatsoever to support this claim.

'It didn't suit my game at all,' said Ronnie, forgetting that his six centuries were a record for a Crucible final.

Instinctively wary of established authority, as the experience of his parents had every reason to make him, Ronnie sometimes, as in this case, gave way to paranoia. He liked, at times, to play the victim. 'I know the minute I'm not doing well, or the minute they think snooker fans have given up on me, they'll get rid of me.'

Why on earth would 'they' do that? How would this serve any useful purpose? Why did he need to see WPBSA/World Snooker as some vengeful god? These remarks were so absurd that the snooker establishment did not even dignify them with a response.

Ronnie also favoured his 200,000 Twitter followers, many of them young and impressionable, with an exchange of 'banter' on the theme of auto-fellatio and even allowed a photograph of a man engaging in it on to his page. This offence, for which he was fined £1,000, was reminiscent of the 'banter', also auto-fellatio related, caught on a press conference microphone at the 2008 China Open.

Incidents like this were clear breaches of the disciplinary code whereby players 'shall at all times (whether at a tournament or not) behave in a proper and correct manner consistent with their status as professional sportsmen'.

The question was: Why did Ronnie need to do it? Was he oblivious of the effect it might have? Was it an attempt to shock in the same way that a seven-year-old might wish to by daringly saying 'tit' or 'bum'? Was it a legacy of the family pornography business in which this kind of thing was unremarkable and all in a day's work?

To complete a hat-trick of disciplinary offences, Ronnie posted that he had taken pills to assist his performance, thus casting doubt over the credibility of snooker's anti-drugs procedures. This appeared to be a reference to taking Prozac during the 2001 World Championship, although neither this drug nor various others that were prescribed for him was on the banned list.

Ronnie took offence that these disciplinary cases were prosecuted against him. After winning his fifth Masters title in 2014, he tweeted, 'I just want to thank the WPBSA disciplinary for motivating me to do well at last week's Masters. Another just before the World Championship would be handy.'

All that the WPBSA was doing was applying its rules. Ronnie was determined to believe that some sort of vendetta was in play but, regardless, he won his four matches at the Masters by a frames aggregate of 28-7. In his 6-0 quarter-final win over Ricky Walden he set a new record of 556 unanswered points, surpassing Ding Junhui's 495 against Stephen Hendry in the 2007 Premier League.

Describing Ronnie as 'unplayable' on the day, Walden said, 'If he can carry on playing like that, he'll win every tournament he plays in for the rest of his life.' Even Ronnie was pleased, although he did not know and did not care all that much about the record. 'My standard is pretty decent most of the time but every now and again you can put in a performance and you're even excited about it yourself.'

Wins over Shaun Murphy, 6-2, and Mark Selby, 10-4, completed Ronnie's capture of the £200,000 first prize to take his total of majors – as defined by world and UK championships and the Masters – to 14, only one fewer than Steve Davis and only four fewer than Hendry.

'I'm competing with players from the new era and the standard is very high but the way I've played this last couple of years is how I wanted to play for the past 18. Better late than never, I suppose.' By winning the Welsh Open, Ronnie moved on to 26 ranking titles, only two behind Davis but still ten behind Hendry; with his twelfth 147, he overtook Hendry's 11 maximums, a striking way to finish off Ding 9-3 in the final.

Ronnie certainly played none the worse for having 'only played three or four hours in a month' after the Masters. As long as no one caught him cold after a period of minimum practice, it seemed to suit him to come into a tournament, if anything, underdone rather than overdone. A frames tally of 36-10 for seven matches at Newport supported this theory. Ronnie did not enter two tournaments in China, claiming he was 'not into long-term travelling', and would not have taken up his entitlement to compete in the Players Championship play-offs either if civil unrest in Thailand had not caused the event to be re-routed from Bangkok to Preston.

There, though, he fell victim to an inspired performance from an unheralded Chinese, Yu Delu, who beat him 4-3 in the last 16. 'I played OK but Yu is a very good player. I started slowly and that shows that if you're not sharp from the start, you get punished.

'Sometimes the odd defeat can do you a bit of good because after winning the Masters and the Welsh, I was wondering when the run was coming to an end. I can knuckle down now and get my game in shape for the Crucible.'

Chapter 25

[2014/15]

PRIOR to and during most of the 2014 World Championship, a large section of the print media seemed to believe that only Ronnie could really play the game and that his sixth world title was therefore a formality.

It did not turn out that way. The general standard amongst the other contenders had risen so much through intense competition that some could often match Ronnie for effectiveness, if not for flair and style. In addition, Ronnie's rivals recognised that the championship was not only a test of skill but of stamina.

Robin Hull, beaten 10-4, caused him no alarm but Joe Perry, who led him 5-3 after one session, 9-7 after two and 11-9 midway through the third, played the match of his life. Having spent a decade either just within or just outside the top 16, Perry was sufficiently experienced to play each shot on its merits and forget who he was playing except, possibly, to a small degree when the winning post came in sight. He had a couple of half chances before Ronnie levelled at 11-11 and was then pinned in his chair as Ronnie seized the remaining two frames with centuries, 124 and 113.

'I just stayed determined right to the end,' said Ronnie. 'It was hard because I was coming from behind all the time and he was playing well. Every time I got close, he'd pull away. I was missing a few shots and he got on top of me, so I had to draw on all my experience. I had to use that as my ace card and stick in until something happened.

'The fans certainly got their money's worth. It was a more exciting match than any of the finals I've had. It was one of the most exciting matches I've ever had at the Crucible and Joe played his part in a great match.

'That's the closest I've been to going out for quite a while. You realise you're in control of most matches but I wasn't in that one. I knew I could only win it if it went close because he was playing too well. I knew I had to be patient and make him earn it.'

Perry said, 'I got blown away by the best player there's ever been. I had him under a lot of pressure, I gave it everything but then he produced that at the end, so what can you do?

'He played fantastic snooker when it mattered. I'm pleased with my performance but I'm gutted because I had him where I wanted him. Five years ago, it might have been enough to beat him but he's a different animal now.'

Ronnie afterwards revealed that he had suggested to Dr Peters that he should not attend the Crucible for the first two sessions of the match so that he could concentrate on another client, Liverpool FC, who were in contention for the Premier League title.

'I've got friends from Liverpool and I'm mindful that I don't want to take up all his time, but really I made a mistake,' said Ronnie, who requested his presence for the final morning.

'He said a couple of things that I should take on board and I did and it made a massive difference.'

Shaun Murphy had little to offer in the quarter-finals as Ronnie progressed 13-3. Barry Hawkins was also dismissed with a session to spare, 17-7, but this extra rest did not prove enough of an advantage even though, in the other semi-final, Mark Selby was pressed to 17-15 by Neil Robertson in a 12-hour epic.

It looked as if Ronnie would retain the title when he led 10-5 in the final but Selby's boundless tenacity reduced this to 10-7 at the close of the first day's play.

The next day's afternoon session was such a long, predominantly tactical affair that it had to be curtailed two frames early to give the players time to prepare for the final night. Of the six frames, Selby won five, including the last, which took 50 minutes and was resolved by a battle on the colours.

Ronnie potted brown and blue but, having done the hard work, carelessly missed the easiest of pinks to a middle pocket, playing it with pace, and it was Selby, with pink and black, who led 12-11 at the adjournment.

Ronnie started the last session with 100 but lost the next two frames and was always at least one behind before Selby assembled a three-frame winning streak through runs of 127, 87 and a black ball win to pass the post at 18-14.

It was a mark of the extra layer of maturity that Ronnie had acquired through his work with Dr Peters that his acceptance of defeat was realistic and generous, with no hints of retirement or that the outcome had been affected by off-table pressures. Here was a player who had done his utmost but had simply been defeated by an opponent whose range of qualities over the two days had overcome his own.

Ronnie's warm words in the aftermath of defeat came from the heart. 'Mark had me in all sorts of trouble for two days and I was just numb. I gave it my best but he's a worthy champion. He out-fought me, out-battled me and I've got no complaints. I fought my hardest. That's the nature of sport. If you buy a raffle ticket and sign up to be a sportsman, you accept the losses as well as the wins. You can't have it all your own way all the time. I've had some great wins here but losing is part of the sport and you accept it. You have to go away, lick your wounds and try and go one better next time.

'It wasn't the most free-flowing match. There were a lot of long safety bouts and I got dragged into it. I tried to make something happen, open balls up, but when you try and force something it never happens. Everything I did, he had an answer for.

'I was finding it hard to put any momentum together. You can never count Mark out. He's the type of player who

271

seems to thrive when he's behind. He's a modern-day Cliff Thorburn. He'll never give in. He's a winner.'

As for Ronnie, he had rediscovered his love of the game and relish for competition. He had found the frequency of tournament play that best assists him to produce his best. He had come to see snooker for what it is.

'Now I can play and not feel my self-worth depends on winning,' he said, referring to his work with Dr Peters.

'Ronnie's a brilliant student,' Peters enthused. 'I challenge people when I first meet them and when Ronnie came to see me I just said, "If you're really serious, go away and write me some questions and come back. If you're serious, let's see some work."'

'He came back with a hard-backed book and started asking questions. After about an hour, I said, "Can I just ask, how many questions have you got?" There were 20 pages of questions. I knew this was a guy who meant business.'

O'Sullivan's underlying problem was allowing his emotional side – described by Peters as his 'chimp' – to overwhelm his rational, calculating analytical side.

'He knew what he wanted and he knew how he wanted to play. Calm and collected, enjoying his snooker. When I first met him, the chimp aspect was absolutely terrified by the whole thing. Fear of failure. He was paralysed by this.'

This was why, in the middle of a match, he might walk out – as he did in his best-of-17 UK quarter-final in York when he was trailing Hendry 4-1 – or find some other, less obvious way of beating himself as if, in his own tangled mind, losing was not really losing if he was not trying full out. Or even displace all his anxieties on to an apparent search for the perfect tip, trying about 20 in 2010, the year he collapsed in his semi-final against Graeme Dott by losing the penultimate session 8-0.

'But,' said Peters, 'Ronnie said to me, "I don't want to be doing this. I don't understand why I'm doing it. It just overwhelms me."

'Ronnie takes it seriously. He comes and stays at my house and we do night-time sessions. We go through it all and he writes down what we do. Then he goes away, writes it up, picks the bits he thinks he's relating to, then he comes back and challenges me. Then we do practical applications of it. The next day, he leaves.'

Of course, some of the game's best coaches, like Terry Griffiths, combine technical expertise with emotional knowledge based on experience. Griffiths may not know much about the dorsolateral prefrontal cortex of the brain but before, during or after a match, he can be counted on to say something likely to be beneficial.

The chances are, though, that Griffiths would have been ultimately defeated by the deep-seated nature of O'Sullivan's problems. Furthermore, it is sometimes essential to consult someone with a high degree of professional detachment.

'You can move between being "human", being "chimp", or you can go to "computer",' said Peters. 'And in most sports, the ideal is "computer". When one starts losing it emotionally, we become "chimp-like" and there's a lot of scientific evidence for this. If you learn to recognise these three systems within yourself, and can choose, that is an advantage.'

The success rate among Peters's best-known patients shows the value of his consultations in helping them not only to maximise their abilities in competition but to make them happier people.

Jim White of the *Daily Telegraph* made much of the conjunction between O'Sullivan's defeat by Selby and Liverpool's squandering of their Premier League title hopes by throwing away a 3-0 lead to draw 3-3 with Crystal Palace. White actually wrote, 'Monday night was not the best advertisement for Dr Peters' work.'

On the contrary, it was, for in helping Ronnie unravel his tangled psyche, he had not only given him his best chance to win, relative to his technical ability, but assisted him to the sense of proportion that made him a better balanced and generally more contented person.

'I can't make people win,' said Dr Peters. 'All I can do, with their help, is increase the probability of winning. You can't guarantee, otherwise sport wouldn't be sport.'

Chapter 26

[2014/15]

LACK of proper recognition for snooker in general and Ronnie in particular prompted him to say on his new Eurosport blog that he would not attend BBC's flagship *Sports Personality of the Year* evening, either in 2014 or any future year.

His capture of the 2013 world title, having played only one competitive match that season, was a remarkable achievement by any standard but did not help him to earn a place on the shortlist. His name had been on the longlist but was quickly dismissed by a committee who valued heroes from sports more associated with the establishment and the middle class.

It was understandable that the 2014 final list of ten should have been topped by Andy Murray, the 2013 Wimbledon champion, but were the claims of the cricketer Ian Bell, for instance, in a not especially distinguished year for him, really superior to Ronnie's?

The public, when they were eventually invited to express an opinion, did not think so as Bell received only 5,626 votes of the 717,454 cast. It seems certain that if the votes of the public had been the sole determinant, Ronnie would have placed very highly, as had Steve Davis, the 1988 winner, on several occasions and Stephen Hendry, the 1990 runner-up. As it was, Ronnie was ignored and snooker itself was dismissed in nine seconds of a two-hour programme.

Ronnie made his feelings plain. 'I've never been in the top ten nominees when I felt I should have been. I feel that's a bit bizarre because if I can't get into the top ten British sportsmen or women, then I must be doing something wrong. I mean, let's face it, we don't have a surplus of them.

'I've never been to the *Sports Personality* and I've no desire to be part of that club or the clique who go to these things. I just don't really get it.

'If it comes down to a panel of judges, and people in suits, it will all come down to things that don't really have anything to do with personality. Obviously, my face doesn't fit and I don't have the right media persona with the people making the final call. I obviously don't tick the boxes and they don't appreciate the skill of snooker. I just have to accept that it's not the type of award I'm going to win.

'I'd rather win an award that's voted for by the fans and probably ex-professional sports people because they know what it takes to succeed at the highest level. As professionals, they'd appreciate what a sportsman had done for their sport.'

Ronnie's 2014/15 season had started quietly. It is difficult to imagine his heart lifting up at the prospect of travelling to Riga, where he lost 4-0 to Mark Allen in the quarter-finals, Furth, where Tian Pengfei beat him 4-2 in the last 16, or even the Shanghai Masters, where he lost his opening match 5-3 to Alan McManus. He did not play particularly poorly and, in fact, made a 139 total clearance against McManus in the style that people like to see, but there was no spark that would have ignited his best.

This was also true of his 6-5 quarter-final defeat by Mark Williams in China's International Championship in Chengdu.

'We both started poorly and I struggled with my concentration all the way through,' said Ronnie. 'At 5-3 [down] I felt I needed to make something happen and that was the best I felt in the match, but it wasn't to be.'

Williams, meanwhile, was 'over the moon' with his first victory over Ronnie in 12 years 7 months. Acknowledging that Ronnie 'obviously wasn't at his best', he said, 'We're all the same age but he can produce a lot better snooker than me or John Higgins. He's still the best in the world.'

Ronnie was unable to engage his higher gears until his defence of the Champion of Champions title fell due at Coventry's Ricoh Arena. From 4-4, a grandstand finish of 91 and 125 made him a 6-4 semi-final winner over Ding Junhui and four centuries, three of which were total clearances, and a string of sizeable breaks saw him 8-3 up on Judd Trump.

It was a contest that carried a whiff of king versus heir apparent. Trump, a junior prodigy of similar ilk to Ronnie, was making 50s and 60s when he was eight, was English under-15 champion at ten and made a 147 in competition at 14, thus superseding Ronnie as the youngest player to make a maximum. He had come through the professional ranks more slowly than expected but made a significant breakthrough by winning the 2011 China Open and immediately afterwards running Higgins to 18-15 in the world final.

Perhaps not appreciating how much work there was still to do, Trump's progress slowed but by late 2014 he was certainly back on the right track, even if, in that final, he left his recovery very late. It saw him score 362 unanswered points as breaks of 102, 100, 69 and 90 brought him to only 8-7 behind.

It was reminiscent of the 2004 Masters final in which Ronnie had led Paul Hunter 7-2 only to lose 10-9. It looked as if Ronnie might lose the next frame as well until Trump went in-off the green. Instead of 8-8, it was 9-7 and Ronnie closed out his 10-7 win with a break of 109.

'That's one of the best performances I've seen in any sport, so I'll take a lot of positives out of my own performance,' said Trump. 'I just don't remember Ronnie missing a ball. I did well to get back into the game but the way Ronnie can make a break like that under pressure, no one else can do that.'

Ronnie, usually so hard to please, said: 'This is how I played when I was 15. You can't ask for any more than a match like that. I hit one safety shot thick and lost four frames. It's a tough school. Twenty years ago, it would have taken your opponent two hours to get back into it. Now, you boil an egg and you've lost four frames.'

Moving on to York for the UK Championship, O'Sullivan and Trump again worked their way to the final, although Ronnie was in desperate trouble in his semi-final when he trailed Stuart Bingham 4-1 before winning 6-5.

'I think the turnaround came when I actually thought about getting to the final and what it would mean to me,' said Bingham, who was to show at the Crucible four months later that he had learned from this mistake.

It looked as if Ronnie would beat Trump in the final without any similar crisis when he led 9-4 but at 9-9 Trump stood on the brink of completing one of snooker's most astounding comebacks on a major occasion.

His five-frame winning streak began with a disjointed frame 14 but accelerated into a run of 351 points without reply, which included breaks of 86, 120 and 127.

Having not potted a ball for 45 minutes, Ronnie led by 59 in frame 18 but Trump stroked in a long red from which he cleared with 67 and it was 9-9.

With the tide running against him but with admirable composure, Ronnie played a highly disciplined decider, seizing the initiative with a break of 51 and holding on for a fifth UK title to add to his five world and five Masters.

'That's the hardest match I've ever played,' he said. 'I had the upper hand for most of the match but from 9-5 to 9-9 Judd didn't miss a ball. At 9-8, I had a good chance but, to be honest, my mind had gone. I didn't know what day it was.

'The pressure was just mounting and mounting and it's difficult to put that out of your head. I felt really nervous after building such a big lead because you think if you lost it from there, the disappointment would have been unbelievable.

'Judd's a very tough opponent. He's dynamic and explosive, he's got so much cue power and he can pot like you wouldn't believe. He's fearless and that's difficult because he's in your face the whole time.'

Trump said, 'At 9-4, I was kind of giving in but then I managed to make a few breaks and started to feel good. I'm a bit annoyed I didn't have a chance in the last, but I didn't bottle it. I knew I had that form in me but early on Ronnie kept clearing up and that was demoralising.'

Some had visions of a series of O'Sullivan/Trump finals but it did not work out that way. In fact, his Champion of Champions/UK double was to be Ronnie's peak for the season and he did not, by his own standards, do much after Christmas.

His break of 101 in his 6-1 quarter-final win over Marco Fu at the Masters saw him surpass Stephen Hendry's record of 775 centuries in competition, but perhaps this achievement depleted him emotionally more than he might have expected. The next day, his 15-match winning streak was abruptly ended by Neil Robertson, 6-1.

'I knew it was coming eventually because I've been scraping through matches,' was Ronnie's typically harsh self-assessment. 'I missed a lot of balls and made a lot of mistakes. Neil played a great game and had me in lots of trouble. He took me apart.'

For the first time, Ronnie combined competing with Eurosport punditry at the German Masters in Berlin, although there are few instances of a top player maintaining the finest edge of his game once he has embarked on television work on a regular basis.

Nevertheless, Ronnie was by now enjoying fronting his own show for Eurosport – a combination of coaching tips and interviews – and was beginning to be mindful of developing a career outside competition.

However, like many sportsmen who move into punditry, it was only on the table that his deepest emotions were engaged and he was annoyed that he failed to cross the winning line against Shaun Murphy in the German Masters quarter-finals from two up with three to play.

Having made a 51 break in the ninth-frame decider, Ronnie needed only the last red to be sure of a semi-final place. It was a shot that caught him in three minds, whether to play it right-handed, left-handed or with the rest. After much uncharacteristic deliberation, Ronnie undercut it left-handed and Murphy cleared to win 5-4 on the black. Murphy, annihilated 13-3 by Ronnie at the Crucible ten months earlier, described the win as 'special', adding, 'Ronnie *is* the standard.'

Ronnie himself tried to extract a positive. 'I played better here than I did at the UK, so I'm going in the right direction.

I felt I was building momentum. I had my chances but Shaun deserved it.'

There was little sign of Ronnie going in the right direction at the Cardiff International Arena, whose multi-table set up for the Welsh Open he labelled as 'like playing in a shopping mall'. He did not appear at all bothered by losing 4-3 to Matthew Stevens in the last 16, his first defeat at that stage for 12 years.

'I scraped over the line,' said Stevens. 'I was fortunate that Ronnie missed a lot of balls.'

It was, admittedly, only one tournament but there were signs that Ronnie was lapsing into some of his bad old mental habits or was at least not at ease with himself.

Championship League, a tournament exclusive to bookmakers' websites and played behind closed doors, is regarded by leading players as a cross between 'real' competition and paid practice. The winner of each of the seven, seven-man groups goes forward to the final group and, along the way, only the bottom two in each group are eliminated.

It was played at Crondon Park Golf Club, within 20 minutes of Ronnie's Chigwell home, a location that could hardly have been more convenient for him.

Coming in at group 5, Ronnie at times played quite beautifully. Beating Fergal O'Brien 3-0 in 22 minutes with breaks of 128, 97 and 101 was a masterclass but his decision to go for a two-and-a-half-mile run prior to the group semi-finals backfired, much as it had when he competed in the

2009 Norwich half marathon in the morning prior to losing to Murphy in the Premier League final.

Ronnie was 2-0 up in 20 minutes on O'Brien, who had also qualified for the group semi-finals from the round-robin stage, but eventually won only 3-2. Playing Mark Davis in the final immediately afterwards, he again led 2-0 but grew progressively more tired and ineffective as Davis, one of the circuit's soundest and most dogged competitors, beat him 3-2.

As a group runner-up, Ronnie was entitled to compete in the next group over the following two days but minutes after his defeat told the tournament organisers that he would not be exercising this option. He had not perhaps sufficiently considered that he might feel differently in the morning, as indeed he did. He rang the organisers seeking to rescind his withdrawal but by that time a replacement had been drafted in.

Sometimes, Ronnie displays an element of self-sabotage; at others, he makes observations that he must know cannot be borne out by the facts. Donald McRae of *The Guardian* quoted without challenge his remark that 'there's no money in snooker', a surprising assertion from a player who had earned £568,408 in prize money alone in 2013/14. He told McRae that he was practising only two hours a week and 'would prefer to be a pundit rather than a world championship participant'. But, if this was really true, what was stopping him?

It was a familiar story of ambivalence: wanting more major titles to define his ultimate place in the pantheon of greats but not relishing the pressure or looking forward to the intensity of it all. Speaking of his new hobby, of sparring in a boxing gym, he said that he did not mind if his hands were damaged. 'I wouldn't have to play in the World Championship then.'

This smacked of wanting an extraneous force or event to make a tricky decision for him: when to retire. Ronnie also complained that his personal sponsorship deals had become less lucrative than they had been ten years earlier. 'I was on £150,000 before I hit a ball,' he said, although this was in the days before players (due to a previous WPBSA administration) had been restricted to one waistcoat logo of their choice and not, moreover, in conflict with the tournament's title sponsor. He complained that the expansion of the circuit to a tournament virtually every week did not suit him. His sporadic attempts to portray World Snooker's chairman, Barry Hearn, as an intransigent autocrat contrasted with warm words about him on other occasions.

None of this augured well for Ronnie in the build-up to the 2015 World Championship. He did not enter the Indian Open in Mumbai but returned to action in ITV's new World Grand Prix at Llandudno, although he was in an odd mood all week. In the first round against the notoriously meticulous Rod Lawler, he sank lower and lower in his chair and was indebted to a fluke double at 2-2 to give him the impetus to win 4-2. Tetchy spats with a referee and photographers did not suggest a quiet, peaceful mind. Nor did arriving only ten minutes before break-off for his quarter-final against Graeme Dott because he was caught in traffic.

Stuart Bingham's abject performance left him little to beat in the semi-finals and in the final he held promising leads over Trump of 4-1 and 7-4. There were interludes of his sumptuous quality but by his own standards his performance was mostly B to B+.

As Trump grittily overhauled him, accumulating a six-frame winning streak to win 10-7, Ronnie's efforts lacked conviction.

'Judd's a bit like Selby. If you go three, four, five frames up, they seem to play better when they're behind. I fully expected him to come back at me. I wasn't playing well enough to be able to keep my foot pressed on the pedal and I knew I was going to give him chances.'

No one was very surprised when Ronnie withdrew from the China Open, citing a recurrence of the glandular fever from which he had suffered during the previous season. There was no arguing with a medical certificate, although only Ronnie himself – and perhaps not even he – could say what was going on inside his head.

Perhaps he would not have been so confused had he not started to restrict his contact with Dr Steve Peters to only 'two or three times a year now', even though there is always more work to do on the kind of problems Ronnie had been grappling with for 20 years.

'I've probably got about 70 per cent of it right now. That's enough to be successful and to be the person I want to be,' said Ronnie. 'Part of me is not willing to invest more time because I'm playing snooker more for fun these days.'

He could not have meant that. Even if he was right about the 70 per cent, why not strive for more? What did he have to lose apart from fees he could easily afford and a few hours of his time?

Nor had Ronnie seemed to be playing 'for fun' at Llandudno. Snooker is always a deadly serious business for him, the most serious and most defining factor in his life, and it was tempting to see his disclaimers to the contrary simply as attempts to evade responsibility to his own talent and desires.

It was understandable that he did not want to compete every week but to leave enough time to live like a human being in terms of family and personal relationships. His love for and pride in his children, for instance, is clearly immense.

He could say, 'I want my security and snooker ain't going to give me that security', but in addition to his prize money, his security depends on the fame and profile that he has earned through snooker.

Linking up with various management companies to help him with off-table income and profile, he began to appear in general newspaper features, giving his opinions on everything from politics to men's fashion.

His views on the upcoming 2015 general election were forthright and at times hilarious: 'I've been too busy really to make it down to the polling station. The thing is, you vote, and in a way you're becoming part of something that you haven't really got any control over.

'So I vote and the Conservatives get in, what can I do? You're voting for people that you've got no faith in anyway, what's the point in that?'

He evinced no faith in the political establishment as a whole, which he depicted as 'raping the country of millions and trillions of pounds, like the banks and all that. They're all having a good time.

'But you need the politicians, you need all these guys ... they're kind of like "I'll take care of that, you take care of that. I'll bring a law in that stops them doing that so we've got it all sorted."'

On foreign policy he emerged as no great admirer of the former prime minister, Tony Blair: 'He went into Iraq. There were no weapons of mass destruction. He caused the war, him and Bush. And now he's the UN peacekeeper for the Middle East. I mean, how'd he get that job?'

Of Guardian Weekend's picture of David Cameron bottle feeding a lamb he observed: '"The outfit's OK but what's his message with the lamb? I can feed the world? No, I think it's "I'm going to milk the lot of you and look after my wealthy mates so the rich get richer and the poor get poorer."'

Told that Ed Miliband, then the Labour leader, liked snooker, he was filmed playing pool with him and attended a Labour rally in London, not that this did Labour any good at the polls.

On the fashion front, he approved of Shia LaBeouf's ensemble, although he 'wouldn't dream of wearing this. I'm too hairy. I'd look a right doughnut.'

As for Jared Leto, 'he looks a bit weird. 10 out of 10 for bravery, 3 for the look.'

His most substantial non-playing commercial relationship was with Eurosport, for whom he starred in a striking World Championship promo in which he was filmed running hard through a wood.

'It's all about preparation. Focus, concentration and commitment. It's a test of endurance and mentally draining. When you're suffering, you have to dig deep or it's game over. It's a marathon not a sprint,' he said in his voiceover.

No one could have put it better but his own preparation for the 2015 championship seemed to start too late and he was still undercooked when the time came to perform at the Crucible.

His 10-3 opening-round win over Craig Steadman was notable chiefly for playing the sixth frame in his socks. He had worn the same pair of match shoes for ten years but left them in a hotel and had not broken in the new pair he wore into the arena. As a big toe, in particular, started to hurt, he discarded the shoes and appealed to the crowd for a pair of size 8s.

The tournament director saved the day: 'I got a pair of Mike Ganley's stinky old shoes and you know what – they felt great,' Ronnie reported. Good came of this bizarre incident. The shoes were auctioned for World Snooker's official charity, the Bluebell Wood Children's Hospice, and raised £351.51.

Without sustaining his best other than in short bursts, Ronnie comfortably beat Matthew Stevens 13-5, so events seemed to be moving towards an O'Sullivan/Trump semi-final before Bingham ejected Ronnie in the quarter-finals.

Sublime interludes apart, Ronnie was too inconsistent to pull away. He did lead 9-8 early in the final session but Bingham had himself acquired a record, including two world ranking titles, a Premier League, a Championship League and four minor ranking events and was playing so well that he was at last able to dismiss any sense that Ronnie's record, reputation and aura constituted any strength beyond what he was actually producing on the table.

After Bingham's run of five straight frames had given him his 13-9 victory, Ronnie was, as ever, generous in defeat. 'Stuart has been playing some great snooker for the last four or five years. Tonight he was just fantastic and there wasn't a lot I could do. I was just way off the pace and he just pushed me around. I felt second best all the way through the match. I was outplayed.'

Ronnie went home; Bingham went on to win the title with epic wins over Trump, 17-16, and Murphy, 18-15.

Chapter 27

[2015/16]

VIRTUALLY all world-class sportsmen have managers, mostly to take care of their non-playing activities. Ronnie has had several, although he cannot be easy to manage because of his mood swings and a reluctance to do anything he does not want to do. He also remains reluctant to give a manager even a small percentage of his on-table earnings.

This did not apply to his first manager, Barry Hearn, who in the 90s moved out of day-to-day involvement with snooker and, except for Steve Davis, snooker management. Ian Doyle, who was in the opposite position, intensively and virtually exclusively involved with snooker, did much good work for Ronnie.

Looking back several years after his retirement, Doyle said, 'Apart from getting into a few scrapes, Ronnie was no trouble by and large. He wasn't difficult but he was restless, which I think was a consequence of his father's situation. But for his father going to prison, I think Ronnie would be regarded beyond doubt as the best player of all time but if you judge this on titles, which you have to, then Stephen [Hendry] is. Hendry had everything: the game, the mental ability, the work rate.

'Ronnie and his dad were just so close. Soon after he'd been convicted I went to see him in Gartree Prison, which was a hellish place. I wondered how on earth he was going to get through his 18 years but it was his family he was worried about, particularly Ronnie. All I could promise was that we'd do our best.'

Amongst Doyle's more bizarre experiences was a trip to Long Lartin, a category A prison in which Ronnie senior served another part of his sentence. An exhibition featuring Ronnie and Jimmy White was arranged and a table was erected in the sports hall.

Doyle got talking to an inmate, who explained that his situation has arisen from 'nicking a car'. He asked a prison officer if this was true and was told, 'Yes, but did he tell you about the two bodies in the boot?'

At times, Ronnie has effectively been self-managed. Django Fung, a friend who owns The Grove, his practice base, filled this role for a while, then, going upmarket, he signed with Merlin Entertainments. Incredibly casual about this important step, Ronnie did not bother to read the contract and was surprised to discover that a substantial payment was required from him when he wanted to escape from it.

In the snooker world, players tend to have managers who are either friends who know quite a lot about snooker but little about business or businessmen who know quite a lot about business but very little about snooker. Acting on his father's recommendation, Ronnie appointed someone who knew little about snooker and whose vaunted business expertise turned out to amount to ownership of an electronic cigarette shop in Walthamstow.

Ronnie's friend, Jason Francis, promoter of the Legends tours and Ronnie's exhibitions, possessed a credible mix of credentials but was happy to keep their relationship untainted by a close business association and was content to introduce him to James Grant Associates, agents amongst others of the television presenters Ant and Dec.

Francis suggested in his book, *Legends Uncovered*, that Ronnie tends to 'morph into the people who are around him at any one time' and having 'various circles of friends [he] adapts his behaviour to the sort of company he is in'. There were people like his father, family and friends who he had known all his life; he was friendly with fellow celebrities like Damien Hirst, the millionaire artist; when Eurosport gave him his own show he demonstrated an easy affability in interviewing fellow players.

Ronnie's relationship with Francis did cause some friction with World Snooker. Why was it, its executives wanted to know, that Ronnie was always fit to play exhibitions for Legends but not always fit enough to compete in world ranking events that he had entered? Why did World Snooker have such trouble getting Ronnie to travel to China for a world ranking tournament yet there was Francis approaching Chinese television channels offering Legends events featuring Ronnie?

Barry Hearn, on behalf of World Snooker, insisted that he had 'absolutely no problem with non-televised exhibitions organised by you [Francis] wherever they are staged, provided they do not clash with a televised event organised by World Snooker, which might lead to tour players choosing your events over ours.'

It was not, Hearn felt, for him to deny players other earning opportunities as long as they did not have an adverse impact on the bedrock of the game, the tournament tour. For instance, World Snooker granted a sanction for Francis's Legends Cup on Eurosport after the 2013 World Championship and Ronnie played in it.

Fortunately for snooker's overall health, Francis did not seriously pursue setting up a rival tour and rival players' body. He had substantial potential funding to call on but surely would have failed because World Snooker held the aces of the BBC contract and the credibility of long-established tournaments like the World and UK Championships and the Masters. Besides, most players appreciated that Hearn's controlling interest in World Snooker, starting in 2008, had considerably improved their lot and promised the virtues of continuity and stability. Ronnie, according to Francis, was ready to sign for a rebel tour but Francis in any case sensibly decided that he did not want to be known as 'the bloke who tried to split snooker in two and rob it of its prized assets'.

Ronnie did, though, sign up to a lengthy schedule of exhibitions promoted by Francis in 2015/16, as well as playing a few pro-ams in the close season to keep match sharp. The most prominent of these, the well-established Pink Ribbon, at the South West Snooker Academy (SWSA), Gloucester, gave him a first prize of £2,400, of which he immediately donated £400 to the cancer charity the event was in aid of.

'There was some sniping on Twitter about Ronnie being paid to play but he wasn't,' said Paul Mount, SWSA's owner, whose sister had died from breast cancer. 'He paid his own entry fee, his own expenses and put up with some long waits between matches. Ronnie gets some flak at times but he was brilliant.'

It was no surprise that Ronnie did not travel to full-scale ranking events in Australia or China or to minor ones in continental Europe, but it was startling that he defended neither his Champion of Champions nor his UK titles, which offered first prizes of £100,000 and £150,000 respectively.

Ronnie's participation in the Champion of Champions was assumed until he tweeted, 'There's a rumour going round that I'm playing in the C of C. Not true.'

Subsequently, he rang Barry Hearn with the glad tidings that he was intending to play but soon afterwards tweeted, 'I don't want fans buying tickets for Coventry thinking I'm playing. I said I hadn't entered weeks ago. Nothing's changed.'

He then blogged on Eurosport, 'I'm really enjoying the exhibitions with Snooker Legends. The shows have been packed out. Just as much as I'd like to have been playing in the major competitions, my doctor has told me in no uncertain terms that he doesn't think it wise for my health situation.

'I'm finally taking advice from the medical experts. I've had to learn to live with insomnia and I do have times when my sleep is fine, but this is only when I take medication.

'The times when I don't sleep, I can't function properly. I can't even make a 20 break.'

Hearn commented resignedly, 'I'm sorry to hear that Ronnie has another medical condition I wasn't aware of. We look forward to him competing again when he feels able to.'

Frustrated as ITV, host broadcasters of the Champion of Champions, and World Snooker were, there was no point getting upset with Ronnie. He had not entered the tournament so the question of disciplinary action based on withdrawal did not arise.

Ronnie then announced that he would not be entering the UK Championship either. Hearn said that in conversations about this, there was no money issue involved and that his absence was not a prelude to retirement, Ronnie having assured him that he was 'not far away' from returning to competition.

Insomnia was not mentioned in this conversation and there was considerable scepticism within the game over whether it was a serious problem for him. It was not serious enough to prevent Ronnie from fulfilling a schedule of exhibition engagements that featured a 147 break in only 6 minutes 40 seconds at Scunthorpe, another maximum at Newry and five centuries in eight frames at Bangor-on-Dee.

There was, however, speculation that his absence from the tournament circuit had something to do with an attempt to renegotiate his financial settlement with Jo Langley, mother of his two youngest children.

This revolved around an assumption that he had to pay a percentage of his prize money under this agreement. If he was to be depriving her of a percentage, he would, of course, be depriving himself of a larger percentage, but the theory was that if she received no percentage (because there was no prize money), it would make it easier to renegotiate the settlement.

It was also assumed that his Legends exhibitions and his work for Eurosport, for whom he agreed to be a studio pundit during the UK Championship, lay outside this arrangement. Players are not on oath when they speak to the press or issue a press release and it would have been understandable had Ronnie not wished to raise a family issue in public, not least because he would not have wanted to be accused of exerting pressure on Jo through the press. On the other hand, he is a public figure and the public want to know the facts and not be fobbed off with an incomplete or false explanation of an absence from competition. Ronnie's management did not respond to a request for comment.

Ronnie did not hit a ball on the World Snooker circuit until just before Christmas 2015, when in the unprepossessing ambience of the Robin Park Sports Centre in Wigan he beat

Pakistan's only representative on the tour, Hamza Akbar, 5-1 in the first round of the German Masters.

Berlin's Tempodrom could be hired only for five days, hence the need to play the first two rounds in Wigan in order to reduce the field from 128 to 32, with no television coverage apart from internet streaming and not even a charge for admission. This did not produce an atmosphere to inspire top players. Neil Robertson, coming off first prizes in both the Champion of Champions and UK Championship, lost in the first round to Ashley Hugill, an amateur from York, and neither John Higgins, Ding Junhui or Ronnie survived the second.

After he had lost 5-3 to Stuart Carrington, a rising young player from Grimsby who had made his Crucible debut the previous spring, Ronnie blogged on Eurosport, 'I can see where I'm not match tight. I looked too relaxed and not taking enough care over my shot. I suppose that's a combination of no matches and a lot of exhibition stuff. I actually played better than I thought I would. I knew I wasn't sharp but had to do the best with what I had.'

Just when his profile was at its lowest, Ronnie was made an OBE in the New Year honours list. When he was inexplicably not included on the shortlist for the BBC's *Sports Personality of the Year* award in 2013, having won his fifth world title after a whole season out of competition, this was widely interpreted not only as a slight on Ronnie but on snooker as a sport.

He had commented at the time, 'I don't really need any awards to be happy with myself. I don't want an OBE or MBE either.' Nevertheless, he was pleased when news of his OBE came through.

'I'm grateful for this recognition, which is a great honour and has made both myself and my family very proud. It came as a great surprise,' read the statement he issued.

Whether or not a renegotiation of his settlement with Jo was achieved or was even an issue, Ronnie obviously could not stay on the sidelines forever if he still wanted to earn substantial money. He confirmed his participation in the Masters and entered Championship League at group 1 in preparation for it.

If he was still rusty, it did not show as he made seven centuries in winning his six round-robin matches, his semi-final and the final to take his career tally to 802. (There was also a curio in that he won a frame without potting a ball as Ricky Walden was called for three consecutive misses from an unsnookered position.)

'Eight hundred centuries is a nice milestone to get to. A thousand would be good but I'll probably have to play another three or four years to do that,' he said. 'I played some decent matches. I didn't feel I played all that well but my scoring would suggest otherwise.

'I felt I could cue a bit better but my focus was good, my mental approach was good and that's probably what held it together. My mental skills are good and that helps me in the game these days and my ability to score amongst the balls always gives me a chance. There are areas of my game that need improving on if I'm to dominate and win how I used to win, but maybe I shouldn't be thinking about that. Maybe I should be just enjoying this new phase.'

He certainly enjoyed his two days at Crondon Park Golf Club, where Championship League was staged behind closed doors. A week after tweeting from the PDC World Darts championship that he would 'like to play in that atmosphere' – an extremely raucous one – Ronnie tweeted, 'Nothing comes close to Crondon Park. Pure snooker. Cue out and play. No faffing about. How it should be.' Part of him was even disappointed, he said, that he had won the group as he would have liked to have played in group 2 as well rather than go straight through to the winners' group several weeks later.

No amount of practice or exhibitions is any substitute for matchplay, so without Championship League sharpening his game it is very doubtful whether Ronnie would have won his sixth Masters to tie Stephen Hendry's record.

He was 4-2 down to Mark Williams in the first round and at 5-5 coolly won the decider with a 62 break after Williams had failed with an all-or-nothing plant when 27 in front. 'If the plant had gone in then I would have won but I knew I was sending the reds everywhere.'

'I got out of jail today,' Ronnie reflected. 'I didn't feel nervous and it was nice to make a break in the last frame. I played a few exhibitions over the summer and I was playing well, but then I hurt my back and now I can't get on the shot right. Maybe I'm just going through a period of playing poorly but that seems to have coincided with the back problem.

'I'm not in pain but I don't feel balanced on the shot, there are too many moving parts. I'm not able to rip into the ball the way I like to. I'm tentative and I'm dollying the ball rather than punching through it.'

It seemed strange to close followers of the game that Ronnie had been so expansive about the insomnia cited as his reason for missing the Champion of Champions event when, in those three months, he had made no public mention of any back problem.

A 6-3 win over Mark Selby, a persistent thorn in his side who had come from behind to beat him in two Masters finals and one at the Crucible, gave him a semi-final place. A performance featuring six half centuries was topped by a wonderful match-clinching clearance of 73 from 0-70.

Pleased as he was to win, he had his reservations. 'I don't feel that good and I can't lie and say I'm confident, but at this tournament you've got to play as if you are confident. You won't do any good being defensive or protective. You've got to go for it and that's what I did.'

No lack of confidence was apparent to anyone else, of course, but he did have a point as he continued, 'My attitude was definitely the key. I was really pleased with it. Five, ten years ago, if I wasn't feeling good, I'd have lost 6-1, 6-2 and been out of there. Today I just kept going, trying really hard and motoring all the way to the line. My long game was very good and I stayed patient.'

Ronnie also acknowledged that he had learnt something as a Eurosport studio analyst for the UK Championship. 'I was working on the UK Championship and watched a lot of Mark's matches. It made me realise that he's granite against everyone, not just me, and that I shouldn't take it personally.

'We've had a bit of grudge and needle over the years but not any more because I know Mark's a great player. I've got massive respect for him and I admire his tenacity and will to win.'

On the face of it, Ronnie was in good form and progressing smoothly but his mood was that of someone sensing, for no apparent reason, that something dreadful was about to happen. Towards the end of his 6-3 semi-final win over Stuart Bingham, he grew increasingly tetchy.

'If Stuart had played the way he did at Sheffield [in their world quarter-final], he would have beaten me 6-1. It's difficult at times because my touch and feel were so bad. I'm butchering everything and feel embarrassed. I'm not sure if it's my back problem but my body and cue feel disconnected. I'm scared of going out there because I'm struggling with my game. I'm petrified but I've got to go and do it. I'm like a golfer who faces a seven-foot putt and hits it eight foot past the hole.'

Ronnie's dismissive opinion of his game and his unrealistic fears sounded so exaggerated that they attracted considerable criticism from the twitterati, although one tweeter, Steven James, showed more insight. 'Ronnie's constant self put-downs are just part of his mental depressions IMO.'

Depression is often marked by a huge, if irrational, sense of worthlessness. In his everyday life, Ronnie was in his best psychological shape for 25 years but at times, particularly under the added external pressures of matchplay, which dented some of his defences, his old problems still bubbled up.

His sense of certainty and security, it had long been accepted, had been shattered when Ronnie senior received his 18-year prison sentence in 1992. On a snooker table, Ronnie's sense of certainty, it seemed, could be shattered by missing shots he reckoned he would never miss or by playing below what he thought of as his normal standard.

Dr Steve Peters, who had helped Ronnie and many other top sportsmen, arrived in time for the final, although, as it turned out, Ronnie had little to beat. Barry Hawkins, euphoric with his performance and 6-4 semi-final win over Judd Trump, was emotionally spent and offered little resistance as Ronnie beat him 10-1 to turn his eleventh Masters final into his sixth title.

'Steve Peters gave me some things to work with and it made sense. I was able to contain my emotions and not think about the importance of the match. I relaxed into the game and played well in spells. This gives me more confidence because it shows that I don't have to be at the top of my game as long as I'm mentally on the ball.

'Steve helped me refocus on what needed to be done and in particular there was one bit of advice that got me through on the final day which I prefer not to divulge. Again, I really did feel like my mind was going. I was on the edge and I was about to tip over to self-sabotage mode. Thanks to Steve, I didn't. I owe Steve for this one and many others, too. I love working with him. He's on another level and if I could afford him to be around every day, I would pay it.'

Mark Williams, a frequent tweeter, showed some irritation with Ronnie's familiar and excessive self-deprecation earlier in the week. 'Is this the same interview here or a new one? It's hard to decide cause it's the same old bull every time.'

Misunderstanding this remark, one tweeter labelled Williams, a model sportsman, 'jealous', an accusation he quickly refuted. "Take a bow Ronnie, you too good for any of us playing okish. We are all playing for second place at Sheffield.'

Chapter 28

[2016]

AFTER playing only exhibitions for the next month, Ronnie was immediately in the headlines after beating Barry Pinches on the opening day of the Welsh Open at the Motorpoint Arena, Cardiff. His fourteenth 147 in competition appeared to be beckoning until he elected to play for pink from the fourteenth red and cleared up with 146.

'I could have done it but I didn't think the prize [£10,000 plus £2,000 for the highest break] was worthy of a 147, so I've tried to let it build up until it is worthy and then go for it.'

At the time, there had been 116 maximums in professional competition, 83 in ranking events, 61 on television and, most relevantly, 47 since 2010. Such frequency made maximums uninsurable except at prohibitive rates. The days of a £147,000 bonus for a maximum at the Crucible had clearly long gone.

World Snooker decided to operate a snowball, offering £5,000 for a maximum at each ranking event until one was achieved. This had reached £40,000 by the time of Neil Robertson's 147 in the UK Championship two months earlier, or, to put it another way, it had cost the Thai left-hander Thepchaiya Un-Nooh £44,000 an hour earlier – the £40,000 snowball plus £4,000 for the highest break – for missing the final black on 140.

Even if Ronnie had completed a 147 in Cardiff, there would have been nothing to stop him pocketing another bonus for a maximum at another tournament down the line. Of course, with so many players capable of one, there was no certainty of a bigger snowball actually accumulating – as Ding Junhui was to prove with his own 147 later in the week.

The incident was a virtual action replay from the 2010 World Open in Glasgow when Ronnie, in protest that there was no prize for a 147 beyond £4,000 for the highest break, declined to pot the final black until pressed to do so 'for the sake of the fans' by the referee Jan Verhaas.

There may well have been fans in Cardiff who would have very much liked to witness a maximum 'in the flesh'. Ali Carter tweeted that if Ronnie really had wanted to make a point about a 'cheap' bonus, 'he could have made the 147 and given the money to charity'. The next morning, Ronnie agreed. 'When I woke up I thought it would have been wonderful [to have done this] but I wasn't thinking out there,' adding that his comments 'shouldn't be taken seriously' and that they were 'only a bit of fun, a bit of a laugh'.

They did not originally come across like that and in any case the public surely had a right to expect that Ronnie, or any other player, would say what he meant and meant what he said. For World Snooker, Barry Hearn described Ronnie's actions as 'not a crime but a shame' and at root 'disrespectful' to the public. Maybe Ronnie had made so many maximums in practice and competition that his satisfaction in the feat itself had become so diluted that he needed to make them special in some way.

Ronnie's unusual 146 break brought a deluge of comment, much of it unfavourable, but it had no effect on his performance the next day as breaks of 110, 90, 112 and 102 saw him overwhelm Tian Pengfei 4-0 in only 39 minutes.

Prompted by a question about his 146, he said, 'Once I step over that line when I'm ready to play, I go into a mindset that I have to be myself. Sometimes I get it right, sometimes I get it wrong, but over the course of my career I'd like to think I get it right more times than wrong. I've already had 13 maximums, five world titles, six Masters, five UK championships and hold the record for the most centuries. I think I've done some good things.

'If I was to go out there and think about charities, mums, dads, my children, what my cleaners are doing, whether I've paid my bills, what Barry Hearn wants me to do, what the public wants me to do, I wouldn't be able to perform. I'd be too worried. When you cross that line, you have to back yourself. You need to grow shoulders to deal with whatever is put in front of you.'

Still in prime form and in only 55 minutes, Ronnie made breaks of 94 and 131 in despatching Jimmy Robertson 4-0 and 96, 132, 70 and 66 in swamping Yu Delu 4-1. His 5-1 quarter-final win over Mark Selby featured breaks of 93, 61, 75 and 132, although this was not a runaway in the early stages as Selby won the opening frame and had a shot at the black for a 2-1 lead.

Ronnie said that his approach was 'to go for everything' in line with a supposed intent to use the tournament to sharpen his game for forthcoming exhibitions. It rang more true when he added, 'If you think of it like a match, you can start to not enjoy it.'

Surely all players feel less pressure when they are playing so well and winning so comfortably that the result is not at the forefront of their minds.

The next day, after his 6-3 semi-final win over Joe Perry, he took a different tack. 'The matches are getting harder but I felt I scored well.

'I was nervous because I'm playing well and I want to stay in the tournament.

'At the Masters, I wasn't nervous at all because I expected to lose. This week, I've played six unbelievable matches and I'm waiting for the bubble to burst.

'In the past three or four years, I've been expressing myself and produced the same type of snooker I played when I was 14 or 15.

'Now it's about my legacy and leaving a mark on the game. Not so much in terms of titles but in the way that I play. I like to think I've played snooker that no one else has.' He was right about that.

Throughout his career, the result had become more important for Ronnie the further he progressed in the tournament, as if he did not want to waste his investment of effort over the week by falling at the last fence.

Neil Robertson led him 5-2 in the final but Ronnie won the last frame of the afternoon and all six in the evening to prevail 9-5 and join John Higgins and Steve Davis on 28 ranking titles, with only Stephen Hendry's 36 in front of him, a total all the more remarkable in the light of withdrawing from or not entering quite a large number of tournaments.

'Record books don't bother me. I'm not really interested in that,' said Ronnie. 'I'm interested in just enjoying the game as I have this week. Even if I'd lost in the final, it would still have been a great week.

'Neil steamrollered me, kept me tight and played some hard match snooker. I just hung in there in the first session because nothing quite happened for me. I tried to stay positive, using all the skills I've learned from Steve Peters over the last four-five years. I only got going towards the end.' In fact, frame-winners of 67, 70, 61 and 141 accounted for the last four frames.

If Ronnie had not won the Welsh Open he would not have qualified for the World Grand Prix, which was restricted to the top 32 ranking points earners for the season. In the intervening three weeks, he played only exhibitions and the two-day winners group of Championship League, in which he won six of his seven matches before losing 3-2 to Judd Trump in a high-quality final, an acceptable reverse as best-of-five is very much a sprint at top level.

What he was not prepared for in Llandudno, though, was an inspired performance from Michael Holt, a talented if volatile player habitually ranked somewhere between 20 and 30, who played superbly to lead him 3-0, making breaks of 88 and 119 as he restricted Ronnie to 16 points in this period. Ronnie won the next three frames in only 28 minutes but Holt, after a protracted safety duel in the decider, made an admirably composed 76 to win 4-3.

'I gave it my best and I was pleased by the way I stuck in there and tried to turn it around. I couldn't have got any more out of myself. My game just wasn't strong enough to override whatever Michael was doing. He scored well and I didn't get much of a look-in for the first three frames. He deserved to win.'

If this was going relatively easy on self-blame, he heaped it upon himself retrospectively. 'I won the Masters even though I was abysmal that week, then I had one good week at the Welsh Open. I've just been papering over the cracks and I just need to find some sort of consistency if I'm to have any chance of a decent run in Sheffield. I need to do some work over the next few weeks.'

But that was it for matchplay prior to the World Championship. Not having competed in any of the minor Eurotour events during the season, he had no means of qualifying for the Players Championship in Manchester, which was won by Mark Allen, and he had never intended to go to the China Open. He was still the bookmakers' favourite for the world title but, as he was to admit, his shortage of matchplay undermined his challenge.

David Gilbert, runner-up in the International Championship in Chengdu earlier in the season, proved a tough first-round opponent. Apart from losing the opening frame, Ronnie was never behind but 10-7 was his closest first-round margin at the Crucible since defeating Liang Wenbo 10-7 in 2010.

'It's probably the best I'll ever play and not win,' Gilbert reflected. 'Ronnie's all-round play is unbelievable. His tactical brain is just brilliant. He's so clever.'

What Ronnie thought about the match had to remain a matter for speculation as he failed to comply with his media obligations even if, under the terms of World Snooker's players' contract, he could not be fined for his first such offence of the season. By utilising this 'free pass', this may have been a continuation of his guerrilla warfare against World Snooker, some of whose fines he felt to have been unjust, and also as some sort of retaliation for – as he saw it – low prizes for 147 breaks.

Although there had been no sign of anything untoward as he engaged in friendly tableside conversation with Gilbert after the match, something must have upset him because, within a couple of minutes of returning to his dressing room, 'banging, crashing and swearing' emanated from within it.

It was not until Victoria Derbyshire asked him about this incident in a wide-ranging interview on her morning BBC show in July 2017 that a fuller version of the truth emerged.

'I didn't intentionally smash [my dressing room] up. I was suffering. I'd had a massive workload, the pressure of the tournament was a lot. I smashed my cue against the wall. John Parris put it together,' Ronnie said.

'[After the match] I was driven down to London and I was in hospital for four or five days. I was physically exhausted. It was touch and go whether I'd play in the second round. I was having a bit of a breakdown. I was in a bad place [but] I've been in worse places. One of the doctors gave me some medication to slow my mind down.' Later in this interview, he admitted, 'The pressure can make you cave in a bit sometimes.'

On the face of it, though, there was no reason to expect Barry Hawkins to beat Ronnie for the first time in 14 years. Ronnie had beaten him 18-12 in their 2013 Crucible final, 17-7 in their 2014 semi-final and 10-1 in the Masters final only three months earlier but, as it turned out, the only time Ronnie led was at 3-2, having made breaks of 139, 88 and 103 to one of 102 by Hawkins in a breathtaking opening.

The remaining three frames of the day were not of this quality but Hawkins won them all and crucially snatched the first of the middle session after Ronnie had got in first with 68, needing only a red to middle in addition. This was very tricky because cue ball and object ball were so close together. In danger of making a push shot, Ronnie barely hit the cue ball. Hawkins gradually clawed his way back into the frame and won it to lead 6-3 instead of 5-4, as had seemed likely.

Ronnie responded immediately with 118 and recovered to only 8-7 but missed some chances in the last frame of the day and trailed 9-7 overnight, a two-frame gap that was maintained when Ronnie won the first frame of the final session with 93 and Hawkins the second on the black after a prolonged tactical battle on the colours.

Hawkins also won two of the next three frames to go three up with four to play. Ronnie had been looking increasingly subdued, almost resigned to his fate, but came to life with 124, 88 and 63 to take the contest the full distance.

The nature of the decider, a tactical battle of 25 minutes' duration, suited Hawkins. 'It settled me down, having a safety exchange and in the end I made a decent break.' This 56 was not arithmetically decisive but with the remaining balls very awkwardly situated, one more mistake from Ronnie was enough for Hawkins to pot the few remaining balls he needed.

Ronnie agreed that the decider wasn't my type of frame. If there was a weakness in my game, it was definitely on the tactical side. I lost all the frames when safety was involved. I was like a golfer who birdies 15 holes, then gets triple bogeys on the last three.'

In response to inevitable questions about the media blackout that had followed his first-round match, Ronnie apologised to the assembled journalists but did not fully elaborate on the factors behind it.

'For various reasons, I wasn't in a fit state to speak. It wasn't that I was being arrogant. I don't handle the responsibility that I carry very well. I find it difficult being the figurehead for the sport. All the attention is on me and there are high expectations from everyone, including myself. I want to manage the pressure and stress that I put on myself. The media make out I've won this tournament before I even turn up and that can be difficult in such an intense environment.'

It was the first time in seven years that Ronnie had failed to reach the quarter-finals.

His season did at least end on a pleasant note with an appearance at Buckingham Palace to receive from Prince Charles the OBE he had been belatedly awarded in the New Year honours list. He described the experience as 'surreal' and 'one of the best moments of my career'.

As to his career, he told journalists, 'I'll maybe [in the coming season] play less exhibitions and a few more tournaments. Once I get the right balance and I've got the right attack and the right defensive game, I'll be better equipped to win tournaments if I'm not playing at my best.'

In upbeat mood, Ronnie contemplated the possibility of playing for another ten years but in the meantime he embarked on 'Ronnie O'Sullivan's American Hustle', a series for the History Channel that showed him interacting with a variety of characters from the world of pool and enjoying features of four of the chief American cities.

In one sequence, he visited Ellis Island where, in the heyday of the immigration that helped build America, 5,000 immigrants a day for 12 years presented themselves, fresh off the boat, to the authorities. Bearing in mind his own Irish-Sicilian heritage, Ronnie reflected, 'I wouldn't be here if England hadn't let immigrants in.'

He disclosed a dislike of heights extending to a dislike of flying. 'I once went by train to a tournament in Germany. It took 14 hours.' Unselfconsciously, on a trip to Alcatraz, the prison that used to house America's most notorious criminals, he revealed that his father sampled 26 prisons while he was serving his 18 years but that he had some happy memories of visiting him – 'two hours of making me laugh'.

Throughout the series Ronnie came across as bright, cheerful, good company and interested in the world about him as he furthered the process of developing his off-table profile, using his fame as a player for non-playing projects of the sort that would keep him usefully occupied approaching and beyond retirement.

Chapter 29

[2016]

NO one believed that Ronnie ought to have been as low as tenth in the world rankings at the start of the 2016/17 season but he had missed so many tournaments in this rolling two-year period of assessment that his need for ranking points was now acute. Looming up, when his points for winning the 2014 UK title were to be deleted, he was in danger even of losing his place in the top 16.

He did enter more tournaments but, in the British summer of 2016, not those in Hyderabad, Riga or Yushan. He did travel to Shanghai but almost lost his opening match to Liang Wenbo.

'Being 4-1 down isn't the ideal situation but I thought I just had to try my best and see what happened. I won a couple of frames and the match turned around,' he said after his 5-4 win.

'I need to start putting more time in now. If I want to compete with the best players in the world, I need to play more. I think I have four or five very good years left in my career.'

However, when Ronnie was derailed in the second round by Michael Holt, who had also beaten him 4-3 in the World Grand Prix in Llandudno a few months earlier, his lack of match tightness was emphasised when he missed two vital and intrinsically basic blacks from their spot in the sixth and seventh frames, the latter allowing Holt to clear with 64 to the pink and win 5-2.

Ronnie's defeat was not entirely self-inflicted because Holt, who throughout his career had always had all the shots of a top player but not the temperament, was becoming a much more mature competitor under the mentorship of Terry Griffiths, the 1979 world champion, who had become a highly respected coach of professional players.

'When you play Ronnie or any of the big players, you've got to stand up and not allow their reputations to make you play worse,' said Holt. 'Although Ronnie is obviously better than me, he's not so much better that I don't have a chance to win in a one-off game.'

Ronnie was philosophical. 'There are so many tournaments that you're bound to play well in some of them,' he said, and duly did so in the next one, the European Masters in Bucharest. 'Last season I had a lot of stuff to sort out away from the table. I got myself into a bit of a twist. Hopefully, I can put that behind me now and play a proper schedule. As long as I put the work in, I'm sure there will be one or two tournaments where I catch fire and pick up some silverware.'

As the week in Bucharest progressed, Ronnie began to find his higher gears more readily but it was not until his 45th tournament frame of the season that he recorded his first century, 129, to complete his 4-1 quarter-final win over Mark Davis.

In this vein, he took only 74 minutes to trounce Neil Robertson 6-0 in their semi-final as breaks of 118, 79, 92, 63 and 96 rolled off his cue. It seemed probable that he would win the title when he stood two up with three to play against Judd Trump in the final only to be robbed first by ill luck but mostly by his opponent's brilliance.

At 8-6, Ronnie expertly split the pack of reds from the green only for a rogue red to find a corner pocket. From this, Trump embarked on a 109 clearance, glued together early by an inspired blue, powering it from its spot to a distant baulk pocket and screwing back amongst the reds. It reminded those with longish memories of the all-or-nothing blue that Alex Higgins had potted in his match-saving 69 clearance against Jimmy White in the penultimate frame of their 1982 world semi-final.

'I just thought I'd go for it,' said Trump after prevailing 9-8. 'After that, I didn't miss and that's a good feeling.'

'I don't think I did a lot wrong and towards the end he just dominated the table,' said Ronnie. 'I battled it out and at least I played six matches this week, which is exactly what I need.'

Although Ronnie, approaching his 41st birthday, still had his own ambitions, there was a sense that he would be happy if Trump came to be regarded, as he himself had been for 25 years, as the favourite of the large section of the public that sets most store on dash, flair and eruptions of genius.

Having practised extensively and played many exhibitions with him, Ronnie said, 'I think Judd's got the talent probably not to dominate snooker but to be the best in the world and he's got time on his side.'

It also became clear that Ronnie had formed an avuncular relationship with another frequent practice opponent, the Chinese left-hander Liang Wenbo, the surprise winner of the circuit's next event, the English Open at Event City, Manchester, by beating Trump 9-6 in the final.

Ronnie himself had to dig deep for his 4-3 second-round win over Zhao Xintong, a Chinese teenager he described as 'an amazing talent with fantastic technique and touch', but then fell 4-3 to Chris Wakelin, who was virtually unknown to the general public, as many middle-ranking players are, but very capable nonetheless.

'You've got so many tournaments it's not really a bad thing if you lose,' Ronnie rationalised. 'It's like a bus. You think there's going to be another one coming along soon. I didn't really care if I won or lost. I know it might sound strange but that's how it feels.'

This did sound a little peculiar. Ronnie had tried to win, selected all the right shots, but perhaps treated it as just another day at the office until the onset of danger and was then unable to summon up the form he needed. He did, though, continue to enjoy his role as a Eurosport pundit, which did not carry the inescapable pressure of competing, proving himself a shrewd analyst with a distinctive turn of phrase on occasion.

During the final, he observed that Liang needed to avoid repeating past mistakes. After his triumph Liang, on the verge of tears, expressed his appreciation of Ronnie's guidance. 'He has done so much for me. I eat with him. I practise with him and I have learned so much from him in the past two years. He told me to look back at the [2015] UK final [which he lost 10-5 to Neil Robertson] and see what I could learn from it. I knew I needed to be more controlled this time.'

A few days later, the tour was in Daqing, where Ronnie was pushed to 6-4 both by Xiao Guodong and Kurt Maflin before losing for the third time in succession to Michael Holt, 6-4 in the last 16.

Despite his best efforts, Ronnie's need for ranking points was not being adequately satisfied. Nor was his temperament suited to play week after week. He passed up the opportunity to compete for a £200,000 first prize in an invitation event in Guangzhou the following week in favour of resting up for the Champion of Champions at Coventry the week after. There were unconfirmed reports that Ronnie would have played in Guangzhou if his request had been met for a £30,000 appearance fee, double the £15,000 first-round losers had been guaranteed. On the other hand, asking for such a virtually prohibitive fee could be interpreted as not having a great desire to stay in China for another week anyway.

Arriving at the Ricoh Arena without his dress shoes, he purchased a new pair in necessary haste that were, he said, 'like wearing a pair of radiators', but coasted through his first two rounds and beat Mark Allen 6-2 in the semi-finals with a display comparable to his very best. Allen made two centuries, 100 and 109, and Ronnie one of 130 before the intermission was taken at 2-2 but in only 28 minutes, through breaks of 73, 124 and 109, Ronnie outscored Northern Ireland's number one 317-7 in leading 5-2. In the next frame, with the cue ball tight on the baulk cushion, Ronnie potted a long red to start his clinching run of 59.

'A few times tonight I felt quite in control of my game because it's been a bit of a struggle lately,' he said. 'I felt my all-round game was in good shape and in balance. You have to keep persevering and when the form comes, it comes. You can't turn it on like a tap but that was better.'

A reminder of the maxim that a century wins only one frame came in the other semi-final when Ding Junhui made four only to lose 6-5 to John Higgins, who went on to beat Ronnie 10-7 in another magnificent episode of their 25-year rivalry.

With a break of 130, Ronnie led 7-6 but potted only one ball in the remaining three frames as Higgins surged past the post with 76, 86, 40 and 58 to win 10-7.

'I just want to say well done to John. I tried to hang in there and I think the score flattered me. I think he's the best player in the world at the moment. I need to find consistency if I'm going to win tournaments again. You can play in spells some of the time [and win] but not against world-class players like John.

'I missed too many balls and made too many mistakes. You can't afford to do that against him.'

Moving straight on to Belfast for the Northern Ireland Open, Ronnie was untroubled as he dropped only two frames in his first three matches but then fell victim, 4-3, to Kyren Wilson, whose Shanghai Masters title the previous season had been among his six ranking event finishes in the quarter-finals or better. In taking a 3-0 lead, Wilson's long potting was outstanding but a hat-trick of centuries, 108, 117 and 126, saw Ronnie level at 3-3 before Wilson made 70 in the decider to go through.

'I brought the best out of Ronnie and he brought the best out of me,' was Wilson's summary.

There was nothing for Ronnie to put his finger on to explain why he had lost. It is not every day that a player makes a hat-trick of centuries in a best-of-seven and still loses. It was a result that perfectly illustrated how fine the balance was between winning and losing at elite level, particularly over the relatively short distance of best-of-seven.

Prior to the UK Championship, Ronnie tweeted some quasi-religious musings couched in the form of dialogues with God.

'I have conversations with God and he said to me, "Jack snooker in mate, you're better off as a pundit" and I was like,

"Hold on, we will have to have a proper conversation about that".

'It's not my last tournament until God puts his foot down. He is the boss and I don't want to take liberties with him.

'God has told me I should not play snooker no more. But I've put that on the back burner for now.

'This is like a bit of a hobby. Getting my cue out is a bit of a pleasure whereas before, when that's all I had to do, I felt I was trapped in a prison. Now I feel like it's a bit exciting and I treat it as a bit of fun. My proper job is my punditry and doing all my other bits. That's my salary but this is a bit of a bonus now.'

Amateur psychologists, and perhaps professional ones, might deduce this was Ronnie's way of reducing the pressure on himself by making it look as if he did not care about his results, but of course he still did. He simply regarded them with a sense of proportion absent in his worst days.

Having another function when he was away at a tournament usually reduced his spare time hanging about between matches, periods that gave him maximum opportunity to think negative thoughts. The more he was in the moment, the better. There was also, in this remark, a hint of returning to his young, innocent days when he was entranced by the game, with tournaments a welcome challenge rather than a potential occasion for disappointing the expectations invested in him.

His first three matches at York were exhibitions of sublime skill as he beat Boonyarit Keattikun, Thailand's world amateur champion of 2016, 6-0 in only 56 minutes, a promising young Scot, Rhys Clark, 6-0 in only 73 and a former world under-21 champion, Michael Georgiou, 6-1 in 84, making five centuries along the way.

Georgiou described Ronnie's ability as 'not human'. Ronnie accepted the compliment but emphasised 'the hard work and discipline' that backed up his natural ability. When people talk about it being natural and effortless, I find that insulting because I work as hard as anyone. Someone once asked Muhammad Ali about his natural talent and he said it only looks that way because he gets up at 6am and spends the whole day running and training.'

Ronnie's fourth-round match was a sterner test, although he beat Matthew Stevens, not the player he had been in his prime years in which he won both a Masters and a UK title, comfortably enough 6-2. 'Matthew made it tough for me. He's got the pedigree and that presence where at any minute he could click into gear. I've got a real dilemma because when I play open, flowing snooker I enjoy myself but I know it can be risky. When I try to tighten it up and play more conservatively, I can't seem to make more than 20 in the balls.'

An exaggeration, of course, but with a grain of truth.

An old adversary, Mark Williams, held Ronnie to 2-2 in the quarter-finals before he pulled away to the 6-2 win that earned him his 64th ranking semi-final appearance from his 100th such quarter-final. Unusually but justifiably, Ronnie criticised the playing conditions. 'The table was really heavy. You couldn't get any bite in the cue ball but I stayed professional and if I did get frustrated I didn't let it affect my next shot.

'It wasn't the greatest of performances but you have to do what you have to do and I played some good safety to put him under pressure. I'm sure my game will get stronger. I'm a fighter and I'll keep fighting until it happens. Mark didn't play anywhere near his best but I was happy with the professionalism and attitude I showed to get the job done.' Williams saw it differently, remarking, 'That's the worst Ronnie's ever played against me and he still won 6-2.'

With Ronnie having amassed a frames tally of 30-5 so far and his next opponent, Marco Fu, reflecting that it was the first time in his career he had got to the semi-finals of a big tournament 'playing my B or C game', the portents were that Ronnie would reach the final much more comfortably than he did after going from 4-2 up to 5-4 down.

In the tenth frame, Fu had two match-winning chances. The first, very early in the frame but with the balls invitingly spread, foundered on a vicious kick on a short-range red that he would otherwise not have missed in a month of Sundays. The second came when Fu, in potting the last red, left himself not at the friendly angle on the pink he had intended but on the green, for which he required the rest, to obtain necessary position on the yellow.

'I just twitched a little bit under pressure,' Fu admitted after Ronnie cleared for 5-5 and killed off the decider with a clearance of 130.

'You just find something sometimes when you have to,' said Ronnie. 'I tried the whole match. I stayed focused. I stayed professional. I didn't beat myself up. I did everything that was in my control to do but sometimes it's either there or it's not there and I just have to grind it out.'

How much this struggle depleted Ronnie's reserves for the next day's final against Mark Selby must remain a matter of conjecture but after starting with a break of 124, he became progressively more ragged as a remark he had made after beating Fu seemed to turn into a self-fulfilling prophecy. 'I'm nervous because I've got self-doubt. I've gone a lot of tournaments without lifting a trophy and you start to wonder whether you're good enough any more. I don't want to spend the next few years delusional.'

When his deficit grew to 7-2 in the evening, a heavy defeat loomed but was averted with three excellent frames from Ronnie, including a break of 134, before the intermission halted his momentum and gave Selby time to gather his thoughts.

'I was thinking to myself that if I was playing anybody else, I wouldn't panic but they don't do it as quickly as Ronnie,' Selby said. 'Because he's so quick, before you know it, he's right up there with you and your head is spinning. I just tried to stay in the moment, remember that I was still in front and just take one frame at a time.'

On the resumption, Ronnie scattered the bunch from a testing red and Selby's ensuing 137 gave him breathing space at 8-5, but Ronnie still had the heart for another recovery.

Breaks of 130 and 82 brought him to only one behind but Selby responded in kind with 134 and 107 to win 10-7 and frustrate Ronnie's bid for a sixth UK title.

The magnificent final session had produced five centuries but Selby emphasised the importance of the afternoon. 'Ronnie missed a few and wasn't really on his game but tonight he put me under a lot of pressure, asked the questions and I was really pleased with myself how I held up at the end.'

Ronnie accepted his first defeat in six UK finals with his customary grace. 'Mark was the best player all week and deserved it. I missed too many easy balls when I was in and you can't do that against the top players or they will annihilate you.

'I think that the fans here enjoyed it and the people watching at home as well. Of course I'm disappointed but I was pleased with my attitude and pleased that when I came to the table I just played the shot required and didn't get bogged down looking around too much, which can happen in long frames.'

He clearly realised, in addition, that whoever was world champion or world number one, any tournament or any match in which Ronnie was involved would inevitably revolve around him. 'As long as I continue to play, whoever I play, it'll be big. People like playing someone who has won so many tournaments. It's like Nadal, Federer and Djokovic in tennis.'

Straight on from York to Glasgow, Ronnie was a 4-2 first-round winner over Matt Selt but admitted, 'Three finals this season isn't bad but I'd like to have won at least one of them.

The first two I didn't believe I was playing well enough to win. Since Belfast, I've found my game a bit and I'm more optimistic. It would really help if I could win a tournament. At the moment, I'm in the habit of losing. I've won matches and got to finals but it gives you a different and deeper feeling when you get the silverware.'

After beating Adam Stefanow 4-1, he was forced to change his tip overnight. This did affect his performance, although he made a century, 114, in beating Jimmy White 4-2. 'When you're on the start line, you go with what you've got. You don't make excuses.'

Even so, the tip was too soft – 'like playing with a pillow on the end.' Another new tip was much more satisfactory. Ronnie went 2-0 up in only 16 minutes with breaks of 104 and 103 and beat Mark Allen 4-2, although he reflected that he 'made a few mistakes from 3-1 up'.

With this tip starting to bed in, his quarter-final against John Higgins was eagerly awaited, as matches between these two all-time greats of the same era invariably were, but it proved to be an anti-climax. Higgins was scathing about the conditions. 'There's just no grip on the cloth,' he said. Nevertheless, he acknowledged that 'any time you beat Ronnie it's a special result, although today he wasn't at his best.' Poor conditions or not, Higgins completed his seventh win in his last eight attempts against Ronnie with a break of 104. Ronnie's highest break of the match was a modest 41.

'John's all-round game was strong,' said Ronnie. 'He's a class act and very difficult to break down. You always have to feel you can get back into it, otherwise there's no point, but when he's playing like that he'll win a lot of tournaments and he's hard to stop.'

Additionally, this was a week in which Higgins, on home ground in Glasgow's Emirates Arena, was especially highly motivated. Events seemed to be moving towards him receiving the new Stephen Hendry Trophy from the seven-times world champion himself, but despite opening with a hat-trick of centuries, 126, 101 and 100, he was beaten 9-4 by Marco Fu, who in this part of the season was producing the snooker of his life.

In his role as a Eurosport studio analyst, Ronnie summarised Fu's vital technical change. 'He's lengthened his backswing and ripping through the ball.' But much as he enjoyed this work, he did question its effect on his game. 'It means I can't always prepare as well and focus on tournaments, but it's the best option for me.'

For whatever reasons, though, including the performances of his opponents, Ronnie had reached Christmas 2016 without having won a title for ten months.

Chapter 30

[2017]

RONNIE'S seventh Masters title, superseding Stephen Hendry's six as the record, seemed a long way away when, on the first day at Alexandra Palace, Liang Wenbo lined up the black that everyone expected would make the defending champion a 6-4 first-round loser. As it was, China's number two, overcome by the enormity of this impending win, put the black on the near jaw and seven days later, having enacted Reprieved Man Syndrome, Ronnie was lifting the Paul Hunter Trophy.

He had to struggle against adversity almost all week. Still suffering from the remnants of a heavy cold (or virus) against Liang, he continued to play against the grain in his 6-3 quarter-final win over Neil Robertson and achieved a sustained burst of his inimitable excellence only in turning a 4-3 deficit into a 6-4 win over Marco Fu in their semi-final. To do this with an emergency new tip, applied after the third frame, was remarkable, even for him, although we are talking here about someone who won the 2009 Masters with a new cue after snapping his existing one in frustration on the eve of the tournament.

On the day of the final, he was in such a good mood that it almost rebounded on him. Doing more pre-match talking that he was to admit was good for him and busy getting tickets for friends, he was not as fully focused as he should have been on the early frames and was 4-1 down to Joe Perry before managing to reach the interval at 4-4. Perry's wins over Stuart Bingham and Ding Junhui, both by 6-1 margins, had been followed by his epic semi-final recovery from three down with four to play and needing a snooker against Barry Hawkins. However, his early lead in the final seemed to change his psychological perspective because Ronnie exudes such an aura that beating him on a major occasion is a very big deal. Perhaps, at his core, Perry could not quite see himself lifting the trophy, although, from 8-4 down, he won three of the next four frames before succumbing 10-7.

This was a landmark win for Ronnie but it did not presage a period of dominance. He did not win another tournament on the road to the Crucible and showed just how highly strung – and sometimes paranoid – he still could be with some of his remarks to the media.

The one that brought most trouble on himself came after his Masters semi-final win over Fu when he scathingly criticised the referee, Terry Camilleri. 'How is he refereeing in the semi-finals of a major tournament? We've got some fantastic referees. In an event like this, you need your best guys out there.'

In the absence of specific examples, the consensus amongst snooker insiders was that this was somewhere between excessively harsh and totally unjustified. Undeniably, it was contrary to his obligation in World Snooker's players' contract to show 'respect' to match officials and everyone professionally involved in the tour.

It was easier to sympathise with Ronnie when, as the post-match press conference was breaking up, he said to a photographer who had distracted him when he was in play, 'You're a fucking nightmare, mate. You obviously don't know not to move in the player's eyeline when he's on the shot.'

When Ronnie received a notice of possible disciplinary action from the WPBSA, it sent him into paranoid mode, claiming that 'free speech' was being stifled and adding, 'The people who run things are looking for any little excuse to throw the book at you. I know how they try to bring certain people down but they'll never take my soul. No one is going to take my freedom.'

His attitude was that of someone needing a target on which to discharge all his negative feelings.

Creditably, ahead of the Masters, where one of his guests was Ed Miliband, the former Labour Party leader, he had shown his warm heart and a developing interest in politics that focused on the injustices in contemporary society. 'There's too much of a divide. We're all human beings, we all have a purpose in life, we all want to enjoy this time on the planet. There's enough in the world for everyone to have the basic needs.

'I believe a lot of our illnesses and struggles and suicides and drug addictions and whatever are brought on by hopelessness. I come from a working-class background. My parents worked hard and got up the ladder. In the 80s, you could do that but since they took away the unions and people power, people are fucked basically. They have nowhere to go.

'"The more you crush someone, the less hope they've got. They become numbed down and they give up. You kill them so much that they think "fuck this, we can't win."'

Ronnie's subsequent suggestion that snooker's lower-ranked players were being downtrodden was not convincing since professional sport is a classic capitalist construction, dependent entirely on results: the weak go to the wall (or at least have to find another job) while the successful enjoy the spoils. It cannot work any other way.

'I'm not going to support a system that doesn't benefit the bottom-ranked players,' he said. 'There's no trickle-down. All the top players get everything and those at the bottom are in poverty, keeping them in debt.'

This contrasted with his previously expressed view. 'The tail is wagging the dog. There are a lot of players out there and they can't play. They're never going to be good enough.'

Ronnie's estimate that players ranked between 30 and 45 would clear around £30,000 a year was pretty accurate but was he really, if he stopped to think about it, in favour of subsidising mediocrity? Furthermore, his attack on WPBSA board members for 'flying business class, drinking red wine, schmoozing and wearing nice suits' was at least a decade out of date.

As it transpired, World Snooker did not pursue disciplinary action against him with a formal referral to the WPBSA, the disciplinary authority. It was easy to agree with Barry Hearn, World Snooker's chairman, that there was 'no singling out of Ronnie' for disciplinary action; if anything, some perceived the reverse, that he had got off lightly in relation to his initial disrespectful remarks about Camilleri.

It was not easy to see why, in the next few weeks, Ronnie chose to turn most of his media interviews into a farce. At the World Grand Prix in Preston he responded like a dalek, or a speak-your-weight machine, to basic questions Neal Foulds put to him on behalf of ITV, the host broadcaster; at the Players Championship in Llandudno, he replied to every question put to him by Phil Yates for ITV by saying that his waistcoat was too tight; and in ITV's studio he referred everything to the birds tweeting and his latest training run. In a BBC Wales interview, he gave mostly one-word answers and sang a few lines of the Oasis song, 'Wonderwall'.

Since he was no longer facing disciplinary action, why was he doing this when, in any case, the press had merely reported what he had said. Reasonable answers to reasonable questions should not have been too much to ask of him.

On table, he suffered some surprise defeats, starting with a 5-4 loss from 4-1 up to Mark King in his first match in Berlin in the German Masters.

'Ronnie and I have got plenty of history, which people don't really know about, since we were kids,' said King. 'It's not a needle match but it's always nice to beat him.'

At the World Grand Prix, Ronnie bookended his 4-2 first-round win over Yan Bingtao with breaks of 137 and 128 but then lost 4-1 to Neil Robertson who, he said, 'played well and deserved to win'. Ronnie added, 'Not a lot went right. It just didn't seem to happen for me. Best-of-sevens are tough but they're tough for everyone.'

In the second round of the Welsh Open in Cardiff, Ronnie smoothly went 3-0 up on Mark Davis but then came to a standstill as he lost 4-3. He made two centuries, 118 and 101, in despatching Liang Wenbo in Llandudno but for the third time in succession lost to Judd Trump, 5-3.

He travelled to Beijing for the China Open but lost his second match 5-4 to an inspired performance by Mark Joyce, the world number 51 at the time, who thus became the sixth player ranked outside the top 16 to beat Ronnie in a ranking event in the 2016/17 season. Ronnie seemed to be suffering from one of the first symptoms of decline that all great players display: a tendency to miss what for him were shots well within his usual range of ability for no apparent reason at key moments.

Two such mistakes cost him the fifth and seventh frames and by the time it came to a ninth-frame decider, he was looking tense and even playing faster than normal. Clearly under pressure, he failed to exploit two chances of the sort he had habitually put away throughout his career and Joyce, despite his anxiety in trying to nail the best win of his career, managed to get over the line.

Such performances did not augur well for Ronnie's chances at the Crucible. Even in the Joyce match he had made two sublime centuries, 106 and 132, but not every frame can be won in a single fluent visit and in those involving more toing and froing, he was simply making too many untimely mistakes.

Ronnie arrived in Sheffield after a seven-week practice regime for which, for the first time, he had kept a diary. 'I didn't seem to be getting anywhere but after five weeks I noticed I was sharper,' he told his friend, Matt Smith, for Eurosport. He felt that the diary had been useful but added that 'I couldn't do it year-round'.

His first-round opponent was Gary Wilson, the 2004 world under-21 champion, whose professional career highlight had been a run to the final of the 2015 China Open. He had fallen back into the shadows but performed very impressively in qualifying, in which he had made eight centuries, including a 147.

A total clearance of 122 helped Ronnie to a 5-1 lead but otherwise he did not look entirely comfortable and was reliant on unforced errors from his opponent to win at least a couple of these frames.

Those of us who expected to see Ronnie pull away into a commanding overnight lead instead saw Wilson make breaks of 64 and 63 in winning the next two frames and add the last of the day after needing a snooker.

Wilson therefore resumed only 5-4 adrift and also opened the scoring with 50 in the new session only for no pottable red to present itself when he split the pack. No subsequent opportunity came his way in this frame. Ronnie closed the gap with 38, laid a fiendish snooker on the yellow that extracted 24 points in fouls and ultimately yielded a chance to pot the yellow, which by then was the only ball he needed.

This left Ronnie 6-4 ahead when it could so easily have been 5-5. Wilson's break of 100 halved the gap but Ronnie's fusillade of 124, 74 and 83 took him within a frame of victory at 9-5. Fighting it out to the last, Wilson won two more frames, the latter with a break of 103, before Ronnie applied the closure at 10-7 with a run of 90.

In 25 years, Ronnie had been a first-round loser at the Crucible only three times – to Alan McManus (1993), David Gray (2000) and Marco Fu (2003) – but his unusually exuberant fist-pumping celebration underlined both how well Wilson had played and Ronnie's relief at overcoming this early challenge.

While Wilson took consolation from 'getting so close' and that 'I put up a bit of a fight', Ronnie had nothing to say about the match and instead resurrected his feud with World Snooker, which was chiefly reported as a personal clash with its chairman, Barry Hearn.

A verbatim transcript of his diatribe read:

> 'I get myself in hot water and I get a letter through saying that I need to respond in 14 days the day before

a tournament and to be fair it kinda messed up my last 3–4 tournaments, I didn't win a match really and I just thought it's not fair on my fans, it's not fair on the people who have invested in me and I don't really think I have done a lot wrong so I think it is important now for the rest of my career that I stay ... I just don't want it to happen again, it has cost me three tournaments, I'd rather not, I've got people dealing with it, I've got some good lawyers that are making sure that I am OK ...

'I phoned Barry up four weeks ago and said look Barry, I'm done mate. I'm done with you and your board of people. I've got a very good friend of mine who said let your lawyers deal with it and I won't get involved with it no more because I'm not getting bullied, I'm not letting people do that to me ever again. I'm not and I'm just fortunate I've got a very good friend, who has got very good lawyers, and they've got my back and I just want to play and have fun. I like Barry but I'm not being intimidated or bullied any more.

'To me, to go in there with all that in my head having to go see lawyers, having to fight off something that I thought I shouldn't have had to fight off, for five, six, seven years, I'm done with it. They pushed me a little bit too far and if I didn't have good lawyers to deal with it I'd probably walk away because I'm too old to be dealing with things like that, it's not that important ... I'm not going to do it and have someone or people trying to intimidate me and bully me, I'm just not having it so whatever they throw at me, I'm equipped to come back because I'm not living my life like that.

'I'm just not prepared to put myself in a position where I'm in breach of the game, if I say something bad about the refs, the players, the venue ... there are so many things there, I'm tarnishing the sport, I'm like, you know what, just drop me out. I've given 25 years' service to this game, I think I have given enough to this game, I think I've done my bit, I think I've helped, I don't need that, not at 41. I don't need you, you probably don't need me but I just want to enjoy my life and I'm not putting up with someone thinking that they can threaten and bully me – ain't happening. They can maybe relax a little bit and chill out and stop being so precious about everything ... I don't want to play with disciplinary hearings over me all the time. The language can be quite threatening and intimidating and it can be unsettling for me and I feel happy, I'm a happy guy.

'I've got a lawyer on it and they realise that I'm not just going to be bullied about and then they back off. It takes that for them to think hold on we can't bully him, but I'm just not prepared to be bullied any more.'

Hearn did not let this pass, taking particular exception to Ronnie's charges of intimidation and bullying on the grounds that such 'unfounded allegations are damaging to World Snooker's reputation as well as my own'. He also reported that no communication had been received from Ronnie's lawyers.

For the rest of the tournament, Ronnie resumed normal relations with the media.

Unlike Judd Trump, the pre-tournament favourite in the eyes of many, who had talked up his chances before the championship and taken victory somewhat for granted against Rory McLeod only to lose 10-8 in the first round, Ronnie played down his prospects even after disposing of Shaun Murphy relatively comfortably, 13-7.

'I've become like a band or a singer nowadays. When they do a world tour, they pitch up and play and there isn't pressure there. If you have a good night or a bad night, it doesn't really matter. I enjoy being in that position more but I have a responsibility to try and play to a certain level, for myself as well.

'I've practised for this tournament for six or seven weeks. It doesn't mean I'm going to play well but I've put the work in. I come here in a little cocoon and do what I've got to do, but it's very hard. The championship is a long slog for me mentally.

'I haven't had the greatest of seasons but it's not been a bad year. I just need to be a supporting act here. I've never been driven by records and titles or being the greatest player on the planet.

'I just feel lucky and privileged to play snooker and not have to get up at six in the morning to get on the Central

Line in London and do a nine-to-five job. I'm truly blessed for that.'

Murphy did not subscribe to this 'not being bothered' stuff that Ronnie comes out with, insisting, 'He's still the benchmark by which we all measure ourselves. He played really well in the whole match and if he plays with that level of focus, I think he'll win it.'

To independent eyes, Ronnie had indeed played pretty well, certainly at the start in opening up a 5-1 lead and well enough to snuff out a couple of promising rallies from Murphy. With a 10–2 win/loss record against Ding Junhui, including their last seven matches, he was expected to equal Stephen Hendry's record of 12 Crucible semi-final appearances.

It did not work out that way. A player does not perform at exactly the same standard throughout his career. Marginally, he will improve or deteriorate. One player in awe of another may one day come to see him simply as a formidable but nevertheless beatable opponent.

For years, it had been too easy to forget just how young Ding still was and therefore not fully equipped to carry the burden of expectation that his extraordinary talent had created, not just among his millions of fans in China but within himself. But he was now 30, having learned many lessons of experience, and ready to dethrone a king who was not the reigning world champion but nevertheless regarded by most players as simply the best the game had ever seen.

In contrast to their previous matches, Ding made a flying start as breaks of 71 (twice) and 128 quickly put him 3-0 up. Ronnie responded with a winning sequence of his own, 63, 99, 65 and 37 to level and took command of the seventh frame with 69, but could not obtain position on the penultimate red and shortly afterwards missed it from distance. Ding cleared with 43 to tie and when Ronnie bungled his safety on the tie-break black, potted it to lead 4-3. Had Ronnie won it, it might have given him the impetus to lead 5-3. He did take the remaining frame of the session but was never able to get in front. The first two frames of the second session were shared but Ding took a stranglehold on the match by winning the next five as he exploited Ronnie's uncharacteristic series of errors.

The first warning sign arrived in the eleventh frame when Ding's overcut pink to middle left Ronnie a clear-cut chance not only to clear but to get ahead in the match. On 31, though, he heavy-handedly overran position for black from the last red and conceded when he overcut it.

In frame 12, Ronnie jawed a short-range red from which Ding ran 67 and then made 120 to lead 8-5. Worse still, with chances to clear, albeit from a long way back, Ronnie failed with two rest shots in frame 14 and did not score in the next as his arrears grew to 10-5.

Perversely, Ronnie seemed liberated by the likelihood of defeat. His break of 104 in just under four minutes, completely at odds with his earlier struggles, reduced his deficit to 10-6 and the next day a full-scale revival was under way as his yellow-to-pink clearance and a break of 97 saw Ding's advantage reduced to 10-8.

Apart from beating Steve Davis from three down with four to play to win the 2004 Welsh Open, Ronnie had no great reputation for winning matches from significantly behind but, perhaps not fearing defeat in quite the same way as he might have done in the past, he seemed to relish the challenge.

Ding extended his lead to 11-8 but at the outset of frame 20, from tight on the baulk cushion, Ronnie stroked in a long red to embark on what looked likely to become his fourth 147 at the Crucible and fourteenth in professional competition.

So relaxed was he that after potting his twelfth red, he amused the crowd by playfully lining up to pot the blue before changing his stance to pot the black and keep his maximum attempt on track. With the remaining three reds and all the colours in open, pottable positions, it did not seem that he would have any further difficulty but perhaps his uncharacteristically jocular interaction with the crowd prior to potting his twelfth black jogged his concentration off full beam.

Coming slightly the wrong side of his thirteenth red, he powered it to middle but did not quite get hold of the cue ball enough to generate the sidespin he needed from the side cushion to obtain black ball position. Forced into taking the pink instead, he duly completed his 146 to earn a roar of acclamation and the £10,000 highest break prize.

Perhaps inevitably, because of his 146 at the 2016 Welsh Open, when he had ignored the probability of a 147 in protest at what he considered a derisory bonus for a maximum, there were claims on social media that he had done so again, although these were rebutted by knowledgeable observers and indeed by Ronnie himself at his press conference.

After those four spellbinding frames, Ronnie was still in it, only two behind at 11-9, but needing to win four of the remaining five after the intermission. Instead, Ding was fortunate enough to leave him with awkward cueing from distance for what would otherwise have been an easy red. When this went astray, Ding made 87 to go three up with four to play.

Still Ronnie was enjoying the battle and when Ding was positionally unlucky on 63 in the next frame, he cleared with a breathtaking 73 as if this was not potentially the last frame but the first.

Ronnie needed Ding to falter – and after such a frame some players might well have done – but there was no hint of this as he ran in 117 in the next frame to cross the line at 13-10, his first victory over Ronnie in ten years.

Ronnie could not have accepted defeat more sportingly, hugging Ding in a warm embrace and whispering words of congratulation and encouragement in his ear before walking out of the arena to uninhibited cheering.

'As I was coming off, it felt really emotional. It was nice because he's a special lad and a beautiful guy. He hasn't got a bad bone in his body and he wants to win this title so badly,' said Ronnie, who then recalled the 2007 Masters final in which he drubbed Ding 10-3.

'Ten years on from that match at Wembley when he was in tears, he's hugging me and beating me. Last time it was me beating and hugging him. It's a decade on, he's in a great place and I wish him all the best.

'I've never been one for chasing records and I won't stop playing just because I'm not winning tournaments. I'll just keep playing because I love playing. I've had the best year of my life and not won many titles. I love what I do, so why not do it. All the stuff that comes with snooker is the bonus. The real love is just getting the cue out of your case.'

Their respect was mutual. 'Ronnie has always been my hero. He is the reason I work hard because I want to play like him and be the best in the game. That is the only way I can get close to his level. It is always a good feeling to beat him but here makes it special for me. I played great,' said Ding.

'I don't have a good record against Ronnie. Every time I had chances but I used to think too much about it, but this time it was quite easy to think well. I'm very proud of the result. This is my dream from when I was a child.'

In the semi-finals Ding fell 17-15 to Mark Selby, who then beat John Higgins 18-15 to win the title for the third time in four years. Even on the morning of the last day, when Higgins was about to resume with a 10-7 lead, Ronnie tweeted, 'If you want to win events you need to play like Selby. It's the new modern way of playing.'

No fan could have enjoyed the final more than Ronnie did. 'I want this final to last seven days. It's gripping.'

And then another Crucible, another season, was over. Ronnie finished a deceptively low fourteenth in the end-of-season rankings, largely due to competing in very few events in the 2015/16 campaign, the first on the two-year ranking cycle, but was third in the prize money list with £472,750, behind only Selby's record of £982,875 and Higgins's £650,075.

Ronnie remained attracted not by titles for the record books but for the feelings they give him in the doing. 'I'll keep playing because I love playing. If you could play like me, you'd love it as well. I always try to play the game in the most beautiful way I can.'

Chapter 31

[2017]

CONTINUING to diversify into income-bearing off-table projects, Ronnie was announced as the author of a crime novel, *Framed*, publicity for which was the ostensible purpose of a lengthy interview by Victoria Derbyshire on her BBC morning show.

It was not easy to imagine him tapping out 100,000 words on his own but not difficult to picture him talking extensively to a ghostwriter and/or editor to produce something publishable.

'Doing the book has been one of the best things I've done,' he said. 'I love the process. Most of it is based on my life.' The central character, Frankie, 'puts his life on the line because his father is in trouble'. When his brother also gets on the wrong side of the wrong people, he steps in 'out of loyalty to his family'.

These are very much Ronnie's own values.

There is very little snooker in the book but the depiction of the Soho scene, in which his parents worked in their younger days, comes across as authentic.

'Too much of one thing can be dull and boring,' he said of his need to give snooker a rest from time to time. His body no longer allowed him to train as he used to when he was on the fringe of the Essex cross-country team but cooking, going to the gym and spending time with his children helped keep him occupied.

Perhaps most importantly of all, Ronnie said he was 'aware of what's going on around me'. His growing interest in politics, particularly in the area of social justice, was stimulated by his friendship with Ed Miliband, the former Labour leader, and he found Labour's subsequent leader, Jeremy Corbyn, 'someone people can relate to [and] people can see he's a decent person'. Ronnie was also to tweet his best wishes to him for the 2017 General Election. In another tweet, about the Grenfell Tower disaster, he said: 'They can't allow another cover-up. This Grenfell enquiry needs to be speedy with the right people being accountable.'

He took most of the summer off, although he did make seven centuries in nine frames, including a 147, in an exhibition at Lincoln University and also travelled to the Hong Kong Masters, an eight-man invitation event offering £20,000 even for first-round losers. Wins of 5-4 from 4-2 down over John Higgins and 6-5 over Judd Trump, after needing a snooker with two reds remaining in the decider, assured him of £45,000 but it was Neil Robertson who took the £100,000 first prize by beating him 6-3 in front of 3,000 spectators in the Queen Elizabeth stadium.

Ronnie was pleased with his win over Higgins ('For my first match since the World Championship I felt pretty good') and with his match-winning green-to-black clearance in the decider against Trump ('I was really pleased that I held myself together. You have to let instinct take over in that situation').

His feelings about the final were more equivocal. 'If you'd have told me at the start of the week that I'd be in the final, I'd have taken it, so I have to take some positives out of it. I don't usually make excuses but my cue, well, I'll be setting fire to it as soon as I get home. It's finished. There were certain shots I just couldn't play. It's had some work done to it and it's not the same.'

Three weeks later, he was back in Asia for the China Championship in Guangzhou, making a couple of centuries, 124 and 100, in despatching Sam Baird 5-2, one of 130 in beating Dave Gilbert 5-3, clearing green to black to prevent the contest requiring a ninth-frame decider, and one of 139 to round off his 5-0 win over Graeme Dott.

It looked as if his twenty-ninth ranking title was about to arrive, all the more so when he led Luca Brecel 4-1 in their quarter-final, only for this to change into a career landmark 5-4 victory for the 22-year-old Belgian, whose comeback started with back-to-back centuries, 110 and 103, and led to a nervy conclusion in the decider, in which Ronnie missed both green and brown.

'It was unbelievable,' said Brecel. 'Against most players, you think you can come back from 4-1 down but against Ronnie you don't fancy it because he's so good. When I made a century, I started believing again.'

Ronnie did not reveal his true feelings in his press conference. 'Hopefully the fans enjoyed the match. There was a lot of excitement there. As long as the fans go home happy, we should all be happy.'

Brecel certainly was when he went on to win the title, his first of ranking status. While he was in Guangzhou, although he knew nothing about it until it was safely all over, Ronnie's girlfriend of five years, Laila Rouass, found herself in the middle of a terrorist attack in Barcelona, forced to take refuge in a nearby restaurant when a white van ploughed into a crowd of tourists, killing 13.

'Hiding in a restaurant freezer. Praying for safety of everyone here,' she tweeted from the scene, adding later, 'Gunshots just heard. Armed police running down the street looking for someone.' Thankfully, no harm came to her but the scary experience served as a stark reminder that the snooker bubble is not insulated against the harsh realities of the modern world.

Ronnie skipped the Indian Open in Hyderabad, the World Open in Yushan and, more surprisingly, the European Masters in Lommel, Belgium, explaining that he disliked playing a first round in qualifying venues like Preston, Barnsley and Wigan alongside what he called the 'numptys', a description – partly perhaps tongue in cheek – that he tends to apply to some lower-ranked professionals. He also stated that the European Masters promoter had declined to pay him an appearance fee.

Snooker had long since moved on from the days when there were so few tournaments that it was unthinkable for players to miss any earning opportunity, but with the calendar overflowing with events players can pick and choose rather than exhaust themselves playing in everything. Neither was there anything to stop Ronnie requesting, or a promoter paying, an appearance fee. Indeed, he revealed that he would be receiving one for the Shanghai Masters, although its late insertion into the schedule meant a daunting workload of three tournaments in three weeks: the International Championship in Daqing, the Champion of Champions in Coventry and the Shanghai Masters.

Prior to this, Ronnie brought his A game to the English Open in Barnsley and departed with his long-awaited twenty-ninth ranking title, tied with John Higgins, superseding Steve Davis's 28 and behind only Stephen Hendry's 36. Only a month short of his 42nd birthday this was a player recapturing his prime, delighting crowds and viewers with 12 centuries and several near misses with his unique brand of fluency, flair, touch and invention.

More conscious of the game's records than he had ever previously been, he increased his total of centuries to 894 and said that he would like to top the thousand. 'I wouldn't say that I don't want to break all the records because who wouldn't? The important thing is to enjoy it. I know getting to a thousand is there for me, so every time I have a chance to make one I really try to take it because I want to get there before my eyes go. I know that this isn't going to last for ever.'

All this came after an ankle injury, sustained in a training run, had made him a doubtful starter for his first match. 'I didn't think I was going to be able to play. This morning I couldn't really walk. I went to the Star Academy to hit a few balls and the Sheffield United physio had a look, gave it some treatment and bandaged me up. It's not too bad now.'

After a trio of 4-1 wins, Ronnie was never in front of John Higgins until his 91 from his first visit in the seventh-frame decider gave him a 4-3 win. By defeating Jack Lisowski 5-2, he reached his first ranking semi-final for ten months. He had not lost one since the 2012 Welsh Open and after leading Anthony McGill 3-0 and 4-1, he snuffed out a promising revival from the young Scot by clinching his 6-4 victory with a 133 total clearance.

Already, Ronnie had frequently pushed the boundaries of excellence but in beating Kyren Wilson 9-2 in the final, he made any conventional superlatives seem inadequate. Breaks of 115, 54, 131, 77, 87 and 96 marked his progress to a 6-2 interval lead and with a mesmerising 50 clearance and two centuries, 127 and 132, he made it a short evening. In recording a 98 per cent pot success rate, he missed only six balls all day. Jimmy White, a close friend well placed to know how Ronnie was really feeling, told Eurosport viewers, 'His mindset is the best it's been for years.'

Even Ronnie, his own harshest critic, judged his performance 'very, very good', adding, 'I felt really good amongst the balls. I keep driving myself on to reach the highest standard. I'm enjoying the challenge of hanging in there against the young players.'

The question was: how long could this level of performance be sustained? Eight days later in Daqing, Ronnie lost his opening match in the International Championship 6-1 to Yan Bingtao, as promising a 17-year-old as the game had seen since Ronnie himself had become UK champion at that age 24 years earlier.

Although Ronnie had won three titles in China relatively early in his career, his dislike of flying or being so far away from home were factors in either not entering these events or not performing at his best if he did. On this occasion, his sole success came through a break of 111 in the third frame but in the remaining four he totalled only five points as Yan raced to victory with runs of 68, 89, 91, 52 and 73.

'Maybe only Stephen Hendry or John Higgins have played that well against me before,' said Ronnie. 'I didn't do that much wrong apart from missing a couple of balls. He [Yan] has presence around the table. To be a champion, you need to portray that image. All the great players won tournaments when they were 17 or 18, so if he's going to be a great player then he'll win one soon.'

As it turned out, Yan beat Higgins 6-2 in their quarter-final but lost 6-2 to Mark Allen in the semis. Mark Selby, who had broken his big toe by dropping a heavy glass ornament on it in the summer, beat Allen 10-7 for his only title in the first half of the season.

Ronnie's early exit at least gave him a few days' respite before the Champion of Champions in Coventry, a tournament he described as 'a numpty-free zone'. After a 'pretty solid day' in which he beat Neil Robertson 4-1 and Higgins 6-0, he was a 6-2 semi-final winner over Anthony Hamilton, making breaks of 124 and 109 to reach 900 centuries in professional competition.

'He's the best. He's always been the best,' said Hamilton. 'You sit there watching him play and it's hard to concentrate. He's so good, he bamboozles you. When you get to the table, you feel like an idiot.'

Carrying a 16-3 frames tally, Ronnie was a warm favourite to beat Shaun Murphy in the final, all the more so when breaks of 97 and 98 gave him a 2-0 lead, but a surprising failure on the last red in the third frame, when needing only a colour in addition, shattered the illusion of easy dominance. Suddenly, Ronnie was making all sorts of mistakes as Murphy found his game. Ronnie lost the next four frames, levelled at 4-4 but Murphy took the last frame of the afternoon on the black in a mutually nervy finish to end the session 5-4 ahead.

Many thought there was every chance that Ronnie would regain control in the evening but in its first frame he was unlucky, on 39, to split the reds only for one of them to crawl into a pocket. Murphy cleared with 86, added two more frames to go 8-4 ahead and by sharing the next two stood four up with five to play.

Ronnie kept his discipline to a degree that his younger self probably would not have done. After a mid-frame 54 had been key to winning the next frame, Ronnie ran through two more with breaks of 108, 68 and 38 to reduce his deficit to 9-8, a point at which Murphy afterwards admitted that he had begun to fear the worst. 'Ronnie's not the kind of player you want charging at you. If he gets momentum, no lead is big enough. We call it the dead man syndrome. People play like that when they have nothing to lose. He started going for shots we know he can get and they started going in.'

In losing eight of their previous ten matches Murphy had seemed, particularly at the Crucible, more in awe of Ronnie than was desirable for a player who then stood fifth in the rankings and had the 2005 World Championship, the 2008 UK and the 2015 Masters on his CV. Against Ronnie, Murphy seemed to change not so much his game but his mindset and found it very difficult to get over the line.

Leading 49-0 in frame 18, he unexpectedly overcut a red to corner. Ronnie edged back, then embarked on a 47 break that took him to the verge of 9-9, pulling off several pressure pots en route, until he did not finish quite right on the frame-ball green and missed it to middle. Murphy dredged up sufficient composure to clear the remaining five colours to win 10-8 and leave Ronnie to say, 'Shaun played a better match than me so well done. I was just trying to hang on and hope that something happened. I wasn't scoring well and missing far too many balls, and although I found a bit of form towards the end it wasn't good enough.'

Little more than 48 hours later, Ronnie was back in action on another continent, beating Gary Wilson 5-2 with the aid of a 144 break as he began his challenge for the Shanghai Masters. He then flew past Joe Perry 5-1, Barry Hawkins 5-0, Mark Williams 5-1, John Higgins 6-2 and in the final Judd Trump 10-3 to win his thirtieth ranking title, his first in China since the Shanghai Masters in 2009.

'I haven't done well at events in China in the last few years, so I wanted to make these tournaments the most important of the season because I've had such fantastic support over here and I owe the fans. My mind has probably been as good as it has ever been this week. I feel a bit tired but I don't mind that if it means I'm winning tournaments. In Barnsley [at the English Open], that was as good as I've ever played. This was a different kind of performance. I didn't feel as though I was on autopilot.

'I kind of had to think and when I'm playing my best, I don't think. You can't always be at your best. Sometimes you have to work things out. It was skill, experience and a lot of it was being mentally sharp.'

Going straight to the Northern Ireland Open in Belfast on his return, Ronnie beat Lukas Kleckers 4-1 and Duane Jones 4-0 but he was running on empty, 'absolutely shattered' as Jimmy White told Eurosport viewers, as he lost 4-1 to Elliot Slessor, the world number 82.

'Elliot played really well and handled the situation,' said Ronnie generously. 'He potted some good balls. He was solid and sometimes solid is enough. I'm a bit fed up with playing, all the travelling and going from one country to another. It's greedy really and I'm not greedy.'

It took Ronnie only a few days to recover in time for the UK Championship in York, where the 16-year-old Welsh prospect, Jackson Page, held him to 2-2 before Ronnie clinched his 6-3 win with a break of 105.

'He's by far the best British player I've seen in his age group,' said Ronnie encouragingly. 'He's a raw talent and there are things he has to work on like his positional play, but they're things which are easy to improve. He's got a great temperament and he enjoyed it out there. Some of his safety was fantastic.'

Ronnie's 6-1 wins over Michael Georgiou and Michael White were routine. 'My game has started to feel good again and I think I owe it to myself to give it a good go,' he said, explaining his decision to undertake a relentlessly hectic tournament schedule. 'I just want to play for the enjoyment of it. I find it tough sometimes. I just have to manage it as well as I can. I keep it as businesslike as possible. I don't want to get too emotionally involved.

'This game is like golf. If you're not set up right or not in line, it can affect everything. We all go through that and some of us can go through that a little better than others, like Seve Ballesteros or Tiger Woods. They're able to get it round sometimes and that's what I was able to do today. It's part of the art of the game. I've won a lot of my matches and tournaments having to do that. It's great to play fluently but that's not always the case.'

Ronnie's fourth-round win against Akani Songsermsawad (known within the game as Sunny and adopting a professional name of Sunny Akani) was anything but straightforward. Akani's inspired performance saw him lead 2-0, 4-2 and, with a 128 break, 5-4. A monumental upset loomed and on the verge of it Akani saw the chance to clip the blue away from the baulk cushion in potting the green while retaining position on the brown. Cruelly and almost incredibly, the blue ran along the baulk cushion into a pocket. Ronnie potted the colours he needed for 5-5 and somewhat shakily added the decider.

'I feel sorry for Sunny because he deserved to win. I feel like I've robbed him. It was my lucky day. Sunny is a great character, a beautiful lad, and I hope he has a fantastic career but I don't care who I play next or whether he comes out tomorrow with three heads. If I play like I did tonight, I won't get through.'

As it transpired, he played considerably better, starting with two centuries, 107 and 106 in leading Martin Gould 5-0. Faced with an impending whitewash, Gould contributed three frame-winners, 101, 61 and 70, to put Ronnie under at least a modicum of pressure but he responded forthrightly with 94 to win 6-3.

'I just battled, tried to be professional and leave every ounce I've got in me on the table. I've given up analysing it any more. I just go out there and try to do my best. I'm kind of detached and I won't allow myself to get sucked in. I'm just playing one ball at a time because I'm not playing well enough to think too far ahead. I'm not playing fantastic but I'm competing and trying my hardest. If something clicks, great, but if it doesn't then I'm going to have to be scraped off the table,' he said.

Ronnie's semi-final against Stephen Maguire followed a similar pattern as he led 4-0 and 5-2. Maguire reduced this to 5-3, and with a total clearance of 129 to 5-4, but was denied any clear-cut chance in the tenth frame as Ronnie's 61 settled the issue, 6-4.

'I just tried to keep my patience and wait for the chance to pounce,' Ronnie said. 'I've got lucky that other players have struggled against me this week and I suppose to get to the final having not played my best isn't a bad thing.'

Maguire reflected, 'At the end, I fancied the job when I got in the balls. It was just a pity that it came too late. It would have been nice to get [to] 5-5 and see what happened because he was obviously starting to rock a little bit.'

The afternoon session of Ronnie's final against Murphy was split 4-4 but at 5-5 he engaged overdrive with three frame-winners, 104, 76, 103, cleared with 86 from 0-49 and passed the post with 59 and 49 to win 10-5, equalling Steve Davis's record of six UK titles.

'The milestones are all good and they're testament to how long I've been in the sport and persevered at it. They're great records to have,' said Ronnie. 'I could never say, "I'm the greatest." That's not in my personality. I'm just pleased to put in some great performances over the years. I'd say there have been 10 or 12 tournaments where I've played unbelievably well. That's something that'll stick with me more than records.

'I just went out there and tried to be professional and ignore how I was feeling. I missed a lot of balls throughout the tournament and you don't expect to win titles unless you're 70 per cent or 80 per cent on your game, so I'm a little bit surprised to come out on top this week. It's just nice to get my hands on another trophy but I don't really feel excited by it. I don't get too emotionally involved now. Playing snooker keeps me out of trouble. If I wasn't playing, I'd probably be going off the rails. As long as I play snooker, it'll keep me reeled in.'

Murphy was much more upbeat about Ronnie's performance. 'Ronnie's the greatest player we've ever seen. For him to still be winning majors and equalling records when playing against opponents who are so much better than they ever were in snooker's perceived heyday is a massive feather in his cap. The difference today was his safety. It had me in real trouble most of the time. I'm not the world's best tactical safety player and he exposed those weaknesses as true legends do.'

Straight up to Glasgow for the Scottish Open, Ronnie swept past Michael Georgiou and Robert Milkins with a pair of 4-1 wins, making three centuries, 136, 112 and 101, but this still left him hard to please. 'I can't divulge what's wrong with my game but let's just say all sportsmen have that. You're always working on getting technically better. I'm a better competitor than I used to be, probably not a better player, just a bit more patient. I used to get a bit fed up and wanted to go home but now I try my hardest every time I'm out there.'

How could he be so critical of his standard of play after winning three of the previous five ranking tournaments?

Li Hang, one of many very able Chinese, led him 3-2 in the third round but could not quite cope with the prospect of the biggest win of his life as Ronnie's 65 and 80 in the last two frames respectively got him through 4-3. Michael White also seemed somewhat overawed as Ronnie beat him 4-1 but John Higgins showed that he was an opponent of an altogether different stamp as he brought Ronnie's 11-match winning streak to an emphatic end, 5-0.

Since winning the Indian Open in early season, Higgins had not enjoyed the best of seasons by his own high standards and had lost all four of his matches against Ronnie. A crisis of confidence had been brought to a head by the manner of his defeat by Mark King in the UK Championship a few days earlier, which made him wonder whether it was 'the beginning of the end'.

Back in Scotland among friends and family, though, Higgins was again his old self, fired by a desire to reassert his authority on the table and inspired by 'a brilliant atmosphere, like a football match, when we came out. These are special occasions to play in.'

Ronnie did not need to make many mistakes. There was one in the opening frame when Higgins cleared with 55 from 31 behind and another in the last when he cleared with 71 from 0-60, but the three intervening frames were accounted for by a hat-trick of centuries, 109, 117 and 105.

'John's a class act and an amazing player. He has touch, power and skill. If you're going to build a snooker player, then you'd build John,' Ronnie said. 'He played fantastically well. No excuses. I was here to try and win the tournament. It just didn't work out but I'm kind of relieved I don't have to come back and play another match. I'm looking forward to getting home and not having to pack my suitcase.'

It seemed to be in the stars that Higgins would win the tournament but he lost 6-3 in the semi-finals to Neil Robertson, who came from four down with five to play to beat Cao Yupeng, yet another highly capable Chinese player coming through the ranks, who in the penultimate frame was within a couple of pots – and subsequently only one – of winning the title.

Citing medical reasons, Ronnie withdrew from the qualifying round of the German Masters in Barnsley. He was simply snookered out after giving his all for eight high-pressure weeks. Nor was he the only one to be looking forward to a Christmas break, although no one would have voted for a return to the bad old days when, under a different administration, the circuit consisted only of six ranking events plus the Masters.

Chapter 32

[2018]

IN Ronnie's world, there is always a conflict between a need for repose, a life as normal as it can possibly be for a superstar, and an opposing desire to fulfil himself as a player, which might require him to go to the very bottom of the well of his mental resources.

Enjoying Christmas as it gave him relief from a tournament schedule that had left him emotionally exhausted, he tweeted that he might not compete at the Crucible but instead film another series of *Hustle* in Australia. Actually, he was not due to start filming until after the championship but it did give him the opportunity to describe the World Championship as 'too long', 'boring' and 'my least fave event' – and play with the idea of relief from all the pressures he would have to cope with.

Mark Selby put it nicely in the *Daily Star*: 'When he says he might give it a miss and go and film a TV series instead, that's just Ronnie's style. It's almost to motivate himself a bit. I'm sure he'll be at the Crucible and not only that, he'll be the man to beat there.'

It certainly looked as if Ronnie would be the man to beat in the January 2018 Masters when he overwhelmed Marco Fu 6-0 in 81 minutes in the first round, outpointing him 649-35, all these points coming from breaks of 120, 121, 50, 74, 112, 75, 44 and 53. It was surprising that he claimed afterwards, 'I feel a little bit dizzy like I'm at the end of a virus. I just had to put my head down and try to make something happen.' These remarks were attributed to Ronnie's contrary nature and inability to feel satisfied with almost any performance, but his self-diagnosis proved to be well founded as he then lost 6-1 to Mark Allen, who went on to win the title. With the exception of his opening-frame 75, Ronnie totalled only 21 points as the symptoms he had previously described left him feeling only '60 per cent'.

'It's not nice to go out there feeling like this and in some respects I'm relieved it's over,' he said. 'I don't think I was physically well enough to go on and win the tournament anyway. You've got to give people every credit when they beat you and Mark deserved his win, there's no doubt about that. He played really nicely for most of the match but I didn't give him much to beat.

'If I was a footballer, they'd have put in a substitute but this is an individual sport and there would have been murders if I hadn't turned up. I just want to go away, recover and get ready for my next competition.'

Because of his withdrawal from the German Masters before Christmas, Ronnie went to Berlin only as a Eurosport pundit, so it was the best part of a month before he competed again at the World Grand Prix in Preston. Yan Bingtao took him to a seventh-frame decider in the second round but his 5-0 dispatch of Xiao Guodong was a sublime solo exhibition that began with a hat-trick of centuries, 105, 102 and 101. He lost position on 48 in the fourth frame but added 56 for 4-0 and completed the annihilation with another century, 106, thereby outpointing Xiao 522-45.

This was as near perfection as anyone could wish to see. It even satisfied Ronnie. 'I do sometimes praise myself and that was a very good match. I can play like that quite a lot of the time, so you can understand when I don't play like that why I get frustrated.

'I think a lot of it is to do with looking after myself. I've been working with a nutritionist and I feel like I've got more energy and feel a lot healthier. I think I have a slight advantage because I don't need to chase ranking points. I'm not motivated by that, so I come in a lot fresher and that's where my longevity will come through.'

In 2004, Ronnie lost twice to Stephen Maguire in eight days and predicted that he would 'rule the game for the next ten years', but he never quite progressed to that level. Ronnie went on to lead their head-to-head record 16-4 but still retained a considerable respect for him, as their UK Championship semi-final a few weeks earlier had shown. This time he was 4-2 down before prevailing 6-4, having been frustrated by his inability to produce the kind of form he had shown against Xiao.

'Early in my career, I'd probably have lost that. I would have given up. I still have those thoughts but these days I don't act on them. You have to win tough matches like that to win tournaments. You can't always cruise through. I've long ago accepted that I'm not going to be brilliant all the time,' he said.

'At 4-2 down, I knew I had to try and up my game and make something happen but I was cueing so badly I didn't fancy potting anything over six feet. This game is easy when you're cueing well but when you're cueing round corners, it's so tough. Early on, it felt like I was sitting in my chair a lot and that was a bit of a drag. I looked at my watch and it had taken us about an hour and a half to get to the interval. I'm usually done and dusted by then. I just had to draw on all my experience because I couldn't seem to get going. I hustled my way through the match. There wasn't really any good ball-striking. I've had to reinvent myself because I can't attack as much as I'd like to. I have to find ways of breaking my opponents down, a bit like how Roger Federer has done in tennis.'

For all his dissatisfaction, Ronnie made frame-winning breaks of 72, 83 and 128 in turning 4-2 down into 5-4 up before running away with the remaining frame he needed.

The tournament timetable gave Ronnie a full day's rest before the final whereas Ding Junhui had to suit up scarcely 12 hours after his 6-5 semi-final win over Mark Selby, which had taken him 4 hours 38 minutes of intense application. This appeared to erode his resistance after the first four frames had been evenly shared and once Ronnie struck the front with back-to-back centuries, 124 and 105, the outcome looked inevitable. Ronnie's third century of the session, 120, one of ten he made during the tournament, saw him 6-3 up at the interval and it took him less than an hour in the evening to apply the closure at 10-3.

Ronnie did not share the common view that this had been a brilliant display. 'I think I dragged him down to my level and did it in bits and pieces. I wasn't flying but Ding was struggling. I just tried to stay professional and give it 100 per cent. I think my cue ball control is so good, I can disguise my performances and where I'm going wrong.

'That was like a golfer having a low score scrambling from the rough and the trees all the time, like Tiger [Woods] or Seve Ballesteros. I'd rather be doing it from the middle of the fairway, if you know what I mean.

'I've re-dedicated myself to the game, I'm having fun and getting a few results. It's been a good season and whatever I'm doing is working.' Even so, he contradicted the widely held opinion, one that he had shared not long previously, that he was playing better than ever. 'My best was probably from 2011–2015. At the moment, I'm just about finding ways to beat people. I don't think I'm capable of doing this at the Crucible. I can do it over a few days but not 17. Winning there is all about consistency, stamina and power. It's not suited to my game. I think I'm too old.'

Some saw Ronnie's progress as irresistible and the following week, with a walkover and three 4-0 wins in the Welsh Open, it was, until John Higgins, an altogether higher class of opponent, beat him 5-1. Perhaps Ronnie's edge had been blunted by too many matches. For whatever reason, he did not seem to be fully up for it and was well below not just his best standard but his basic level of form, failing to make a 30 break after taking the opening frame with one of 64. His series of uncharacteristic errors included, most unusually, some failures of touch as Higgins started his five-frame winning streak with a break of 113 and concluded it with one of 101.

Ronnie should have levelled at 2-2 when he led by 24 only to go in off in potting the green, which would otherwise have left Higgins needing a snooker.

'The fourth frame was massive. He'll probably wonder to himself what he was doing even coming close to the middle pocket. That's what will be pickling his head tonight,' said Higgins. 'To beat Ronnie is always a great win. He didn't play great tonight and I was a bit surprised by that. In my eyes, Ronnie will always be the best. I'm more of a working man's player. I don't have the same flair but I give it everything.'

Ronnie indicated that his great rival's self-assessment was too modest. 'John's just different class. He's just a brilliant player. I'd recommend anyone who's a snooker fan to come and watch John because it doesn't get any better than the way he plays.'

Higgins maintained his momentum to win the title by beating Barry Hawkins 9-7 in the final, his 30th ranking title.

Ronnie passed on the One Frame Shoot-out, the Gibraltar Open and a new invitation event, the Romanian Masters, so he was again fresh and eager for the Players Championship in Llandudno, which was restricted to the 16 players who had earned the most ranking points during the season.

'A lot of the other players are burned out. I just chip up now and then and nick a few trophies,' he said. 'I look at myself like a Ferrari. You can't keep driving it every day. You have to polish it, clean it, keep it in the garage and keep the miles down. If you put too many miles on the clock you'll wear it out pretty soon, so I try to keep my mileage down.'

In the second round, Ronnie trailed Ding 2-0. This should have been 3-0 but Ding missed a simple pink and after a safety battle on the last red Ronnie took the frame, the crux of a match in which he made three centuries, 134, 100 and 121, in securing what was ultimately a comfortable 6-3 victory.

'I'm pleased with how I changed the way I was playing after going 2-0 down,' Ronnie said. 'I decided to play aggressively, as if I was playing against a load of numpties in an exhibition, going for my shots and not caring if I missed. When I play my best that's how I'm thinking, playing the first shot that I see. The key for me is to find ways to enjoy it, motivate myself and find that spark.'

Ronnie also fell 2-0 behind to Judd Trump in a semi-final that produced breaks of 143 from Ronnie and 109 and 123 from Trump, who led 5-4. Whereas Ronnie is almost always clear headed in killing off winning positions, Trump tends to dive in, perhaps excessively conscious of how significant he would consider a win over Ronnie to be. At 5-5, he immediately lost black ball position with a winning break laid out in front of him and went in off in a middle pocket, playing up for blue. Ronnie did not give him a chance of redemption, making 67 from the long red this left him to win 6-5.

Suffering from persistent neck and back pain, Shaun Murphy had been a doubtful starter for the event, having been forced to withdraw from the Gibraltar and Romania tournaments of the previous two weeks. Extensive physiotherapy eased his pain and, without practice, he did exceptionally well, particularly in his 6-3 semi-final win over Mark Williams, to reach the final but could not reproduce this form against Ronnie, who was not at his most imperious but nevertheless won comfortably 10-4.

'For the last six years, I've been playing some good stuff but now I'm more focused on matchplay snooker,' said Ronnie after securing his 33rd ranking title, only three behind Stephen Hendry's record of 36.

This left only one more stop on the long road to the Crucible, the China Open, which for the first time offered a £1m prize fund. It was quite widely believed that it did not pay realistic world title contenders to expend too much mental energy in Beijing, although Mark Selby had completed the China Open/world title double in 2017. Maybe because he is more highly strung, Ronnie does not possess Selby's inexhaustible mental stamina and clarity of focus, so his second-round defeat by Elliot Slessor in Beijing at least gave him more time to rest and prepare for the rigours of 17 days in Sheffield.

This was arguably Ronnie's worst performance of the season. Perhaps he was more mindful of the challenges of the Crucible than those immediately at hand. At any rate, he started very poorly and was soon 4-0 down as Slessor, as Ronnie put it, 'kept potting balls and there wasn't a lot I could do about it'.

Bizarrely, Ronnie made a 147, his fourteenth maximum, in the first frame after the intermission but this was the only time his intensity was switched on to full beam as Slessor, one of a raft of capable middle-ranking professionals, kept his head to close out his 6-2 win.

Chapter 33

[2018]

IN the week before the World Championship, it is pointless to leave ten centuries a day on the practice table. The better someone is playing, the less he needs to practise, enough to keep in trim but not so much that he is jaded before he even sets out for Sheffield.

Some mornings Ronnie played a few frames with Judd Trump at The Grove, a spartan practice facility in Romford owned by Trump's manager, Django Fung, but in the main he lived a quiet private life with the objective of relaxing into his optimum state of mind. He posted a picture of himself preparing a curry in his kitchen and another one of enjoying a restaurant meal with his two youngest children and his father.

'To me, the snooker part is the easy part,' he told Peter Carline of the *Daily Mail*. 'The hard part is getting me to practise and getting me into the right frame of mind. Once

I work on that, then I'm excited to be at the tournament and playing.

'Really, snooker is something I do because I want to do it, not because I have to do it. I've got snooker just where I want it right now. There's a working life [for me] outside of snooker whereas before I thought, "what else am I going to do?" I can never visualise what my life would be like without snooker.

'I love the punditry. It's one of the best things I do now. I never used to watch snooker but I was forced to watch it because of work. You get so involved in it. Anything where there is no pressure is fun. Come the tournaments, that's a different ball game.'

He travelled to Sheffield on the Friday, the day before the championship, in time for the press conference that all the Crucible players have to attend. He checked into a hotel by the river, although he used this room only for sleeping and for keeping his clothes. For most of his off-duty moments, he preferred to relax on his houseboat.

Ronnie's first-round match against Stephen Maguire, twice a semi-finalist and three times a quarter-finalist, was set for the afternoon on the Saturday and the morning of the Sunday. The draw had Ronnie, as world number two, at the bottom and Mark Selby, as defending champion and world number one, at the top, an implicit scenario for a Ronnie v Selby final, although this possibility was halfway out of the window on the first morning as Joe Perry led Selby 7-2 at lunch and in the evening was to go on to beat him 10-4.

Ronnie would not have been sorry to witness the exit of one of his most respected and dangerous rivals, although there were some suggestions that it might have shifted his own mental perspective. Whatever the reason, Ronnie's game was, in Jimmy White's words, 'all over the office' in the early frames, wayward in his long potting, hitting several safeties badly and missing some easy balls.

'Try and be as relaxed as you can. Try to be in a good place and ready to go,' was how Ronnie told Eurosport he would like to feel. But Joe Johnson, the 1986 world champion, commentating for Eurosport, thought that this had gone too far. 'Ronnie's too relaxed, as if he had no nerves, and you need nerves. He's trying to get in the groove without having to work to get there.'

Maguire had breaks of 101 and 95 in leading 4-0. Ronnie – highest break so far 28 – settled to one of 54 in the first frame after the intermission and was suddenly into full stride with back-to-back centuries, 118 and 100, but Maguire took frame eight, in which his chief contribution was 24 in penalties, and their last of the day with an 84. The next morning, in contrast to the first half of the opening session, Ronnie was intensely focused, brisk and businesslike as he attacked his 6-3 deficit, sweeping in a long red with his first shot to start a break of 41 and adding 35 to clinch the frame. From 0-49, he cleared with 86 to reduce Maguire's lead to 6-5.

Ronnie led by 27 in the next frame with only 27 (the combined value of the colours) remaining but, in failing to escape from a snooker, developed the pink from a safe to a pottable position. This gave Maguire a glimpse of a 7-5 lead but, forced to attempt the pink down a side cushion with the rest at pace for position on the black, he wobbled it in the jaws of a baulk pocket to allow Ronnie to level at 6-6.

With an 84 break, Maguire regained the lead at 7-6 but after Ronnie had shut him out of frame 14 and cleared with 53 from 38 behind to go ahead for the first time at 8-7, Maguire seemed to sense that his train had departed. When he split the pack in missing a black in the next frame, Ronnie went to 9-7 with a run of 77 and converted this into victory at 10-7 by comfortably winning the remaining frame he needed.

Ronnie afterwards agreed that he did not feel the nerves he needed in the first session. 'It was so embarrassing. I felt like giving the fans their money back. I wanted to battle through and make the scoreline a bit respectable. When I got three frames on the board, I went home thinking "I've had a result really." It gave me a little bit of belief. Sometimes you can play your way into a tournament.' As for Selby's exit, he said, 'You'd have to be stupid to say it doesn't change things a bit.'

Maguire, whose worst fault is excessive frustration with his own shortcomings, said, 'I only had the lead because Ronnie was so bad yesterday. I was under no illusions that I was playing well enough to be 6-3 up, so I wasn't surprised when he came out today because I knew he'd improve and he did while I stayed the same.

'There were two frames that I could have nicked to make it 8-5 but that doesn't mean I'd have won the match from then.

Ronnie never gives up against me. I've seen him in matches throwing in the towel. I wish he'd do that with me. He's given me some hidings in the past which were good to watch, but that match was there for the taking if I'd stepped it up.'

He had nevertheless given Ronnie a scare and activated his adrenalin and survival instinct.

Having completed his match on day two, Ronnie was not due to start his next until day six, morning and evening, with the finish on the afternoon of day seven. He went home for a few days, had a day's practice but found himself wanting to be back in the thick of it.

Everyone expected him to reach at least the quarter-finals as his head-to-head against his next opponent, Ali Carter, stood at 13-0, including comprehensive wins in the world finals of 2008 and 2010.

A long-time sufferer from Crohn's disease, who had survived two serious encounters with cancer, Carter had done well to recover from 6-2 and 7-6 down to beat Graeme Dott in the first round.

'I've been through a lot in my life,' he said. 'I've been very ill and overcome it and I wouldn't have got over that if I didn't have that personality and fight in me. I used that today.'

He was also determined not to be intimidated by Ronnie's skill, reputation or charisma, as he had been in the past, and also raised the stakes by complaining to World Snooker that Ronnie, after his first match, had been slow to vacate the same dressing room that Carter had been allotted for the next session, leaving it unacceptably untidy.

'It's the Ronnie O'Sullivan show, isn't it?' he complained. 'I turn up to my match but he's still in the dressing room after he's won, so I've gone in the [tournament] office and said, "what's going on? where's my dressing room?"

'They said, "We're sorry but he's doing interviews." Well, he's had his match. I've got a match now but everyone's like "I don't want to upset Ronnie".'

This incident may have inflamed Carter's rivalrous feelings to his advantage. Certainly, he was to play to his best standard with maximum intensity.

In the opening session, Ronnie won three frames with sizeable breaks – 121 in the second, 61 in the third and 96 in the sixth – but Carter, who also made a century, 115, to lead 3-2, was superior in broken play. From 3-3, Ronnie started to struggle and trailed 5-3 at lunch.

When this became 8-3 early in the evening, it was clear that Ronnie was in serious trouble. This three-frame spell had seen his pot success rate at only 73 per cent and his long potting at only 30 per cent. Carter was potting well, keeping it tight and testing Ronnie's patience. Already up against it, Ronnie's promising 25 in frame ten died when an untimely kick cost him position to continue. A multi-ball positional cannon early in frame 11 left the cue ball close to a side cushion and led to Ronnie missing the black from its spot to let Carter in for 72.

Five frames behind, Ronnie made a break of 55 in each of the next two frames as he reduced the gap to three. He never backed off from playing the right shot in the hope of short-term benefit, but the impression he conveyed was of struggling against the grain.

He did seem to be loosening up in frame 14 until a kick stopped him in his tracks on 54. Carter replied with 22, refused a dangerous cutback in favour of safety and got in again to clear with 51 for 9-5.

After he had been well on the way to only two behind at 8-6, this was a body blow but Ronnie responded with his most fluent form of the session as breaks of 79 and 106 restricted Carter's lead to 9-7 overnight.

It was highly desirable that Ronnie should start the final session well, and when Carter missed on 37-0 he completed a 66 clearance to trail only by a single frame.

There was a lengthy safety duel early in the next. Ronnie had Carter pinned to the black cushion with no safety available. Knowing that Ronnie would probably level at 9-9 if he missed, Carter stroked in a very tough red to middle and made 63 to go two clear once more.

Although it had little or no bearing on the result, frame 19 produced the incident that commanded most of the press coverage the next day. Trailing by 26 with only the last five colours remaining, Ronnie needed a snooker and during his attempt to lay one collided with Carter in the tight confines of the Crucible's two-table set up.

'You're Mr Angry,' Ronnie said with a wink. 'You shoulder-barged me. I thought I'd give you one back.'

'Thank you very much. Very nice of you,' Carter replied with a grin.

Some spectators thought that this was friendly banter but Paul Collier, the referee, sensed something different and called upon the players simply to play.

'Yeah, I'm cool, cool as a cucumber,' was Ronnie's parting shot.

Carter then led 10-8, increased to 11-8 after a 28-minute frame of bits and pieces. Ronnie seized the last before the intermission with 59 and 71 and was well in with 54 in frame 21 until he took an elementary blue to middle for granted. Three more pots would have brought him within striking distance at 11-10. Instead, Carter recognised that this was a key moment and produced a 51 clearance to win on the black and go three up with four to play.

Carter then opened what proved to be the last frame with 51. A ghastly miscue on a simple ball sealed Ronnie's fate and with a professional handshake and a congratulatory tap on the chest, he left Carter to his triumphal celebrations.

Afterwards, Carter dismissed the barging incident as 'nothing really, no big deal' but Ronnie revealed a twinge of resentment about its origins.

'We had a shoulder-barge earlier in the match and I just decided that I wasn't going to bend out of the way again, so we just sort of collided,' he said.

'When someone starts complaining about not getting out of your dressing room early enough, you have to wonder where that's coming from. It seems more like he has a problem with me rather than I have a problem with him. I don't have a problem with anyone on the circuit.

'I don't want to dwell on it. It's not that important. Just think of Syria and all these terrible things going on in the world and we're sitting here talking about a shoulder-barge.

'He was the better player throughout the whole match. I was just hanging on to him really. I made a few clearances to keep in it, battled back last night, but I was second to the punch every time. He did a [Floyd] Mayweather on me.'

'Snooker is a sport like no other,' he said after moving from the arena to the Eurosport commentary box. 'You practise right, you prepare right but sometimes it doesn't happen.' This seemed to reflect not just his own experience but that of countless other players frustrated by the disparity between their practice form and what they could bring to their most important matches.

Even so, to give yourself your best chance, 'you have to live the life', always treating your game as your top priority without too many holidays or off-table distractions. As he had once previously put it, 'You never know when you're [suddenly] going to play well.'

The World Championship is unique in its demands: best of 19 for the first round, the same length as for most world ranking finals, followed by two best of 25s, a best of 33 and a best of 35 for the final. 'This tournament is such an animal. It's not always the best player who wins it, it's the most consistent. You've got to squeeze every bit of water out of that sponge when you're out there. It's not just your best sessions that win matches for you, it's when you get out 4-4 when you should have been 5-3 down.'

After 15 days at the Crucible only Mark Williams, trying to win his third world title 15 years after his second, and John Higgins, going for his fifth after holding off Judd Trump 13-12 in the quarter-finals and Kyren Wilson 17-13 in the semis, were left standing.

After several mediocre seasons by the standards of a former world number one, Williams had revived his career – he had not won a ranking title for six years – through adopting Steve Feeney's Sightright alignment method.

'He's more over the ball,' Ronnie said. 'He's been in the doldrums for six years but he's always been grafting, living the life, and now Sightright's given him a new lease of life. He's a born-again snooker player.'

The final, engrossing for three sessions, was viscerally gripping as it came to its climax. Some players, Ronnie among them, had expressed the view that the World Championship should be slightly shortened, but each year the champion must complete the marathon of the mind that his predecessors have, a marathon designed to test his strength on the run-in when he has to scrape out the last knockings of his resources.

Both finalists did this magnificently. When Williams, leading 17-15 and in on 63, agonisingly sent a slowly rolled pink wide of a corner pocket – championship ball barring snookers – Higgins summoned a 65 clearance to renew the possibility that he might again be lifting the 91-year-old trophy. Instead, Williams somehow pushed his horrible mistake to the back of his mind, potted an exceptional red at the start of the next frame and made 69 from it to secure the record £425,000 first prize.

If Ronnie had won his sixth world title, he would have become the first player to top £1m in prize money in a single season.

As it was, having risen to second in the rankings behind only Mark Selby, he grossed £831,000, having equalled the record of five ranking titles in a season, jointly held by Stephen Hendry, Ding and Selby. Of the 17 ranking events in the whole campaign the class of 92 had won ten, Ronnie's five, three for Williams and two for Higgins, testament not just to their superlative skill but their staying power. In 1992, they were three exceptionally talented kids; in 2018, they were all-time greats with kids of their own.

Higgins spoke for them all after the Crucible final. 'It's heartbreaking to lose a final, let alone two, but it's like a drug this game, and that atmosphere. It's what we play for. If I never get this again, at least I can say I've sampled it a few times.'

Ronnie's season had ended in disappointment but not devastation. There was no hint of retirement. He will surely go on playing until his ranking or his pride of performance tells him he should stop. Standing on 5 world titles and 33 ranking titles in all, he could surpass Hendry's 7 and 36 but his motivation is not records as such but experiencing the feeling of absorption in the process and the satisfaction of grappling with and sometimes accomplishing something very difficult.

He loves the game but is not enslaved by it, as he sometimes was in his troubled younger days. He would like to have triumphed at the Crucible again but his attitude when he lost echoed that of Terry Griffiths when he fell at the first fence in defending his 1979 world title. 'It's not the end of the world. It's just the end of the World Championship for this year.' Even the best do not win all the time.